Promise of a Dream

SHEILA ROWBOTHAM

Promise of
a Dream

Remembering the Sixties

ALLEN LANE
THE PENGUIN PRESS

ALLEN LANE
THE PENGUIN PRESS
Published by the Penguin Group
Penguin Books Ltd, 27 Wrights Lane, London w8 5tz, England
Penguin Putnam Inc., 375 Hudson Street, New York, New York 10014, USA
Penguin Books Australia Ltd, Ringwood, Victoria, Australia
Penguin Books Canada Ltd, 10 Alcorn Avenue, Toronto, Ontario, Canada m4v 3b2
Penguin Books (NZ) Ltd, Private Bag 102902, NSMC, Auckland, New Zealand

Penguin Books Ltd, Registered Offices: Harmondsworth, Middlesex, England

First published by Allen Lane The Penguin Press 2000
1 3 5 7 9 10 8 6 4 2

Set in 10.5/14 pt Linotype Sabon
Typeset by Rowland Phototypesetting Ltd, Bury St Edmunds, Suffolk
Printed and bound in Great Britain by The Bath Press Ltd, Bath

A CIP catalogue record for this book is available from the British Library

ISBN 0-713-99446-0

Contents

List of Illustrations

Acknowledgements

My thanks go to Tariq Ali and Richard Neville, who inadvertently sparked off this book. In an unusual coalition, they got me on to a Radio 3 programme about the sixties which provoked the idea of writing down my story. Nikos Papastergiadis's interest in the artistic movements of the decade inspired the realization that I could take a new slant on my own memories, while Mike Savage reminded me of Walter Benjamin's metaphorical ' "labyrinth" where all kinds of lost dreams, hopes and artefacts, swept aside by more recent fashions and developments, resided'. The image became my standard as I wrote and rewrote.

My agent, Faith Evans, encouraged me to begin writing and was constantly supportive as I meandered through version after version. She gave me detailed editorial comments on the first draft I considered 'finished', combining much-needed firm criticisms with reassurance. Her skill and experience have been crucial factors in enabling me to find my way through an unfamiliar form of writing and I owe her a great debt.

I am similarly grateful to Tariq Ali, Vinay Chand, Barbara Davy, Monica Henriquez, Roberta Hunter Henderson, Tony Kaye, Marsha Rowe, Lynne Segal, Hilary Wainwright and Susan Watkins, who from the outset communicated a cheering faith, regardless of the lack of palpable evidence, in my capacity to write personal history. Their belief in me and in the value of doing *Promise of a Dream* was more vital to its completion than any of them realized. Along with Sally Alexander, Robin Blackburn, Nigel Fountain, Tony Garnett, Lindsay Harford, Hermione Harris, Jane Harris, Adam Hart, John Hoyland, Alison Light and Roger Smith, they also gave their time when I pestered them for facts and dates. Thank you to Stuart Hall, Hermione Harris and John Hoyland for photos and posters from their private collections and, for permission to reproduce their work, Red Saunders, Irving Teitelbaum and Arnold Cragg, who took the picture used for the cover. Ros Baxandall, John and Joan Bohanna, Barbara Davy, Stephanie Hunt and Hilary Wainwright all read parts of the manuscript at various stages and gave helpful comments. Monica Henriquez also read an early version with the graphic eye of a film editor and, with a few deft and imaginative suggestions, made me understand how to begin and how to connect crucial bits of the text. She made explicit for me what was buried and implicit.

The late Marc Karlin's enthusiasm for my return to discarded memory sites was inestimably precious. Before he died in January 1999, he was beginning to make a film about radical history which was to include the writing of *Promise of a Dream*. We had time only for a preliminary discussion. As I completed the manuscript for the last time my thoughts were with him in a continuing unanswered conversation.

I am grateful to Dorothy Thompson for permission to quote from two letters of another friend, the late Edward Thompson, whose astute criticisms and generous-hearted praise in a succession of missives over three decades educated and sustained me.

I received wonderful help and support from my editor at Penguin, Margaret Bluman. Like my copy-editor, Lesley Levene, she responds with zest and an ebullient commitment well beyond any call of duty. Both have that great and miraculous gift of making a writer feel wanted and are a delight to work with.

Some of the material which went into *Promise of a Dream* was rehearsed in talks: the day event on radical film 'If Only . . .', organized by the British Cinema and Television Research Group from De Montfort University in Leicester, Kent University's Conference on 1968 and a seminar for Manchester University history graduates. Thanks to the participants for the feedback they gave me.

Introduction

A Guinness advert fascinated me as a child. 'Don't look now but I think we're about to be swallowed,' one drink declared to the other, an uneasy grin on its frothy cream head. I can recognize its discomfort now. Like many people who have lived through the sixties, I feel that my memories of what happened then have been swallowed several times over. This disjuncture between memory and interpretation is not only an inevitable consequence of time passing. It has arisen because, as the hopeful radical promise of the sixties became stranded, it was variously dismissed as ridiculous, sinister, impossibly utopian, earnest or immature. The punks despised the sixties as soppy, the Thatcherite right maintained they were rotten, the nineties consensus was to dismiss them as ingenuous. Dreams have gone out of fashion, making a decade when they were very real appear incongruous and elusive.

Then, even as the political and social radicalism of the era was being buried deep under the waste deposits of Conservatism, sixties pop culture was sent off to rehab. A sanitized 'sixties' were to re-emerge, glossily packaged as the snap, crackle and pop fun time, to be opened up periodically for selective nostalgic peeps on cue: the pill, the mini-skirt, the Beatles, Swinging London, Revolution in the Streets. As if anything was ever so simple!

Alternately reviled and idealized, the sixties remain the controversial decade you are expected to see as all good or all bad. By wrenching aspects of experience out of context, this dichotomy inevitably distorts and so this is a book that refuses to be either 'for' or 'against'.

By writing my own story of the sixties, I want to evoke what it felt like at the time, situate responses and relate my subjective take on events to a wider social picture. Of course a personal narrative is by definition partial, but it can also introduce unexpected slants by looking at what occurred from a point of view which has not previously been taken. The return to a specific source can move the angle of vision, skew the existing record and lay a new trail.

Sixties radicalism has become retrospectively incomprehensible because the framework of assumption has been so thoroughly eclipsed and because the record has been so often filtered through sneers or a bluff historical patronage. These derisory stances cannot adequately explain *why* thousands of us marched in protest against nuclear weapons or the American government's bombing in Vietnam. They have been unable to either comprehend our motives or communicate what we feared or opposed.

Many obvious questions about the left in the sixties have simply never been asked and many areas of political and social experience have been curiously ignored. For example, amidst all the words expended on the sixties, women make very limited entrances, usually as legs in miniskirts. Radical young women suddenly arrive in the record during the seventies as the Women's Liberation movement emerges. But what of us in the sixties? Where did all those ideas about reinventing ourselves come from after all?

My generation in the sixties was living through big social changes: the expansion of higher education, the opening of new employment opportunities, the increase in consumption and the growth of the media. These were combining to alter the boundaries between public and personal aspects of life. In a general sense it is not difficult to see that such large-scale structural transformations were likely to have an effect upon women's identity. However, it is much harder to pin down their effect upon specific individuals.

Running through the outer story of my own political radicalization is a troubled questioning of what it meant to be a woman, long before women's liberation surfaced as a movement. Young women like myself, on the nexus of popular culture and left politics, were profoundly affected by the broader shifts in society. At the same time our beliefs and activism meant that we were caught in an uncomfortable gap between the manifold aspects of 'femininity' – our personal destiny – and a public discourse about democracy and equality. This divide was lived and experienced as a private discordance which seemed apart from politics. The contradictory personal perceptions which resulted, and were working their way beneath the surface of many women's lives, rarely appear in historical accounts of the sixties.

If radical middle-class women's consciousness has been bypassed, the views of the working-class women and men who took part in strikes, demonstrations and community struggles have been more or less completely ignored. The sixties saw the beginning of a politicized labour *movement* which spilled over existing institutions and was to mobilize on a bigger scale during the seventies. It was also the period when the first indications of the changes in the working class can be detected. Women were beginning to play a more confident part as trade unionists; there was a new presence of Asian and Afro-Caribbean workers in the unions and in community politics. The course of their activism, along with that of the organic intelligentsia within the various currents of black radicalism, has been only sketchily recorded.

Not only have particular groups been written off, the connections between movements and ideas have been largely missed. In an era of expanding radicalism like the sixties, individuals criss-cross over boundaries. Contrary to many abstract theories *about* social movements, actual social movements in the sixties were not completely distinct from or absolutely opposed to 'labour'. The grass-roots movements of the sixties, from CND to Women's Liberation, were not simply composed of the middle class and there was considerable interaction between the working-class left and young middle-class radicals like myself.

Reflecting from three decades on, it is apparent too that the radical ideas associated with the sixties go back much further than the arbitrary boundary stone of 1960. The decade tends to be treated as intact, but the people who inspired me and many others – Brecht, Sartre, de Beauvoir, Gramsci – had been writing much earlier. We were assimilating the ideas of a great crowd of left-wing thinkers from the past at high speed – philosophy, psychology, politics, aesthetics.

I discovered as I wrote how the currents which flowed into left social movements permeated the culture much more than I had realized at the time. Looking back, it became evident how oral life stories on the radio, realistic TV drama, a dynamic view of class in social history, a sociological interest in the marginal, the stigmatized and disregarded had all shaped sixties New Left politics.

Tracing the convergences and counter-eddies of lifestyle and culture which affected me and the people I knew, I was frequently surprised by the extent that cultural attitudes and radical politics intermingled. Debates in the arts, for instance about 'authenticity' and 'the real', or the emphasis on fluidity and on the 'living', along with a fascination with synchronicity and simultaneity, all found political echoes.

In both the visual arts and drama during the sixties there was also a preoccupation with process which passed into the student movement and then into the libertarian left and feminism during the seventies. This was marked by the desire to dissolve demarcations between forms, an impulse to auto-destruct rather than be compromised, along with the often contradictory commitment to extend participation through mutual ways of working.

Our concern about *how* was of course partly a political revulsion against Stalinism, but equally it was embedded within the material and social changes occurring around us. As the influential Marshall McLuhan insisted, the medium shaped the message, and the medium of communication was being materially transformed. In these circumstances a degree of instability was hardly surprising.

Sixties culture oscillated between dramatic lunges towards modernity and nostalgic flirtations with the old which embraced the earthed simplicity of arts and crafts and the exotic coils of *fin de siècle* degeneracy. A similar indecisiveness about the future and the past marked libertarian left politics. We looked backwards and forwards, forwards and backwards as the world spun round. Our sense of crisis, our intensity, our conviction that time was running out, these did not simply derive from a youthful self-importance. We faced the very real problem that capitalism was changing much faster than we were.

A heightened awareness of subjective identity can be seen in both the new radicalism and mass popular culture. 'The personal is political,' declared the American New Left, and the slogan passed into the women's movement. They might have added, 'The personal is also big money.' Ironically, openings created by social movements were to present market opportunities – the slogans transmogrified into designer labels and some quick-footed 'alternative' capitalists emerged from the mêlée. Yet the radical dream of the sixties was to be stillborn, for we were not to move towards the cooperative egalitarian society we had imagined. Instead the sixties ushered in an order which was *more* competitive and less equal than the one we had protested against.

It is not then simply a matter of memories having been swallowed; our hopes have been appropriated, our aspirations twisted. In these circumstances, claiming space to remember not only defies an overtly guarded set of political assumptions but also touches the sources of desire. By describing how I thought as I thought and did what I did in personal terms, I hope to bring some of the dreams of the sixties back into view. This is partly because the historian in me is concerned to record and partly because I still believe in their relevance for the future. Retrieval has become an act of rebellion.

Retrieval, however, possesses an undeniable momentum of its own. 'He who seeks to approach his own buried past must conduct himself like a man digging,' said Walter Benjamin. I did indeed dig – sometimes like a rabbit furiously, hind legs vanishing, and sometimes like an archaeologist, sifting, noting layers of deposits. At the very beginning I could remember only in snatches, making little lists in a notebook. Then I was drowning in memories. Some were triggered off by reading; others by talking to friends. Some were sought out by that strange and often disturbing process of focusing upon a particular period; others would literally spring to mind when I was not thinking about the book at all. These were stray, short-lived, wandering thoughts which dissolved unless I wrote them down. So I remembered and forgot, struggled to remember, was surprised by remembering too much and finally came gasping up for air.

In the course of writing, I had to unlearn some habits. Instead of the sources being external, as they are in writing history, a personal account required that I look inward, giving rise to an uncomfortable feeling of turning my insides out. Subjectivity is of course always there in writing history, but it is continually being pushed aside, held down. You learn to suspect your immediate response, hold it in check, remove yourself in order to enter and tell other people's stories. It took many drafts before I could relate a personal story because I was so accustomed to recording from without rather than within.

Another problem was self-imposed. I had sought to find words which could express inner feelings, while reaching towards outer worlds of politics, social existence, culture. This is much easier said than done and two contrary anxieties kept presenting themselves. I wondered sometimes whether the sensations I was recounting were so uniquely peculiar to my own experience that they could be of no interest to anyone else at all. Conversely, as I located attitudes and ideas which I had always assumed to be my own in the wider culture, I began to fret about whether I had anything unique to my name at all. I hadn't bargained for metaphysical angst.

The difficulty in writing was also emotional. The constant returns affected me more than I had anticipated. I re-entered buried feelings over and over as draft followed draft and each time around was surprised by their reawakened and continuing power to touch me. Some made me laugh; others saddened me. For two years I was to feel like a time-traveller and not quite at home in the present. Long-forgotten names came out of the shadows of memory and the faces of people who had drifted in and out of my life appeared with clarity.

Hanging around memories was lonely, but there was also a more convivial side to *Promise of a Dream*. By checking my versions of events with friends, I found people again. Uncannily, people whom I had not seen for many years popped up out of the blue. I discovered more about people I had whizzed by when I was young. Some I met again and some I read more about, piecing together my personal recollections with written material.

As I worked consciously over my life as 'evidence', I was surprised by what I had kept. Documents I held on myself ranged from half a departure note from my first love and a statement of my first part-time teaching pay in further education. I uncovered letters, a diary, notes and some early articles I had written. I returned to books and magazines which had survived on my shelves from the sixties, reading them with new eyes. From material written subsequently, I not only learned more about the period through which I had lived but found myself able to remember things lurking on the sidelines – a film I had seen, a demonstration I had been at. I patterned and repatterned the returning memories many times, moving between what was written in these external accounts and my own reconstructions of what I had been doing and thinking.

The process of re-creating was also one of realization. It often felt as if I was mapping out a mosaic of submerged bits and pieces, buried under everything that had happened since. Yet in another sense writing *Promise of a Dream* left me enmeshed in a deeper level of bewilderment, for it revealed the tangle of coincidences which contribute to the particular fatality of living a life.

Writing down memories flouts the linear sequence of time; it seems as if you are living a second time around. This of course is illusion, for writing, unlike living, is just pretend. 'You only live once,' my mother would assert. The person looking back at their own life is not, of course, exactly the same person who lived it at the time. On the other hand, to cut through a fine point, you do know more about yourself than you know about others, and do have a privileged access to yourself as evidence.

I did not know how I would write my story when I began. Nor did I know what to expect in rediscovering myself long ago. In my copy of the *Evergreen Review* for early 1960, I found a quote from Sartre saying that Brecht sought 'to provoke . . . the "source of all philosophy", that is wonder, by making the familiar unfamiliar'. I have pursued this in a double sense, by framing what is familiar to me in a personal narrative and by seeking to subvert some familiar ways of interpreting the sixties.

CHAPTER 1

1960–61

My sixties began far away from any recognizable markers. On New Year's Eve 1959, I was roaming around remote churches near the edge of the North Yorkshire moors together with my friend from school, Barbara Raines. I was sixteen, but Bar, a few months older, had just passed her driving test. This, our first autonomous expedition in a car, was suffused with excited intimations of freedom.

We were searching for Saxon crosses, the rough-hewn signposts of forgotten clusters of humanity scattered around what was then still known as the North Riding of Yorkshire. 'Riding' echoes an Old Norse word meaning 'thirding' and Viking settlers and their descendants, as well as Saxons, had sculpted the stone in the tenth and eleventh centuries.

As the winter dusk closed in, I peered at the coiled, labyrinthine carvings on the grey stone, trying to reach the hand that had crafted them long ago. Someone who had carved old motifs with an accomplished dexterity and then broken away and laboriously chiselled new designs. Someone as unimaginable as the decade to come.

Bar and I were ourselves defying all established patterns of behaviour. What kind of normal people would be wandering through chilly graveyards when there were warm mince pies and celebrations at home? We disdained such mundane conventions, convinced that we were going to live the new decade in ways that had never been known.

Though united in our aspirations, we came from quite different worlds. Bar's background, a wealthy farming family, deeply rooted in North Yorkshire, was remote from my upbringing in a Leeds Conservative lower-middle-class milieu. Her childhood had been shaped by a rural community which was still stratified, fixed and constant in its assumptions and values. In contrast, social mobility was taken for granted amidst the mill chimneys and blackened civic buildings of the West Riding, where I grew up. 'It's not what a man has, but what he'll make,' my father would declare, and he had lived out his own axiom. Born the seventh child in a family of fourteen on a small South Yorkshire farm in 1888, he had won a scholarship to grammar school and trained as a mining engineer, leaving his village for ever to work in the Indian mines in the early twenties.

Grandma Rowbotham had run out of common or garden names such as Charlie and Tommy by the time he arrived and my father was christened rather fancifully as Lancelot. His sisters called him 'our Lance', which suited him better, romance not being something he reckoned highly. His travels had left him convinced that the essence of all that was good centred first on Yorkshire and then on Britain. His Yorkshire was peopled by hard workers with moral integrity who treated others fairly. A Tory with a defiant individualism, my father would pronounce on the world from a core of downright certainty with a series of deeply held convictions.

The gulf between us was extreme. He could express his love for me only as control, which brought us into sustained conflict. This exploded into violence in my early teens when I decided I wanted to be received as a Methodist. In my father's village Methodists had been lower in status than Anglicans and he remained deaf to my theological arguments. I was to continue pitting myself against his sureties, without being aware how I was turning them around and adapting them.

The contradictions in his outlook exasperated me in my teens because I esteemed theoretical consistency. Lacking any sense of irony, he would unselfconsciously declare, 'I'm a very tolerant man but I don't like the Welsh and I don't like Methodists.' In fact these discrepancies in his approach to life were to provide me with the means of escape. For the man who despised Methodists sent me to a Methodist boarding school, Hunmanby Hall, near Filey, in East Yorkshire, where endeavour was valued as service rather than the material accumulation he ostensibly esteemed. Though he discussed women as breeding stock, he was prepared to let me stay on into the sixth form and go to university. Despite his profoundly patriarchal assurance of male control over women, he admired women with 'spirit' and loved my mother,

Jean, an incurable romantic, a flibbertigibbet with a profound inner strength, who perpetually subverted his pomposity.

She was a tiny, dark, mischievous woman with the elegance of inter-war femininity and the flapper's love of pleasure. As a middle-class schoolgirl in Sheffield just before the First World War, she had been forced to write, over and over again, in her copy book, 'The common round, the daily task, is really all we need to ask' – a phrase she abhorred. I remember her in well-cut fifties suits, with stockinged legs crossed, holding her cigarette. 'Allow me, Madam,' gentlemen would say, leaning across with their lighters, in the posh lounge of the Queen's Hotel next to Leeds station, where my mother, reliving her ladylike days as an engineer's wife in India, would occasionally take me for afternoon tea. Resolutely undomestic, she loved Palm Court orchestras, ballroom dancing, romantic novels, shopping and glamour. She exuded a sense of unstated possibilities and deeper meanings – somewhere over the rainbow.

I was a late child. My mother had become pregnant shortly after an operation for cancer in which her breast had been removed. She tried to abort me by falling down the stairs but I had persisted, a mistake, appearing when my brother, Peter, who was to be a remote but revered figure for me as a little girl, was about to leave home for his national service in the RAF.

Already fifty-nine when the sixties began, my mother seemed much younger, being congenitally irreverent and ever ready to assimilate the new. When I decided to put her on a forced course of Simone de Beauvoir, Sartre and Henry Miller, then only obtainable in the green-backed Grove Press editions smuggled over from Paris, she read them with a characteristic open-mindedness, only demurring at Miller's 'bad language'.

From childhood she would tell me stories of her life, the content shifting subtly as I grew older. She had been close to her father, an early amateur photographer who owned a gun factory and loved reading, but remembered her mother as stern and repressive. Despite family opposition, aged about nineteen she had run away with my much older father to India. They were to return during the Depression to digs and poverty in Leeds, until my father borrowed some money to buy a Morris and found a sales job as an engineer. They prospered in the fifties, moving up in the world from Harehills to middle-class Roundhay. One story, however, she never told me. She was never my father's wife. Aged sixteen, he had married a village girl, a Catholic, who refused to divorce him when he met my mother. In leaving with him for India, Jean Turner had virtually broken with her own family and found herself completely dependent for survival upon my father. This explained many mysteries: the remoteness of relatives, the absence of wedding photographs and the intensity in her voice when she expressed the hope that education would enable me to earn my own living.

When I was ten my parents took me in the car through York and Malton and deposited me at Hunmanby. I did not understand why at the time and no explanation was forthcoming, apart from an anecdote about a business acquaintance of my father's telling him that the sea air would be good for bronchial catarrh. 'It toughens them up. Teaches them to be independent,' the adults told one another. My education thus determined, for seven years I coughed and wheezed, with the icy wind whistling across the flat land reclaimed from the North Sea.

The first few years of my life at Hunmanby were spent contriving to defy the weather and the school timetable. I fended off the cold with hot-water bottles and pink fluffy bed socks at night and, by day, vests, liberty bodices and woolly gloves with the fingers cut off, carefully buttonhole-stitched to prevent fraying. My other enemy, the bell, punctuated time remorselessly. It woke us at 7.10 each morning, marked breakfast at 7.45, signalled assembly, lessons, games and prep, and determined each detail of existence: folding back your counterpane, washing, lights out. I developed elaborate devices to steal time, reading after lights in the lavatory or hiding during games. I stored moments, like the cinder toffee and mint Yo Yo biscuits I learned to hide in the stark wooden dormitory cubicles.

We were meant to be pure as well as tough. At school assembly tapers would be lit and passed round from a lamp of purity, instituted at the founding of the school, while we sang a special school hymn about unselfish love and wise adventure. I never *really* sang because I was tone deaf, miming my way through services for seven years. By the late fifties, when I reached the sixth form, the Methodist Church had acquired a liberal intellectual wing that communicated tolerant and inquiring Christianity. One minister with a sense of humour joked about visiting the school during the war when oil was rationed. The then headmistress had proudly displayed the lamp, announcing, 'This is our lamp of purity. We put it out on Friday night and light it again on Monday morning.'

Impure freedom at the weekends was never enough, though, for me and I fantasized for seven years about escaping. Early schemes of raft-building or walking over the Yorkshire moors transmogrified into reading and dreaming. From around fourteen I was hobnobbing with interesting historical figures like Mary Wollstonecraft, Lord Byron and Olive Schreiner. By the time I reached the sixth form I had acquired aspirations towards the contemporary avant-garde. I would sit, wrapped in jumpers and blazers, still with the gloves cut off at the fingers, earnestly following Ken Tynan's theatre reviews or tuning in to Christopher Logue on the Third Programme under the bedclothes after lights out. Imagination being my only form of transport, I would depart in spirit: Simone de Beauvoir's *The Mandarins* took me to Paris, I travelled to San Francisco with Jack Kerouac and dropped in to Chicago and New York when I listened to blues and jazz.

My migratory lifestyle disposed me towards an absolute repudiation of the values of home and school, including the lingering warnings about 'saving' your virginity for marriage which I decided to be irrational. Nonetheless, my pursuit of impurity and unwise adventure remained annoyingly cerebral. When the young Methodist minister who lived next door recruited me for witnessing sessions in the Christmas holidays, I was so impressed by everybody else's sins that I began going to his Methodist youth club. After I declared in a debate there that I believed in sex before marriage, a boy who drove a van kindly offered to teach me the cha-cha-cha. When he fondled my breasts and said he wouldn't kick me out of bed I was amazed. How on earth would we be in *bed*, I wondered?

The seclusion of Hunmanby Hall might have left me unschooled in how people actually conducted themselves in 1960, but it was conducive to intensive scrutinizing of the meaning of life with Bar and my other close friend, Lindsay. Lindsay was from Ilkley and from a professional background. Her father was a lawyer and she was the only person I knew with an educated mother. Neither of her parents spoke with Yorkshire accents and though we both bounced through the Gay Gordons partnered by pink-faced young men with clammy hands, I always knew dimly that there was some nuanced distinction between our families.

By the sixth form of course we disregarded the petty customs of Leeds bourgeois life. But it was not clear how to find an alternative. Lindsay, who was slender and aesthetic, inclined towards a philosophical outlook of ethereal transcendence. It was consequently Bar, dark and unfashionably voluptuous, who helped me to confront the unspoken residue of guilt about the body which had accrued despite my moral iconoclasm. Angst-ridden about most aspects of existence apart from the physical, she possessed a steady acceptance of physicality which I admired. Beneath my overt rejection of conventional morality, I continued to be haunted by the fear of condemnation, a fifties hang-over which remained powerful in 1960. This transmuted into an anxiety that 'sophistication' might eat away the capacity to respond with direct spontaneity. The body too evoked ambiguous responses, suggesting freedom knotted with confinement; while sexual passion held out the contradictory promise of transcendent release and masochistic debasement. Whereupon the image of Mitzi Gaynor shampooing her hair in *South Pacific* and singing 'I'm going to wash that man right out of my hair' would flash into my head. Perhaps some compromise could be arranged on the lines of the character in Tennessee Williams's *Camino Real* who renewed her virginity with the moon. You could gain the wisdom of a life of all-consuming experience and then wash your hair or check the moon and the world would appear as new. This would avoid having to be ethereal.

In our last year in the Hunmanby sixth form Bar, Lindsay and I created a self-consciously bohemian enclave, drinking Nescafé, quoting Baudelaire and Shelley, and debating Bertrand Russell and Sartre. Bar introduced the newly fashionable brown make-up, Lindsay acquired a pair of black stockings and I grew my hair, swelling with pride when shopkeepers on Roundhay parade quizzed, 'You an art student?'

An ally in rebellion was Vivienne Wellburn. A year ahead of us, Viv had gone off to a glittering life at Leeds University, where she was an assistant producer in a participatory student production of *The*

Merchant of Venice starring Ronald Pickup as Lorenzo. Early in 1960 she wrote to me at Hunmanby enthusing about 'Ron', along with *Waiting for Godot*, and telling me to read Ann Jellicoe's *The Sport of My Mad Mother*. Viv was to write several plays herself in the sixties, their themes anticipating women's liberation.

Leeds provided rather more scope than Hunmanby for bohemian exploration. Other worlds came filtering through into a large provincial city, even if they required some searching out. An art cinema showed a dirty film one week and the New Wave *Hiroshima Mon Amour* the next; Joe Harriott came to the modern jazz club down by the station; Wolf Mankowitz's Play *Expresso Bongo* was performed at the Grand Theatre. I would spend long hours leafing through the shiny record covers of labels like Folkways, Riverside, Prestige Bluesville and Topic which began to arrive in the new Vallance's shop in the Headrow. As my fingers touched pictures of wooden houses, railway lines and lonesome roads in the Southern states, I entered distant lives. From the rock and skiffle of Fats Domino and Lonnie Donegan during my early teens, by 1960 I had begun listening to the blues of Ma Rainey and Champion Jack Dupree. Miles Davis, John Coltrane and Thelonius Monk were the badge of cool and thus *de rigueur* – though my own preference was really for the warmth and melancholy of the blues.

Another browsing space, Austick's, the university bookshop, stocked the *Evergreen Review*, the Grove Press arts journal from New York. This served as my beat etiquette manual and I would go right through it with the proverbial toothcomb, taking in advertisements as well as articles and reviews, for the whole magazine promised a happening intensity. In my January/February 1960 copy, for example, along with writing by Jack Kerouac and Allen Ginsberg there was William Burroughs getting off junk, Antonin Artaud's 'Letters from Rodez' and Philip O'Connor's account of being a down and out, later published as *Steiner's Tour*. Jack Gelber's play about a junkie, *The Connection*, was reviewed, as was Norman Mailer's unashamedly boastful *Advertisements for Myself*. Though the *Evergreen Review* campaigned against the US ban on *Lady Chatterley's Lover* and dipped into left politics with Sartre on Brecht, it mainly prefigured that fascination with extreme inner experiences which was later to characterize the underground press. The mystical nihilism and scorn for external possessions expounded in the *Evergreen Review* were to be my lodestones for the new decade.

Judith Okely, in her biography of Simone de Beauvoir, relates how as a young girl de Beauvoir would read books as a means of translating herself into other worlds, employing 'the word *dépayser* (to change scenery or disorientate) to describe what they did for her'. The precision of the French language provides words for mental processes which remain an ambiguous mush in the Anglo-Saxon consciousness. I could not have expressed it so neatly, but this was exactly what I was doing when I set off with the *Evergreen Review*, ready to brave all on a lonely quest for profundity. Though I had no idea what this entailed, I was sure it would involve a profound disorientation from Hunmanby and Roundhay. I would live in some heightened state of becoming, seeing what had never been seen.

Like many other young sixties rebels, I assumed that whatever I had just discovered was somehow new. We saw ourselves at the cutting edge of cultural innovation. In fact we were constantly dipping into earlier decades for inspiration and influences, helping ourselves to French existentialism and New Wave films or to protest songs and rhythm and blues from America. It was not so much the components but the particular fusion that was our own invention. For reasons beyond our control, the mix was to be perpetuated by the growth of a subculture. Structural changes as the decade unfolded were to create waves of dissident young people with some surplus cash for leisure and ideas about their destiny gleaned from growing access to the liberal education of the universities. The ripples persisted long after the sixties were over.

At the age of seventeen, I was of course unable to foresee that this great crowd of outsiders was going to show up, nor could I conceive that they were destined eventually to turn into a greying establishment. Consequently I would work myself into a perpetual pother attempting to lure being and nothingness, by sheer willpower, over the wooded mound where Hun had been allowed to build his settlement by the Viking king.

One sardonic voice did penetrate the ardour of adolescence; the bantering humour of my history teacher, Olga Wilkinson, could make me pause and laugh wryly at myself. Olga, then in her thirties, should, according to the conventions of the time, have appeared ugly. She had a large face, a propensity to sties and a red nose, along with a large, most determined chin. Yet even on wintry Hunmanby mornings, she contrived to look terrific in expensive suits and fashionable black-rimmed glasses. If I had known the word then, I would have said that Olga had style. She liked *Vogue*, stately homes and Baroque architecture. However, from an East Yorkshire Methodist farming family, she was also a specialist in local agricultural history and Methodist architecture. She taught us A-level history by taking us to churches and chapels, Palladian houses and medieval digs. It was a drive in Olga's car along moorland roads thick with fog, to a lecture in Pocklington, which had aroused my interest in the Celtic crosses. Olga's history lessons ingrained the habit of inquiring where things had come from; why someone expressed a particular opinion; why people came to think the way they did. Her scepticism and humanistic tolerance countered beatnik enthusiasm and her deep sense of continuity tempered the attraction of all absolute iconoclasms.

In the autumn of 1960 Bar went off to Bristol to study French, while Lindsay and I stayed at Hunmanby to do the entrance exams for Oxford and Cambridge. I awaited Bar's letters eagerly. She was at university and thus on the front line. Her excitement sprawled over the pages of hastily composed epistles. She longed to be able to talk. She had met a boy who spoke 'our language' – it was as if we were a tribe apart. Finding similar people was delightful, for it meant that our enclaves of oddness began to extend outwards and that existence was about to burst asunder and form afresh.

'There's so much to think about,' she wrote, and the ideas tumbled out about Gide's views on classicism, New Wave films and the Aldermaston march. She had gravitated towards left-wing students from the drama department, several of whom were involved in the Campaign for Nuclear Disarmament. From 1958 CND had begun organizing marches every Easter, originally from London to the weapons-research establishment at Aldermaston, though later the route was to be reversed. They were demanding that Britain should unilaterally 'Ban the Bomb'. CND was the first social movement which broke with party politics and represented a moral cause as much as an explicitly political one to the marchers.

While CND was to act as a catalyst for a counter-culture in which many kinds of youthful dissidence assumed visibility, for me politics remained peripheral. I was preoccupied with new kinds of personal relating rather than commitment to external social change in any conventional political sense, following in the steps of Bloomsbury and the beats rather than Marx and Bakunin. E. M. Forster's *Howards End*, our A-level English set text, had left a strong impression – all the more so because the two main characters doing the relating were advanced young women. As for sex, like many adolescents in this era I had imbibed the torrential and earnest D. H. Lawrence, whose *Lady Chatterley's Lover* had been published by Penguin in 1960. But the evidence was mounting that neither Forster nor Lawrence fitted the dilemmas we faced about how to behave as young women.

Bar's letters puzzled away about the young men she met in Bristol CND or in the university drama department. They were not looking for oneness, nor did they share our intensity about 'relationships'. They were preoccupied with being cool, discarding conventions and living, as far as possible, from day to day. And they wanted sex. She reflected, 'I've come to the conclusion that what's most different in men and women where relationships are concerned is the sense of urgency in women and the lack of it in men.'

Without realizing, she was expressing a turmoil of confusion and a collision of assumptions which many young women like us were facing all over the country. Determined not to follow the patterns set by our mothers in being women, we wanted to relate differently to men, but there were no received assumptions about how this might be. We appeared to have no history, no culture, certainly no movement, just snatches of suggestion to ponder. Too romantic for the cynicism of Helen Gurley Brown's *Sex and the Single Girl*, I made my own compilation of Simone de Beauvoir, Juliette Greco singing '*Je suis comme je suis*', Edith Piaf's wail '*Non, je ne regrette rien*' and Bessie Smith's earthy blues.

Basing your life on faraway echoes could be a little unnerving, so it was a major advance when Bar found lodgings with Mrs Watts, whom I met when I visited Bristol during half-term. Accustomed to 'theatricals', Mrs Watts was the ideal landlady, her qualifications being that she enjoyed chatting about our life and (would-be) loves and seemed unshockable. Nonetheless, despite her racy twinkle, unlike Bar and myself Mrs Watts was a realist. She thought the earnest frankness we applied to sexual relationships was misguided. Untouched by either existentialism or Methodism, she tried to tell us that we should play the field strategically and recognize our power as young women. 'We used to demand a mink at least for what you are willing to do for nothing,' she exclaimed in the kitchen, waving a cup of tea for dramatic effect. Of course we didn't listen. We were going to break all those old irrational rules and restrictions. And what would we do with a mink anyway?

I was still in that concertina time of adolescence and those few extra months at Hunmanby crawled interminably. One day in the school Bible class, which was held in a room surrounded by bookcases looking out on to the stables where Pete, the only sexy young workman in the school, used to take a succession of girls, the chaplain asked, 'How do you feel, girls, personally about this moment of communion – that special moment of contact with God?' It sounded like a line from the satirical script of *Beyond the Fringe*, but I kept a straight face and inquired wickedly, 'Was the ecstasy of communion comparable to orgasm?' When the poor gauche man blushed I felt no remorse, just the rage of a seventeen-year-old against confinement.

To my Leeds townee eyes, being stuck in Hunmanby an extra term was the equivalent of exile in Siberia. The arrival of a new French teacher from Cambridge with a baby, a broken marriage and a duffel coat who was prepared to read *Les Mains Sales* was the only good news. She would struggle across the freezing quad, her long light brown hair escaping from combs and clips in the wind, a harbinger of hope who had miraculously reached Hunmanby.

My own hair growing had received a setback. Olga, who maintained that I increasingly resembled a Pekinese (my layers had to grow out), made a deal with me. If I had a tidy haircut before my interview for Oxford, she would persuade my father to let me go to Paris, to join Bar for several months before the university year started. So a Leeds hairdresser had clipped a tidy bouffant haircut and my aspiration to look scruffy had to be placed on hold.

In my Oxford exam I had answered a question wrongly. '"Age of Faith" or "Age of Reason"? Discuss.' You were meant to do one or the other; I did both. Though I had never studied medieval history, I had read stuff about the Renaissance being preceded by medieval humanism. By a lucky fluke this delighted Beryl Smalley at St Hilda's, who was a scholar of medieval humanism, and I was accepted.

Being given a place at Oxford was an honour, but it left me permanently perplexed by the arbitrary nature of what was defined as 'intelligence'. For years I had been regarded as stupid until I could specialize in history and literature, whereupon I was classed as clever. Now I had done what teachers warned you against and answered the wrong question, and I was being rewarded. It didn't make sense. It never did. However, even at seventeen I could be a bit pragmatic. I proceeded to dump my red-brick 'Angry' credentials for Oxbridge.

It was Lindsay, who didn't get in, who nonetheless managed to have a much more interesting time going for an interview. On the station she met Tony Kaye from a Catholic boarding school, Ampleforth. Tony was tall and extremely thin, with dark hair and glasses, a cross between a Gothic perpendicular church and a daddy-long-legs. He was the son of a bluff Hull tool manufacturer who was undoubtedly perplexed by his bizarre offspring. Thanks to their love affair, I found a soulmate. I regarded Tony as the fount of all scientific knowledge (he was to study psychology at Cambridge) and interrogated him on everything beyond my literary or historical ken, from mescalin (we read Aldous Huxley's *The Doors of Perception*) to the geometrical puzzle of sexual intercourse. He was also wonderfully ready to listen to my latest profound ideas about existence. Bar and Lindsay, who knew me rather better, were inclined to take my theories with a pinch of salt.

Like us, Tony lived in perpetual alienation from where he happened to be. In his case it was Hull and Ampleforth instead of Leeds and Hunmanby. Lindsay and I once visited him at Ampleforth, a vast brooding building of dull dark stone, part monastery, part fortress, rising amidst woodlands and low hills. I'd never seen a monk before and was intrigued by the oddness of men's legs moving in skirts as their robes swished past us in the corridors. I stared at the vigorous faces of sixteenth-century benefactors in the portraits along the walls, pondering their Catholicism.

Despite being so different from Methodist Hunmanby, Ampleforth had somehow produced a similar rebel and the first male addition to our hitherto completely female band. The four of us combined to invent an imaginary space out of our sense of displacement, a realm where existence would be always real, always poetic. We were willing it through talk, like the Parisian intellectuals we admired. But instead of boulevards we had Briggate in Leeds and our Deux Magots was a coffee bar near Lewis's called the Flamenco.

Early in January 1961 Tony, Lindsay, Bar and I sat round a table at the Flamenco in our carefully studied brown and black clothes, bursting with the future. Three of us were relocating physically. Tony had a job as a school assistant in a little place called Bressuire; Bar and I were heading for the Cours de Civilisation at the Sorbonne in Paris, where we would listen to great French professors. We were not just changing scenery, we were cultural migrants.

As the taxi from the airport headed towards the Latin Quarter and my room in a cheap hotel, I watched the meter anxiously. My sense of cities was still measured through Leeds, but Paris went on and on. Suddenly young people were spilling over the pavements of the Boulevard St Michel, their clothes signalling 'French students' with a deft precision. The young women wore dark brown suede jackets in those Parisian styles which made the Leeds ones look clumpy. The young men were in fawn belted macs, some with neat goatee beards or rimless glasses. These Sorbonne *étudiants* constituted a recognizable and unembarrassed section of French society, where education was accepted. In contrast, their English equivalents, either in college scarves and sports jackets or defiantly 'scruffy' in duffel coats, would have been regarded with a resentment mixed with contempt.

As the cab slowed down in the congested traffic I could see exercise books in stacks outside a shop selling those white, soft-backed French volumes along with colourful cheap 'Livre de Poche' editions. My driver pressed his horn. The hooting din all round, accompanied by shouted altercations through car windows and much waving of arms, amazed me. This was definitely not Leeds. I was in France! I sat back, relaxed and breathed freedom, preparing to transmogrify into a cross between Juliette Greco and Brigitte Bardot.

But it was still me looking into the mirror of a small hotel room, the red hair I was intent on growing falling in two wings over my brow, the Hunmanby pink of my cheeks blotted out with pale make-up, which also concealed my lips, while two black existentialist lines accentuated my eyes. I sucked in my cheeks, sighing at my failure to look at all gaunt and raddled. Whereupon I turned to the making of my new ambience, unpacking my white 'modern' fibreglass case and pinning up my postcards of Picasso's blue period and Toulouse-Lautrec, cultural treasures from a school trip to the Louvre. Then I drew back the shutters and looked out over the roofs. I was free – and terribly lonely.

As Bar was living far out in the suburbs and working for her keep as an au pair, I would wander alone around the Left Bank, leafing through the second-hand bookstalls by the Seine, staring at the windows of little shops full of strange objects from Africa, visiting art galleries or laughing to myself at the Ionesco one-act plays in the tiny Théâtre de la Huchette. Monsieur at the reception desk was all insinuating smiles as I came and went. However, Madame regarded me with stony disapproval.

Alone for long periods for the first time in my life, I drew on the inner world I had acquired secretly in defiance of the routines and enforced collectivity of boarding school. I imagined myself as unique; in fact I was an entirely predictable cultural phenomenon. The Left Bank was full of young Britons and Americans drifting through Paris searching for traces of forties existentialists. Among them was Judith Okely, busy underlining sections of *The Second Sex* about the young girl becoming intoxicated by her solitude and promising that the future 'will be a revenge upon the mediocrity of her present life'.

Student life in Paris was not as I had imagined. The great French professors, for instance, were a real letdown. During the week, we foreigners on the Cours de la Civilisation would cram into a vast auditorium at the Sorbonne to listen to them intoning what seemed to me to be platitudes. Everything was cut and dried, without openings for questions. They may have been great minds, but they were not wasting any pearls of wisdom on the students on the Cours de la Civilisation. I slowly realized that paradoxically the regimented French education system was much less open to intellectual inquiry than the teaching I had received at Hunmanby. Our Cours Pratique was even worse: a grammar lesson taught by rote by a man who never smiled.

Cherishing every last moment of freedom before it began, I used to saunter across the Luxembourg Gardens, reluctantly dragging my feet in the direction of the classroom.

After a month or so I gave up, occupying the grammar test by writing to Tony in faraway Bressuire on the square-lined paper I had bought in the Boulevard St Michel. I had been reading Camus's *Les Justes* and was troubled about the revolutionary who believed that the ends justified the means. I admired people who were committed but thought individuals were 'often more attractive than causes'. Was my sympathy for the individual socialist, intellectual sentimentalism? This did not help my French grammar but it was a dilemma that was to travel with me for the rest of my life.

Things were not going at all well on the deep-conversations-on-the-meaning-of-life front, when a group of French students invited me to see Brecht's *The Preventable Rise of Arturo Ui* at the Théâtre National Populaire. I thus stumbled inadvertently upon an adventurous production by Jean Vilar, who was to inspire a new generation in Britain and France with the possibility of a democratized drama. I was already interested in Brecht and could recognize the innovative verve of the performance. But it was very hard for me to follow in French and went on for three hours. So despite my desperate desire to understand, I had to admit to Tony, 'alienation in an alien tongue unfortunately often = incomprehension'.

There was more incomprehension during the interval when the French students chatted together in slangy camaraderie. I was puzzled not only by their French but by their whole approach to plays and books. Unlike me, they did not regard these as containing meanings to live by, vehicles for the examination of the inner soul, but simply as an acceptable veneer for the intelligent bourgeois. In England their equivalents would not have found this easy familiarity with an intellectual culture necessary for small talk. The sexual mores foxed me too. Elaborate rituals of flirtation led more or less nowhere; it was all diversion. The reason was basic and practical. In 1960 contraceptives were still illegal in Catholic France. Moreover, the intact hymen retained some symbolic meaning; older women shop assistants would murmur '*jeune fille*' sotto voce in doom-laden voices when I asked for tampons at the chemist's.

That March, still in pursuit of profound philosophizing, I came across an advertisement in *L'Humanité*, the Communist newspaper which I used to buy from a street seller, more out of a desire for some conversation than from any interest in Communism. It announced that the playwright Arthur Adamov was to speak at a meeting near the Sorbonne to commemorate the Commune of 1871. Adamov was a cult figure from the Theatre of the Absurd to Bar and me. We were unaware that he had changed tack with a play called *Spring '71* in a socialist realist style, in which scenes from the everyday life of the Commune were interspersed with historical commentary.

Drawn by Adamov's esoteric reputation, we sat through interminable speeches in a vast hall until a wiry, dark man with hunched shoulders shambled forwards from the wings. Communism, he told us, would not necessarily make us happy; it *would*, however, enable us to distinguish the problems which were our own responsibility. At last a French person talking like the books! Adamov could have signed me up on the spot on this open-ended promise. But instead he was gone and the hall was echoing with the strains of the Internationale. Nonconformists and non-Communists that we were, Bar and I remained seated as we did for the National Anthem at the pictures in Leeds; no indulgent, hypocritical collectivity for us. Such dissent made us somewhat conspicuous and a young man with a neatly trimmed French student style of beard invited us to have a coffee. He turned out to be a veritable zealot who lectured us about 'the Cause' and – just like the Methodist ministers – decided I needed saving.

Not only was I drawing blanks with my endeavours to find Parisian intellectuals, it was even proving impossible to reflect alone. No sooner had I settled on a bench or down by the *quais* than I would hear a voice in my ear making sexual propositions. I would scowl and try to sound gruff, but as I was not really sure how to be gruff in French, I would usually end up marching off infuriated.

Such incidents were generally annoying rather than alarming. However, one night, returning home along the dark and deserted streets of the Seizième, where I had moved into a maid's room at the top of an old apartment block, I heard steps behind me. The buildings in the area were tall and set back and the pavements empty, as the rich residents tended to drive home in their cars rather than from the métro

Ranelagh. The click, click of soles on the pavement started to go faster. I began moving more quickly. Again the steps accelerated. Fearful that the distance between us was closing, I glanced back. A man was drawing purposefully towards me. It was his intent silence that conveyed menace. At least the ridiculous chat-up lines gave a degree of normality to being accosted. The street was so quiet I could hear him panting as his pace quickened. A cold sweat spread over my brow. I had become prey. Half running, I approached the grey-painted gate on the outside of my building. As I reached the handle, he was so close I could feel his breath on the back of my neck. I lunged through the gate, slamming it behind me. That night even the punitive face of the concierge was welcome.

Terror in a city was utterly unfamiliar to me. You could wander around in Leeds at that time without fear. After a month or so, I tried to copy the Parisian women, walking around head held high, without meeting anyone in the eye, and thus achieved a measure of city-type mobility. But it didn't come naturally, as I remained nosy, keen to know about everyone I encountered. This boundaryless curiosity kept getting me into trouble, but it didn't stop me wanting to migrate into the souls of strangers. My lack of bearings left me with no idea of what was likely to happen next and I was repeatedly being flummoxed by other people's attitudes to sex.

The collision of assumptions I was encountering was not about sex alone. I had arrived in Paris just after the referendum in which the majority in France, weary of the colonial war, had voted for Algerian self-determination. That February, French settlers in Algeria, who were bitterly opposed to Algerian independence, had secretly formed the Organisation de l'Algérie Secrete, the OAS. They were preparing to take up arms against General de Gaulle's government.

My knowledge of the French political situation was hazy and abstract. I had read an exposure of French torture in Algeria, but was confused, knowing that Sartre and Camus, my cultural heroes, had been in opposing camps. As I walked past Algerians held at machine-gun point in the street by the 'flics', I would feel a mute personal sympathy for victims with whom I vaguely identified. Yet in the cafés and the streets, it was the North African workers in France who would be my most persistent sexual tormentors.

'*Tu aimes les Arabes?*' inquired Dominique, one of the French students who had been at the Brecht play, when I confided my anxieties. Perched on a high stool in a café on the Boulevard St Michel, she spat out the word '*Arabes*' like a shot of concentrated bile. Her words made me flinch. They conjured up my father booming across the dining-room table about the British Raj, 'We built them the railroads.' I was startled to hear someone of my own age echoing my father. From Suez in 1956, I had come to regard colonialism as outmoded and irrational, attitudes imbued from Olga's liberalism and the shedding of Britain's imperial past. Former British colonies were gaining independence in the late fifties and sixties and pragmatic Conservatives (unlike Lance Row-botham) such as Harold Macmillan were prepared to accept the 'wind of change'.

My recoil, however, came not so much from any political response, but rather from a psychological repugnance against categorizing people as inhuman which was deeply rooted in childhood. My mother possessed the snobberies of her middle-class upbringing, but nonetheless had persistently challenged my father's verdicts on India and ridiculed the anti-Semitism which was rife in Leeds. The only time she had ever slapped me was when I came home from school aged around seven and parroted 'She's a Catholic' about a girl in my class called Margaret. 'Never say that about anyone.' And I knew she was right. I liked Margaret. I had been mimicking the voice of the crowd, whom I knew from experience could support the class bully. From being very young I was to acquire the conviction that despising anyone could rebound upon yourself.

I looked at the pretty Parisienne opposite me with antagonism and resolved not to meet her again. Whereupon, with a toss of her brown curls, she admonished me, 'You must slap them in the face. Only then do they know that you don't want them.' Despite my emotional abhorrence and regardless of liberal reason, her words hit the buried resentment which had accumulated from all those encounters with the North African men who had pestered me. I left her troubled and uneasy.

Neither my liberal anti-colonialism nor my subjective rejection of racial prejudice enabled me to grasp the seriousness of the crisis in French society caused by the Algerian war. I was only dimly aware of the hatreds and the violence. I had heard, for example, that the French authorities had committed atrocities against prisoners and that student demonstrators for Algerian self-determination had been subjected to tear gas and beaten by the police with lead-weighted capes. Yet I had no sense of the war as an issue which directly concerned me. It impinged on me in a disjointed manner and remained remote. We had been warned sternly on arrival at the Sorbonne not to go on the *manifestations*. Bombs were going off in the cafés of the Left Bank but I disregarded them, assuming I wouldn't be around when one happened to explode.

On reflection it is rather extraordinary that my exceedingly protective father let me go to Paris in the midst of all this. But then I suspect neither the *Daily Mail* nor the *Yorkshire Post* was covering the Algerian situation in much detail. Unwittingly it was to be my parents who were to send me into circumstances in which the contradictions of war really did hit me head on and thus into the only real danger which seriously threatened me during my stay in Paris.

My father had hired a Leeds removal firm called Turnbulls to deliver my school trunk. Unused to international transactions, the Leeds company sent it to a freight company's office on the outskirts of Paris. My journey to collect it took me to the end of the métro line, to arrive in a strange no man's land of half-built skyscrapers and partially built roads surrounded by rough open ground where new suburbs were being built.

As I had never been to the edge of the city and was uncertain where to go, I asked an old woman the way and was a little troubled when she hailed a young North African man, who nodded confidently and said he would show me. I looked at him searchingly. He was tall, around twenty-three, with Brylcreemed hair and a moustache, wearing labourer's jeans. I was not sure what to do, but the politeness ingrained into my petit-bourgeois being, combined with my dislike of Dominique's attitudes, overcame my wariness. It was broad daylight, the old woman had approached him, he was being helpful. Anyway, how else was I going to find my trunk? I hesitated for a second and then followed him.

He led me off the dirt road along a maze of paths through the building site. As we walked and walked, I began to suspect that we were going round in circles. Worried, I looked around. How was I to extricate myself? Who else could I ask? My companion, however, was courteous and reassuring. We arrived at a café. Did I want a drink. '*Non, non.*' However, he had a wine and insisted on getting me something. I had an espresso. We resumed our walking. Another café. I had an espresso. He insisted on paying. As we left he began asking me, '*Tu veux pisser.*' '*Non, non,*' I replied. Why was he going on about the toilet? Hunmanby French had not included slang. '*Tu veux pisser.*' '*Non, non,*' I replied emphatically. I was getting seriously worried. Twilight was falling and I was completely lost in a wasteland. I knew I had to get away from this man. I was going to have to admit failure and give up on the trunk for today. Sounding as decisive as I could, I announced it was time for me to go home. Please would he show me the bus stop? He seemed to concur and said he had to ask someone the way. He headed off across a field. I stumbled after him over the uneven ground, the long heels of my stilettos sinking into the earth.

We were in the middle of waste land when he turned round suddenly, grabbed me hard on the shoulder, bent his face towards mine and tried to kiss me. Dominique's confident pronouncement pierced through blind panic and I slapped him decisively on the cheek. His surprise gained me a second. He loosened his grip. I began to run over the mix of earth and grass. There were some shacks in the next field. I could hear music. Perhaps I could reach people and safety. My shoe came off. I stumbled and fell, and as I tried to get up he came towards me. I was scrambling on all fours over the ground in terror with my shoe in my hand. Then he was on top of me, holding me down. I tried to stab the pointed heel into his head, but he easily grabbed my hand, forcing my arm back. A peculiar relief flooded through me; even in these circumstances the possibility of wounding someone horrified me. I was struggling so desperately I managed to pull both of us a little way over the ground. But he was not letting go of me.

I screamed. I was sure the men in the huts could hear. No one took any notice. He put his hand over my mouth, then his hands were round my neck, holding me down with his body. I kept wriggling and screaming. I could feel his hands tightening around my neck and saw my own panic reflected back in his eyes. 'I'm going to die,' I thought. This had not been how I had imagined my life at all. 'I'm only eighteen.

I've had no time to live. Only Bar will realize how absurd this is.'
Then instead of terror an extraordinary clarity swept through my
consciousness – all those black coffees and the adrenalin of fear. 'This
man is much stronger than you physically,' said a voice in my head.
'Stop struggling. Use your wits. You've been luckier than him in life.
Fight him with the reason you've learned from being educated. Use
the weapons of your privilege.'

Abruptly I stopped screaming and went still. His grip on my neck
loosened. I began to make an elaborate and rational case. Raping me
was unwise and would result in unnecessary trouble for him. The
French authorities were very strict about North Africans in France.
My father was a rich and powerful man in England and would pursue
him in vengeance. I was a virgin. There were plenty of prostitutes who
would not object to sex. I managed to wiggle my hands free and clasped
them firmly between my legs. He was holding me by my shoulders and
having a problem keeping me still, while at the same time moving my
hands away. Each time he tried I wiggled and reasoned all the more.

He had opened the buttons on his jeans. When I looked down I
could see his penis. It was the first time I had ever seen an erection. As
a small girl I had glimpsed my father's stubby penis once in the corridor
and discussed with a schoolfriend a theory that short fat men had
short fat ones and long thin men had long thin ones, a hypothesis
based on our two fathers. When I was six someone's brother produced
one. It reminded me of the tassels on the velour tablecloths old people
still kept in their kitchens. But this man's penis was threatening and I
was repulsed by it.

My dark green check Leeds C&A pencil dress had been pushed up
in the struggle, revealing the black silky underskirt. All my life I had
got into trouble for talking too much. Now some instinct said, 'Keep
talking.' Danger was making my French remarkably fluent. I still had
my hands between my legs, clinging on desperately as I developed
arguments to demonstrate that raping me was not a rational act. We
were in an impasse. Every time he moved a hand from my shoulder to
push my hands away I moved more strenuously. Anything to keep that
horrible thing from getting inside me.

He was becoming annoyed, but my matter-of-fact voice meant he
kept getting drawn into conversation and this seemed to defuse things.

I played for moments with words. Perhaps before time ran out someone would appear and save me. It was growing dark. We continued to shuffle on the earth and grass. Abruptly he announced that he would kill me and then have sex with me. This had not occurred to me. But my response was the absolutism of virginity. I had theorized myself into an intellectual rejection of virginity. But now I felt utter repugnance. I was not going to have this as my first experience of sex. Running out of conversational ideas, I inquired how he would be able to kill me. He replied that he was carrying a knife. Did I sense he was bluffing? I can't be sure. But it was some reversion to the dares of childish gang fights in Harehills which made me command, 'Show me!', at which point he put back his head and roared with laughter.

I felt the convulsion of his body and saw a white, hot, sticky liquid spreading over my black underskirt. I still had my hands protectively between my legs, but he was getting to his feet still laughing. I was bewildered by the sudden change of mood. He stood over me and congratulated me on my courage. I didn't think it was courage. I had resisted him because I couldn't bear not to. Even in shock I could see the irony. The man who a few minutes before had nearly choked and raped me was greeting me as a human being.

He led me over to the corrugated-iron shacks in the next field. Despite being shaken and disorientated, I was sufficiently collected to be appalled by the living conditions of the Algerian workmen. The huts were open at the front with dirt floors; a few had the bright, cheap plastic ribbons you saw in some cafés instead of a door. They had lived all through that winter in these.

A young man stood in front of one, his black hair flopped loosely over his brow. His face was that of a beautiful and delicate bird. He had large dark eyes and long eyelashes. A half-formed thought flickered into my consciousness. What if it had been him? I banished it swiftly, but to this day I am not sure. Was it revulsion against a particular man which had made rape worse than death, or was it a refusal to be compelled? My companion asked him something and I looked hopefully into his eyes, sure that someone who looked so sensitive would help me. His response burned back hatred and disgust. I was contemptible to him. I lowered my eyes. We were enemies, at war because I was a European and thus the same as his French colonizers. I was a woman and a sexually disgraced woman. Some barriers, sometimes, were insurmountable.

My companion, in contrast, had become genial. Very soon we were back in a built-up area with traffic and streets. The normal world had never in fact been far away. I felt bemused by the obliviousness of the familiar. He bent to kiss me at the bus stop. I cringed but the bus was approaching. I was going to be free. I passively consented. He was behaving as though we had been out on a date. As I stepped on the bus I felt somehow implicated and vaguely indebted – he hadn't raped me and he hadn't murdered me. My standards of expectation had been drastically lowered. As the bus drew away I was overwhelmed with relief. I had survived.

My period came early and I anxiously consulted Bar that Monday in the courtyard of the Sorbonne. Did this mean I was pregnant? There were all kinds of tales about sperm getting inside you from your tummy; perhaps they could jump off your skirt. Her term at Bristol had made her more worldly wise about physiology. She reassured me that you only had to worry when it was the other way round.

I was particularly slow on the uptake about the basic mechanics of sex, being devoid of any geometric sense which could relate biological diagrams to reality and short on what was called in Yorkshire 'common gump'. However, I was not the only one. My generation was still being brought up as if ignorance was akin to innocence. Consequently a rebel minority found ourselves crossing from one extreme to the other over a chasm of unknowing. Even though we were rejecting the trappings of traditional forms of protection, bashing our way out of all acceptable modes of behaviour and heading full tilt towards existential authenticity, we continued to contend with a powerful and disturbing undertow. The leftovers of fifties sleaze still lurked around and all kinds of disconcerting, often humiliating reactions were commonplace. It was a kind of cusp in sexual attitudes; prohibition and permission were shifting but had yet to realign.

There were no clear paths for us to take. On the other hand, the entrances towards sexual freedom had opened and were beckoning, not only among the young intelligentsia but in popular culture. The situation in France, which had experienced neither the puritanism of the Anglo-Saxons nor the same earnest reappraisal, was completely different. The French were also less susceptible to American youth cultural influences. Even though the myth of the Left Bank represented freedom, the reality was that young French middle-class girls tended to be more sheltered sexually than the British or Americans, who were seen as easy targets.

Unlike Judith Okely, who decided celibacy was the only dignified solution to the narrow choice of being either sheltered or seduced, my brush with rape and death galvanized me to overcome my shyness. I wanted to wipe out the bad memory of that erect penis on my black silky underskirt by meeting a man. Resolutely I took myself off to a dance club which advertised among foreign students. I hated it. 'Like a market,' I said to the handsome young man who had asked me to dance.

He worked at the airport, embodied Gallic charm and commenced a courtly defloration by taking me to see Andrzej Wajda's compelling film about the Warsaw ghetto *Kanal* – my introduction to the Polish director's trilogy. As I glanced around the cinema in the interval, I felt pleased with myself for braving the terrible club and discovering this well-dressed companion. Yet a nagging sense that things did not seem right lingered. Not only was I realizing that my fashionable – in Leeds – fawn plastic coat was going to have to be dumped, I was troubled by a less tangible perception. I was shamming.

The force of circumstance was to be interrupted by the Easter holidays and the reappearance of Tony from his job as an assistant in Bressuire. His visits to Paris always put him in a good mood, promising decadence and an excess of aperitifs which gave him terrible headaches. On this occasion he was in particularly good spirits, as he was accompanied by his new love, Danielle. I must meet her and some art students from the Slade he had met the night before: 'You'll like them. They're really cool.'

By this time my post-Hunmanby reconstruction job was finally shaping up, my hair having grown sufficiently to resemble long and straight. I had never met any London art students but I was still Leeds enough to want to hold my end up with Londoners – cool or not cool. So I got dressed up in my smart beatnik outfit: high heels, black stockings, C&A tight black jumper over a dark, pleated skirt in muted greys and blues, which I considered suitably subtle and interesting. To these I added my precious Paris purchases, alternative accessories, a dangling string of large dark-coloured bean beads and a long black bag made of strips of soft leather sewn together in a patchwork (which my mother was to call my horse's nosebag).

While we waited in a bar, Tony told me how he had met Dani in the wilds of Bressuire. I listened with one ear, a little apprehensive about the London art students, but reassuring myself that anyone with a discerning artistic eye would note those green and brown bean beads and that Left Bank bag. A Miles Davis record was playing in the background for dramatic tension when, with perfect timing, three young men in black made a rather self-conscious entry. Like Tony, they all wore big black sunglasses – shades, their shields.

Tony introduced first Barry, small with wispy blond hair and a puckish face, and then a dark, sturdy Geoff, who smiled a sensual grin. But it was Bernie Jennings, tall, skinny and pale-faced, like a harlequin in mourning, who provoked peculiar and unrecognizable sensations in me – something between an electric shock and being hit under the ribs. I was drawn to the shyness and pride as much as to the light brown fringe, long white face and black holey sweater. Over the years this kind of agitation would become recognizable as desire, but at just eighteen, I had no reference points, no compass to journey into passion. And I had been programmed since early adolescence to be desired, not to do the desiring.

Intimidated by the cockney voices which prickled with class hostility, I resorted to a Yorkshire no-nonsense manner and teased them about their sunglasses. This cool had to have some cracks. I didn't realize that my outfit, which I imagined was a unique expression of my personality, made me look like a middle-class Hampstead person to Bernie and his friends. But they'd never met one with a Leeds accent and were completely thrown.

I had rejected flirting as akin to that other no-no, prick-teasing, in the cerebral sexual code I had elaborated against convention. Now, annoyed with myself for feeling like a marshmallow, I dumped my own rules and, in extremity, began flirting defensively with Bernie. I was desperate to break through his surface detachment and my sexuality was edged with aggression. Bernie retreated into complete silence, a crab in a cave backing into some place where he could not be reached. But I had found a crack in the cool; I had managed to insinuate myself into one of those imperceptible spaces where the nerves turn tremors into messages. Bernie, who had sat next to me, slowly began rolling Gauloise tobacco into a cigarette. I could feel a contained response rising. Yet overtly none of this was happening. We were a group at a table, having a drink and waiting for Dani.

Tony's ironic panache turned suddenly into a benign grin. A bubbly but resolute-looking Danielle was by his side. I smiled over at them wrapped up together on the seat opposite and the tiny figure in jeans and black sweater chuckled back. How did Tony's Danielle contrive that minimalist chic, I wondered? I could never get it. The flat Leeds accents of 'smart' continued to echo in my head years after I had ejected C&A and Lewis's fashions. It was evident to me, though, that it was not clothes, or even the dark curls peeping from beneath a small bottle-green scarf, which had allured Tony; it was the vitality twinkling in Dani's two large brown eyes.

We all ambled off to eat couscous in the Rue de la Huchette, with Bernie explaining to the Algerian waiter in bad French that we were 'Parti Travailliste'. I don't know what they made of the news that this band of odd-looking English were on the side of the workers, but they saw he was trying to be friends and gave us sweet, sticky, delicious honey cakes. By then Bernie and I had entered into a wordless conspiracy to lose everyone else.

Finally alone, we meandered together into a modern jazz club. We couldn't afford to go downstairs but sat upstairs in the brown, wooden-walled room on a bench, making one drink last for ever. As the music floated up the stairs we sat in silence, listening hard, until the straining notes seemed to be playing from inside my head. Little by little we kept edging closer. I could just feel his shoulder. This slight touch became overwhelming. We were being carried together into some timeless zone, beyond reason, outside day-to-day experiencing.

But time had passed nonetheless. They were putting the chairs on the tables. It must have been around two in the morning when we found ourselves breathing the chilly night air outside. I shivered. We wandered through Paris all that night, behaving like classic lovers while pretending to ignore the cold. It was all most impractical. I had no idea how to get home after the last métro went and was anyway far too nervous to suggest it. Bernie shared a tiny hotel room with Geoff and Barry; we couldn't go back there. Eventually, tired, drained and hungry in the dawn, we huddled over a coffee in Les Halles, desire on hold and overlaid by the shouts of the market men, hauling their loads and wiping their stalls. We were extraneous in the bustle of the early morning.

I have no coherent sequence of memory for the days that followed, only a series of cameos. Bernie and Barry were smoking kief – the green leafy cannabis which found its way to France from Morocco – in their little hotel room and playing *musique concrète* with the bare light bulb. I went out for a sandwich, got lost, forgot the name of their hotel. The streets seemed maze-like and I kept rounding the same corners. Panicking and cursing my hopeless sense of direction, I asked a man the way. He explained with tolerance that there were many possible destinations in the area for one who had no precise notion of what was being sought. I finally unravelled the way back to the hotel entrance and returned to the tiny room, flustered and distraught, to find my absence had not even been noticed. They were still incanting, but in semi-gloom. The light bulb had shattered in a tympanic blow. My anxiety mutated into an irrational fury and I sat glowering at them for no good reason. Barry must have translated this into a message to depart, for eventually he sauntered out.

Neither of us was sure what to do next. I gazed at him, sheepish and uncertain. When you blew all the rules, how did you make a move? 'We could meditate,' he said, showing me how to sit cross-legged on the bed. Neither of us wanted to meditate. He drew me to him and undid my bra. A diffuse arousal spun around my body. 'I'm a virgin,' I said, clumsy, sensing he assumed I knew more about what was happening than I did. He was incredulous. How could anyone be a virgin at eighteen! Girls he knew in Bermondsey were never virgins by then. I'd never been to Bermondsey, but immediately endowed it with drama and life in the raw. Impossible to explain about Roundhay or Hunmanby; how could he comprehend the peculiar difficulties of losing your virginity in such conditions? He offered to take me to the métro. On the way I tried to tell him about my mother, but he was dismissive about middle-class people and described how his mother had brought him up alone. I was silenced by his scorn and felt ashamed by my class privilege.

My virginity seemed to create a sexual pause but I had nothing to judge such a courtship by and accepted the days as they came. Time wafted past in a haze. Bernie declared I needed some proper clothes and the three of them took me off to the flea market to buy washed old Levi's with fly buttons, telling me how to cut them down the leg and sew them up tight. The truth was that a five-foot-three female person with a waist and round hips did not look great in men's Levi's. However, I was to wear them with pride until they disintegrated, convinced that this was the real thing.

Bernie drew tourists' portraits in the squares for money. He looked the part, was quite a hit and we set out happily to eat. On the way there an old tramp put out his hand. Bernie fished the money out of his pocket and gave him half. My small-business Yorkshire self was aghast, but the mystical Methodist in me recognized an economic justice beyond common sense.

Bernie, at twenty, appeared to invent how to behave in every encounter he made. He looked out at the world like no one I had ever met. Through his eyes the ordinary became extraordinary, the mundane miraculous. 'You have such a capacity to wonder,' Bernie announced once out of the blue. I didn't tell him this was called being gormless in Yorkshire. He informed me that beauty could be seen everywhere, pointing to the corner of an advertisement or the patterns left by his espresso coffee on the side of the cup. I was surprised; I'd thought it was in art galleries or Swedish-designed teapots.

One day he took me on a winding trek through the back streets of the Latin Quarter. There was an exhibition he was eager to see in one of the little galleries. Used to the Louvre, I was put out by the sight of creatures made of sacking with cork noses and funny hats around the walls. This was ridiculous. Annoyed to be walking around looking so solemnly at things that kids might make, I growled in irritation. Bernie said this was a good reaction. The artist wanted me to respond. This made me even crosser. I think it was Marcel Duchamp who was responsible for my bad humour.

Knowing nothing about the conflicting theories of aesthetics simmering away among tiny groups in the art colleges, I presumed Bernie's views on art and existence were entirely individual. In fact of course he was communicating to me a mix of attitudes circulating during the early sixties, when the shock tactics of the avant-garde were shifting towards celebrating the popular. Pop Art was to inscribe familiar motifs with new meanings in an effort to break with élitism, only to become rapidly commercialized itself. This tension in aesthetics between separation from mass consumerism and the desire to find a relation to popular culture prefigured a political dilemma for the left which was to erupt in the late sixties and rumble through the subsequent decades.

Only recently did I discover that Bernard Jennings was among the signatories of the Fine Artz Associates' Manifesto from the Slade in 1964, announcing they were going to take 'art back into society . . . and give it a larger public'. It figured. My personal memories suddenly fell into a new relief. They had acquired surroundings. Odd when the social meets the personal unawares, as if two trains enter a tunnel at opposite ends and, instead of colliding, just merge.

Bernie and I eventually managed to make our way back to the Seizième the night before I was to leave on a visit to the Loire home of one of the French students. We stopped in a café and he drank a coffee. I sipped a hot chocolate, reflecting anxiously that he looked so pale and thin he might just fade into the ether. I had known him for one week. It felt much, much longer.

I smuggled him nervously past the concierge, who was luckily snoozing. Up we went in the cranking, creaking little lift, which always had a peculiar effect on my bladder – perhaps because it seemed so unlikely that the ancient thing would make it to the top floor. I opened the door of the little room with its cold mosaic floor, the bidet, the bed, the dresser and my postcards. 'Quite a picture gallery you've got here,' he remarked sardonically, making me want to tear them off the wall. Before he crossed its threshold, nothing had happened in that room. It had been my ascetic cell, where I read or slept or ate bread and yoghurt, watching the elaborate lives and brightly striped sun chairs of a rich French family in the flat across the road.

In bed Bernie produced a crinkled brown object. This antique sheath was so ugly it appalled me. Ignorant and unpractical, I declared I didn't want him to use it and stuffed it under the pillow. I felt a moment of fear. Would I find his penis repellent? I looked down anxiously. There it was, just part of him, part of the skinny body that was utterly unthreatening. I wanted his closeness, loved the touch of him as we embraced. But sex remained a puzzle. Was it just this moving up and down? After all that worrying about your shape, your lipstick, your clothes; after all that prohibiting and whispering and all that longing? Was this it then, backwards and forwards? Could losing your virginity be a kind of non-event? What about all those D. H. Lawrence explosions? Was this really not being a virgin any more? I was far too shy to ask Bernie. Anyway, while he slept I was lying there with other worries. This was the first time since I was a child that I had slept without rollers in my hair. What on earth would I look like in the morning? To my surprise, I didn't look much different. The rollers had got bigger and bigger anyway, to accommodate the natural Bardot look.

I left him asleep in my single iron bed and hurried away, late and flustered, to meet a crew-cut American student who had offered to drive me to the Loire on a scooter. In the métro window I could see my reflection. I smiled the secret smile of a satisfied sinner. These other people in the carriage could not possibly imagine! If it had been yesterday they would have been sitting with a virgin. A unique, momentous divide of before and after had occurred in my life. Or had it?

My geography was little better than my physiology. I had no idea that France was so big. The scooter journey was an ordeal of dust and fumes, hour after hour. That evening, amidst the châteaux and lush countryside of the Loire, surrounded by polite young people making small talk, I rued the dutiful politeness which had made me leave Paris. Pleading tiredness, I escaped to bed.

In turmoil, the following day I wandered down the garden and, finding a stream which ran at the bottom, sat, drawing a strange peacefulness from its flow. Acute, exhausted, the borders of perception seemed to open; it was as if I was seeing the everyday for the first time, through new eyes. The green of the grass, the shine on the wetness of the stones and the moving water became more real than real. I seemed to vanish into them. Ordinary existence melted away, leaving a calm delight, an intensity of joy. And ever since in my life when such moments have recurred I remember being eighteen and so hopelessly in love.

Time was a merciless slowcoach that weekend, but at long last I was back and heading for the Monaco, where I had arranged to meet Bernie. The Monaco was a tiny triangle of a place, near Danton's statue and overlooking the Carrefour de l'Odéon. Round metal-rimmed tables stood outside on the pavement, or tucked themselves between thin pillars inside. The bar was on the left as you entered, backed by the standard mirror. There was little room for anything else apart from an old black and white clock on the wall and a notice board where drifters and bums left messages for one another. The café, now, has been completely refurbished and renamed Le Comptoir du Relais, but in 1961 it was cheap and served as a kind of beatnik social club.

I waited nervously, glancing at the big round clock, pulling my skirt down – that twitchy, on-edge kind of waiting for someone you are longing to see. I was early. The hands on the clock went slowly round. And round. I followed the second hand with my eyes, willing the seconds to become minutes. I was no longer early; he was late. My heart was doing heavy thuds. Then Geoff was leaning at the bar and looking towards me. I started, collected myself, moving forward to greet him, smiling. Awkwardly he handed me a note. Bernie had gone to the Welcome café in Brussels.

I stared at Geoff in dumb incomprehension. All at once nothing made sense. Geoff was looking exceedingly embarrassed and saying something, but I was not hearing conversation normally. His words sank in only after they'd hung for a while suspended in the air. There was thus a delay before I realized that he was offering himself as consolation. Some barely functioning part of my consciousness knew he thought this might cheer me up. But my immediate response was outrage. Geoff shrugged. We were both relieved when Tony strolled in.

Tony walked and walked through Paris with me in the drizzle. Obsessively, I interpreted and reinterpreted – he'd said, I'd said, he did, I'd done, I felt, what did he feel? – until the evening became night. Whereupon Tony sat patiently on a bench with me as I wept and wept, making the misty wet night even wetter. But he had to go back to Bressuire.

Every day was painful afterwards. I staggered through them in a disconsolate trance. Classes and lectures at the Sorbonne had become out of the question. I drifted through the streets of the Latin Quarter. But so many places were haunted with memories: the Rue de la Huchette, M. Pierre's with its sawdust floor where we ate steak and *frites*, and the Monaco itself. I turned over in my head the places he had mentioned. The Welcome café, the Partisan, a left coffee bar in Soho, Sam Widge's café at King's Cross. Perhaps I could find him. I wrote to him at the Slade. I didn't know then that time padded the betrayals of passion, that time would heal the wrenching loss. About a year later he wrote to say sorry. He had 'cut out' because he'd wanted to be a hipster and was afraid of getting involved. He'd visited Giacometti, admired de Kooning, told me to read Wilhelm Reich, listen to Eric Dolphy and take out a sub to *Anarchy*. I was glad to get his letter, but by then I had become another person.

After Bernie had left I settled into the Monaco as a surrogate home, still hoping he might return. The café was frequented by exiles from the Spanish Civil War, a lingering Mau Mau fugitive from the Kikuyus' resistance to British rule in Kenya during the late fifties with a deeply lined, stretched face who sat staring out at the passers-by and never smiled, a despairing Portuguese revolutionary who drank far too much and became morose and self-destructive. Various GIs drifted in. Bums and petty criminals (resting) sat next to writers, artists and musicians.

Two kindly folk singers were the first to befriend me. Wiz Jones, then a street performer, would twang a guitar on which he had written 'Give me a guitar and I'll rock this old town, Archimedes'. Wiz, who had long, curling brown hair, big square glasses and a cowboy hat, played with Clive, a gentle banjo player with pale red hair and a limp. Clive used to sit outside the Monaco and sing 'Blue Moon' over and over again, and a mix of hope and melancholy would float towards Danton's statue to mingle with revolutionary ghosts and the noise of the traffic.

Wiz and Clive helped restore my self-esteem by discovering that I possessed a practical economic skill – taking the hat round when they sang. This was based on experience gained through chapel collections at Hunmanby and speaking French. I was chuffed, for I had quickly picked up that in the gossipy circles of the Monaco, where normal values were inverted, women who could get money were well esteemed. For example, a sensuous White Russian lesbian who lived with her tiny skinny partner in a nearby hotel was grudgingly respected by the men as a good hustler. I was aware that I had no hustle in me at all. Even Lolita, a young Indian woman who was only sixteen, was more worldly wise than I was and took me under her wing. Before she moved on, Lolita wrote me her address on the back of an envelope. Boreham Wood, Herts, was Timbuktu to me, so was the Northern Line and the 52 bus. But she added, 'or leave note in Partisan, Carlisle St, Soho, nr Tottenham Ct Rd tube'. Now I knew how to find the Partisan.

Snobbery being inside out at the Monaco, people who were *already* rich were considered to be the lowest of the low. A member of this despised smart set, a bumptious American artist who reminded me of Toad of Toad Hall, tried chatting me up, boasting that his action paintings had just been exhibited and that he owned an island in Spain. I suspected him of being a 'phoney' – the ultimate moral condemnation – reporting suspiciously to Tony, 'He uses decorator's rollers not brushes and squirts things on to massive canvasses.'

As I moved closer towards the café's social interior, I perceived its factional conflicts, particularly the major schism between drink and dope. I was briefly adopted by the drink contingent. The leading figure, a would-be rock star who had become a pacifist while serving in the British Army in Cyprus, before the country was partitioned between the Greeks and Turks, and then gravitated to the Partisan in Soho, decided to court me. His approach was direct, but miscalculated. He'd just grab my legs under the table and assume arousal would clinch it. Lust, however, was outside my ken. 'Stop being daft,' I'd bark. Eventually he and his friend, a retired safe-breaker who took great pride in his craft skills, while despairing of the fecklessness of humankind because they entrusted their valuables to locks which were so easy to force, adopted me on a younger-sister basis. I appreciated all the advice about how to defeat burglars, but found the firm resolve, which arose from sour grapes, to defend my virtue cumbersome. One night my two protectors took me with them to one of their favourite haunts, an all-night club on the Place de la Contrescarpe. Male prostitutes with breast implants flamboyantly seduced the clientele; a woman danced on the tables; the men shouted and banged their glasses to the music. Everyone got extremely drunk and had a good time except me, who retained my Hunmanby-instilled suspicion of alcohol.

Methodists had, however, said nothing against magic mushrooms. Wiz and Clive, who belonged to the rival dope-smoking clique, held a black American GI called Dave in great respect because he had taken mushrooms, which he said were like the mescalin Aldous Huxley describes in *The Doors of Perception*. Dave and his friend Mel – the son of a Methodist minister from Batley, a little town near Leeds – were reassuringly calm and tolerant when they smoked their kief. Like Voltaire's Candide, I applied the test of experience, sitting around with them observing as they got high. When Dave described taking his mushrooms up some mountain, I decided that this was a profound spiritual encounter, concluding that dope was OK because it encouraged mystical contemplation. I was biased, of course, because Bernie had smoked.

My peculiar new social set at the Monaco was slowly helping me to ease out of my paralysed misery. I wrote to Tony, announcing grandly, 'I exist as a being independent of him. I existed before and I can exist now without him.' Nonetheless, I jumped at Mel's offer to hitch with him to Brussels, thinking that perhaps I might find Bernie in the Welcome café, which, like the Partisan, had assumed a mythical status to me. The expedition proved a disaster; we arrived in pouring rain and could not find an hotel. '*Pas avec une jeune fille!*' How to tell the tight-lipped receptionist that I was just travelling with Mel? We shuddered all night in the station and went back to Paris on the early train.

I was so absorbed in myself and in the micro world of the café that the news on 22 April of an attempted coup against General de Gaulle's government by generals in Algeria opposed to self-determination seemed quite unreal. The surrounding cafés were packed with taut-faced Parisians watching the news on TV, while de Gaulle called on citizens to get on their bicycles and be ready to go to the airport to defend Paris. The Monaco remained an oasis of oblivion. I could not comprehend either rebellion or invasion and simply did not take the political situation seriously.

I knew, but was refusing to know because I didn't want to admit it, that Mel was keen on me. A few weeks after the suppression of the putsch, he suggested that we should hitch down south. He could earn money chalking, I could fill in the corners and my French would be useful. I hesitated. I was nursing my romantic wounds, but I liked Mel and kidded myself that this was going to be a friendly business arrangement. I was weary too of Paris, with its chafing memories, while hitchhiking (despite the Brussels experience) still promised, thanks to Kerouac's *On The Road*, a quintessential freedom.

So I put on my flea-market Levi's and stuffed my favourite tight brown dress and high heels into a little bag. Bar agreed to send on my letters to my parents, in order for it to appear as if I was still in Paris, and, one sunny morning in May, Mel and I took to the road. I had yet to see the fool on the tarot pack setting out with *his* little bag, but he could have been my imago.

We were heading for Lyons, which Mel said was full of very kind French working-class people who gave generously to pavement artists. Hitching has so many dead waiting times, you can learn a lot about someone's view of life. Mel had a clear-cut outlook about people. The rich were bad, the working class good, while *clochards* and prostitutes were the *crème de la crème*, being the people who would help you if you were really starving. He disapproved of my attachment to frippery and always called me 'man'. 'Look, man, if you wear a dress people will think you're a prostitute if you're with someone who looks like a bum.' Mel was invested with considerable authority, for he had been a real tramp before doing his national service. I aspired to become a serious hitchhiker who would not be a burden. On the other hand, I remained far too Leeds not to want to get dressed up sometimes. Anyway, he kept praising prostitutes. 'I don't mind being taken for a prostitute,' I told him, and he grumpily shut up.

Things were going well in Lyons and we took a day off to explore the old town, high up on a hill with tiny cobbled streets and washing stretched across them in criss-cross lines. Mel thirstily drank a bottle of milk in the hot sun. 'That'll give you a fever, that'll give you a fever,' chanted a group of old women in high-pitched warning. They were right. Mel awoke soon after with a raging temperature. He was so ill I worried about doctors. After a few days he was obviously recovering. However, we had consumed our margin of survival. Out of money, we needed to chalk desperately, but luck was against us. The weather changed and it rained and rained. 'We have to get out of Lyons,' Mel announced. Miserable and bedraggled, we tried to hitch, but no one would take us. We had no choice but to return to Lyons, where Mel chalked under a lighted window and I filled in the corners for all I was worth. The good people of Lyons rescued us again.

We eventually reached Marseilles, where Mel drew David (popular there because of the statue). People in the old port gathered around and made flattering comments. I couldn't imagine the English working class getting so involved in the aesthetics of pavement art. Mel and I celebrated by taking a cheap bottle of red wine down to the harbour after we had eaten and I relaxed into the unfamiliar softness of my first Mediterranean spring night. But Marseilles was fraught because of the conflict in Algeria. Flashing searchlights repeatedly prodded the darkness.

Abruptly they stopped, holding us pinioned in unrelenting light. I froze, rabbit-like, my back against the stone wall of the old port. Mel's instruction, 'Don't move else they'll shoot!', was unnecessary. I stayed put for what seemed like a long, long moment, staring at the soldiers' machine guns across the black lapping water. The possibility that I could just dissolve into light, annihilated, flashed through my consciousness and logged into memory. I realized that a faraway reality, which I understood only hazily, could ricochet from an arbitrary hand and explode the disconnected bubbles of personal experience which had seemed to me the sole sources of truth. Then the instant of incongruity and fear vanished into inconsequence; the light moved on. This was not our war.

Our troubles proved more mundane. The truth was that Mel and I were not really economically viable. I increased costs and de Gaulle's regime had tightened up the laws on *clochards*. Chalking was still legal in the old port, but it was packed with competition. With our David and his green backing, we had to contend with a Cuban who did the head of Christ and a gawky Dane who was continually chasing pigeons away from his picture. I wrote a letter to Tony headed 'Pavement, Marseilles', adding, 'The above address is too literal for comfort.' Mel was implacably reassuring: 'Don't worry, man, something will turn up.' His words would return throughout my life whenever things looked really bleak.

I learned to adapt to taking every day as it came, accepting the evenings when we could afford only bread and relishing the pleasure of the good times when money jingled in Mel's pocket and we could get a hot meal in a cheap restaurant. I was developing a few skills of my own. I acquired a sharp eye for the cheapest hotels and restaurants, and my French was handy for the menus – though one dreadful time we ended up eating brains, while another bad guess resulted in tripe. It was in Marseilles too that I taught myself how to be invisible. Mel would be sitting round with groups of men, smoking, and it would be my turn to get the sandwiches. Complaint would have revealed me as a dependent chick, so I would hunch my shoulders, put my head down and, unseen, march through the chaotic clamour of the prostitutes' street to the sandwich stall.

The sun and bustle of Marseilles encouraged light-heartedness. Boatmen inveigled surplus chalkers on to their boats in order to convince tourists they would fill up soon. Impersonating members of the public, we would go rocking contentedly back and forth over the sea to a nearby island. But on the bad days, as more and more chalkers packed into the old port, we could afford only bread and I would feel the hunger pressing against my ribs. Mel tried to get me to play a game he had devised while he was a tramp of imagining menus, but fantasy food was not as good as real food. My time in Marseilles helped to undermine my inclination to mystical idealism and made me see that materialists had a point.

Occasionally my Kerouac hitchhiking androgynous persona would be blown. I was taking the hat round one day when a member of the French Foreign Legion approached Mel. He was offering to buy me for a Foreign Legion 'farm'. I couldn't believe my ears. He pressed a deposit into Mel's hands, telling him to bring me back that evening.

We fled to Toulon, where we ran right out of money but into good luck. Our hotel-keeper was a lovely woman in her forties who happened to have a soft spot for artists. Because Mel could chalk, she supported us with aromatic Provençal stews until Bar sent on some money and we could pay her for the room. While I never met one of the mythical existentialists, my travels with Mel left me with a profound gratitude for the small kindnesses of strangers and an intimation of interconnection. Many years later on a train to Calcutta, I told the sweeper he could keep a plastic pill phial I had thrown away. He took it with delight, saying philosophically, 'We all take a little from one another and give a little to one another in this life.' He had summed up the outlook I had absorbed filling in the corners of Mel's drawing of David.

I was to find my own interpretation of E. M. Forster's exhortation in *Howards End*, 'Only connect', on that journey. My stance in Leeds as the defiant outsider on the margins of society was tempered by the realization that some kinds of social acceptance could be precious indeed. One night in a Toulon bar an American sailor stormed out of the lavatory complaining that homosexuals were in there having sex. The whole bar surveyed him with equanimity. He demanded that the barman should call the police. Slowly the barman responded with an eloquent shrug of absolute indifference. The sailor looked round, expecting support from the crowd. Incredulous and still bellowing in moral disgust, he found himself encircled by ironic smiles. Two men sauntered like lascivious heroes out of the lavatory. The sailor, realizing that *he* was the outcast among these mad foreigners, slunk out of the bar.

There were still many things that perplexed me. Both Bernie and Mel were egalitarian in their attitudes to women, so I assumed that as long as I respected *clochards* and renounced cakes I would be treated as an equal according to beatnik mores. But beatniks had their anomalies. Sitting smoking one night on the beach with a group of young Americans, I was asked out of the blue by one of them, 'Have you always been wild?' Wild? Wasn't he sitting there quietly smoking just like me?

I had drifted into a sexual relationship with Mel based on proximity and affection. I had done with unrequited passion. But I remained as ignorant as ever about sex. Mel was not forthcoming on the topic either; it was sheer luck that I didn't get pregnant. He did make one sexual observation that puzzled me. Once in a bar he nodded towards the prostitutes having a break from their clients. Their tight skirts revealed bulges and Mel maintained their bellies stuck out because they had sex with so many men. This struck me as rum, but I pulled my tummy in. In fact I'd been eating so much bread that I'd put on several pounds. I started doing the Canadian Air Force exercises we had learned at school.

In Nice Mel insisted that we eat in the tramps' restaurant to economize. The food was so bad it made the bread-only days seem a treat. The *clochards*, for their part, considered us a peculiar pair, staring as we walked in – Mel, his long hair and beard even blonder in the sun, and me, ginger and fiercely freckly. Walking along by the sea one day, we bumped into Wiz, from the Monaco, still with his hat and the guitar, but looking rather sheepish and subdued because he was with his mother, a middle-aged English woman with permed hair, a long pleated skirt and a pacamac. The sight of Wiz's mother and her strange entourage striding along the Promenade des Anglais created a stir of astonishment in fashion-conscious Nice.

We headed back to Paris, with Mel singing 'Cocaine all around my brain' over and over again and telling me about the kind of folk musicians he admired. I knew none of the names then – Ramblin' Jack Elliott, Derroll Adams, Davy Graham – all influential in the early-sixties folk revival, the 'missing link' between Woody Guthrie, folk blues and Bob Dylan. But I stored them away, along with the rest of my new-found learning. A few weeks away had turned me into a seasoned, sunburned veteran of the road and I listened wryly as two men walked by debating whether to buy me while we were chalking in Lyons. Shaking their heads, they decided I was too scruffy.

It was late June when we returned to Paris and I rushed off to meet Bar in the sunny courtyard of the Sorbonne, bursting with travellers' tales. I sobered up when she handed me a pile of letters from Leeds. As the weeks had gone by, their tone had become more and more insistent that I should come home. My mother was seriously puzzled. My letters home, all written in beatnik lingo, had failed to respond to her news that my sister-in-law had given birth to a baby girl. I was being recalled.

Back in Leeds, I wasn't in the right frame of mind for Latin translation or Gibbon and Macaulay. In the neighbours' view I had gone to the dogs: 'Sheila's come back all beatnik.' Unfairly, they blamed the French. Tony and Danielle came to visit and we took snapshots of ourselves on the Roundhay lawn in black sweaters and jeans like a plague of big black beetles which had mysteriously landed on suburbia. My father would bristle whenever a shaggy-looking Mel passed his beloved rose bushes on the garden path at Ladywood Road. My mother, however, liked Mel. Beard or no beard, she saw a man who, she decided, had looked after her daughter.

I visited Mel's parents in the Batley manse, where his father proudly showed me his copy of *Foxe's Book of Martyrs*. Sure enough, he began to try and save me, and I reflected on the irony of putting all that effort into distancing myself from Hunmanby's flame of purity to end up with yet another Methodist minister talking about redemption. Listening to him and looking out at the yellow scrubbed steps of Batley, I began to understand Mel's clear-cut take on the world, his reserve about discussing sex and that strain of puritanical severity which his endeavours towards a laid-back lifestyle had not melted.

I was still so intent on shedding the familiar as fast as I was able that it never occurred to me how much I too had assimilated from home and school. Nor did I bother to observe what was close at hand or consider that things might not be as they outwardly seemed. For instance, Olga was to write describing a Workers' Educational Association class that autumn at Hunmanby on 'The Modern Novel and Social Problems' in which the school bursar, a Methodist lay preacher, two teachers, a postman, some farmers and sixth-formers, along with herself, could be found arguing about race relations, totalitarianism, religion, fatalism, capital punishment and sex. I might have made the connection to Sartre's observation on Brecht in my own 1960 *Evergreen Review*, and wondered about 'the familiar'. Though this was to become a preoccupation which pursued me in many guises over the years, it was not for me then. At eighteen the unfamiliar had to be somewhere else.

My sexual miasma persisted. That August I wrote to Tony, inquiring whether ceasing to be a virgin was, 'i) after a penis has gone in, or ii) after there's been an orgasm?' I added, 'Isn't it ridiculous how ignorant people are kept, because people don't just discuss sex naturally?'

I had been talking with Mel, who was about to return to France, and we had both decided that everything would have been easier if I'd been a man. I complained to Tony that women were 'expected to take an interest in cooking and kids, clothes and look attractive'. Moreover, even 'intelligent' people accepted that men could say things about sex which were taboo for women. If women said they wanted sexual relationships, for example, they were seen as whores. I resented having to opt for either being seen as 'nice' and acting hypocritically or getting categorized as 'naughty'. The letter grumbled on, 'No one seems to think about just being honest. I'm beginning to sound like a suffragette or something, but you know what I mean.'

After Mel left that August I began spending time in a café near Ilkley moors, where Lindsay had assiduously assembled a circle of advanced people who wore Chelsea boots and enthused about Gurdjieff amidst the sauce bottles. I found myself between the devil and the deep blue sea, being rather too earthy for their higher planes and too mystical for Viv Wellburn, who had turned into a staunch socialist at Leeds University. Viv was unimpressed by my life and times in Paris, upbraiding me for going 'beat' and letting myself be directed by events. I held Viv, who had had a play put on and a review by Irving Wardle in the *Times Literary Supplement*, in awe. Nevertheless, I found her talk about 'commitment' rather abrasive, writing in protest to Tony that I thought I did control my reactions to events and this, I considered, was all you could hope for.

Even so, when the positive-minded Viv hectored me to create, rather than drifting, I was stung enough to write a short story based on an anecdote I had heard about an anti-Semitic Polish refugee who had found himself in Leeds, a strongly Jewish city. Viv disapproved of the subject matter, but convinced me to send it to a literary magazine called *New Departures*, which presaged the underground. An encouraging rejection letter came back from the editor, Michael Horowitz, and I read out his criticisms to my mother in great excitement. He advised that if I wanted to write about people's strongest feelings I should listen carefully to 'all the stops in Charlie Parker's rehearsals', adding that Jack Kerouac was wrong – it 'won't just come like an orgasm'. 'Fancy writing about orgasms like that to someone you don't even know,' commented my mother in surprise. But she was impressed that a real magazine person had written to me. I was particularly chuffed that he had asked me to send a stamp next time, as this suggested he considered me the type of person who would write some more.

I scuttled off to play Charlie Parker. I was bothered about those orgasms though. How could you even tell that it wasn't coming like an orgasm if you'd never had one?

Michael Horowitz wished me 'Happy New Departures'. That

October, I was indeed to depart from Roundhay to Oxford. There I would quickly start burying recollections of adolescence, embarrassed by that earlier self, adrift without bearings and devoid of points of comparison.

CHAPTER 2

1961–4

The first few days at St Hilda's felt like a tape rewinding. At Oxford the fifties had been preserved and in a women's college I was enclosed once again in an institution which returned me to the claustrophobia of Hunmanby. Certainly here you had your own room and the teachers were called dons, but you were still shut in at night, not free to come and go as you pleased. They called it '*in loco parentis*'.

I had imagined myself meeting students with profound and intense minds, searching for truth and plumbing the universe, unaware that southern public schools and London 'crammers' studiously groomed young women for Oxford and Cambridge along narrowly defined tracks. 'Why have you got poetry?' inquired one undergraduate, peering at the dark-green hardback edition of Christopher Logue's poems, chosen as my school literary prize, and the pale-blue paperback 'Livre de Poche' collection of Rimbaud purchased in Paris. 'Aren't you doing history?'

Feeling deflated, I unpacked my antique washed Levi's, my shift dress with muddy gold and wine stripes bought in the Bon Marché in Paris, and my black tight dress with its halter-neck collar, which, despite its origins in Leeds Lewis's, had an existential look, and hung them in the wardrobe attached to the wall – so like school. They dangled there in culture shock, waiting for someone with the requisite discrimination to open the door and appreciate the nuances of my carefully assembled beat identity.

The first-year college photo caught me staring out like an alien, my hair now long and completely straight. I disdained ordering a copy; no Oxford college camaraderie for me – the lone misunderstood rebel.

In long letters to Tony I announced that I was going to be miserable at Oxford.

I *had* spotted someone with two pigtails and a fawn duffel coat in St Hilda's who looked like a fellow spirit. This austere and beautiful figure, with dark eyes accentuated by black lines, possessed the high, pronounced cheekbones, made the 'in' facial feature by Brigitte Bardot, to which I vainly aspired. Judith Okely and I were to become friends, but our first meeting did not go well. Parrying, we checked one another out: Paris, tick; Camus and Sartre, tick. Then Judith asked me about my politics. Politics! I had been so intent on my beat reflections on the human condition that I had barely considered politics. Politics as I understood them took place in a removed terrain of elections and parties. Clutching at straws, I remembered that Olga had supported the Liberal Party. 'I'm a sort of liberal,' I mumbled. A terrible hush fell. Judith's lip curled and she announced emphatically that she was a socialist. I realized glumly that I had said the wrong thing.

I then gravitated to Anne Henderson from a Bromley grammar school ('Direct grant,' she explained). Anne was completely without any of my pretensions. Not at all existential, she still had the remains of a bouffant hairdo and liked clothes, a chat and a laugh. But the most important thing was that she wasn't posh. Together, Anne and I could take on Oxford, lower middle class and proud. Having put so much effort into leaving Leeds, I set about rediscovering my roots at a distance.

However, while the idyllic working-class hero was just arriving on the horizon in 1961, there was no such romantic literary genre to elevate a lower-middle-class woman. You were presumed thick in Oxford if you had even a middle-class Northern voice and my Yorkshire vowel sounds, which had resisted the best efforts of the Hunmanby elocution teacher, evoked complicit smirks. You were either a comedy routine or you lost your accent and talked posh.

I had no sooner decided to dig myself into a position of uncompromising hostility as a defiant Northerner when Hermione and Catriona, in jeans and dark sweaters with scarves tied under their chins, came to visit my room. They sat on the bed and with many groans, giggles and grimaces told me that they had been 'debs'. I was amazed that débutantes, whom I had read about being received at court and attending balls in Tanfield's Column in the *Daily Mail*, were sitting on my bed and were recognizably normal people. Even though sounds came out of their throats which were unfamiliar – my Leeds voice seemed to use different zones of the larynx – they were fun and I took to them both.

Hermione Harris, who became a lifelong friend, had a dissident Quaker strand in her background and, already at eighteen, looked out at the foibles of the world with an eye of undeceived clarity. Like a character in a Jane Austen novel applying herself to a contemporary setting, she explained that the beatnik-dressed upper-class girls who did the season could be the most 'phoney' people. Appearances, Hermione observed sagely, could be deceiving. This revelation disrupted my social categories. A few weeks in Oxford were making me dither.

In Oxford things were not so clear as they had appeared in Leeds or in the Monaco. This was not simply a matter of my subjective perception. Barriers which would have remained tightly closed anywhere else were exceedingly permeable. The result was a mélange which reminded me of my mother's descriptions of the boat to India. You were together, willy-nilly, for the duration of the voyage. Young women like myself, being of little account within the prevailing masculine ambience, could move back and forth, not only through class demarcations but between sets. Sex clinched this licence to shape-change; a five to one male to female ratio guaranteed a welcome. The advantage was that you could nose around and observe. Fascinated by dissolving boundary lines and ever curious, I found aspects of this social fluidity, inconceivable in most parts of British society at that time, intriguing. Thus, while wanting to be embedded, I also fancied flitting about. This enduring contradiction in my life posed itself as a particularly acute dilemma in my first term at Oxford.

Gadding about was enjoyable, but I was determined not to be mopped up by Oxford, with its amoeba-like capacity to absorb all kinds of bits and bobs in their youth and turn them out stolid and double-chinned with the same creaky accents. The unknown might beckon, but a staunch combination of Northern pride and beatnik principles made me disdain not only the upper-class public school boys in their sports jackets, but the 'smoothies' and 'arty types' who wore corduroy jackets.

Consequently, when I opened my door to an aesthetic-looking young man with light ginger hair falling in that peculiarly upper-middle-class way over his brow my hackles were up. In two bounds he was on the other side of my room and was seated cross-legged on top of the wardrobe, looking down on me like the caterpillar in Lewis Carroll. This was Derek Parfit and my first introduction to that distinctive Balliol confidence and charm. He wondered if I'd like to sell *Mesopotamia*, a satirical magazine which preceded *Private Eye*. In the late fifties and early sixties satire was 'in'; laughing at records of Tom Lehrer and Lenny Bruce or at Alan Bennett and Jonathan Miller's satirical show *Beyond the Fringe* was an acceptable way of demonstrating a radical stance without being exactly political. So off I went, up and down the ancient staircases of that other Oxford outside the snug confines of St Hilda's. By importuning all those lonely-looking, lost young men tucked away in rooms they seemed never to have left, I discovered that I enjoyed hawking things. A youth spent visiting National Coal Board offices with my father, selling Horace Green's pit motors, had incongruously prepared me for Balliol's *Mesopotamia*.

These trips round male colleges confirmed the statistics: there *were* a lot of men at Oxford. However, statistics have their limitations and finding a man you could fancy was far more difficult. My convoluted criteria of correct accoutrements obviously made this particularly tricky, but to be fair I was prepared to modify the clothes inventory after a few weeks. The real problem concerned attitudes. Oxford male students sniggered to me about 'buns in the oven' and told me women were inferior and should be treated like dirt in order to make them crawl back for more. 'I think that's very immature,' I would declare in lofty indignation, beating a hasty retreat. A more liberal slant was that women, like Robert Graves's 'White Goddesses', were essentially different from men, their sexuality closely linked to fecundity. Being put on a pedestal felt uncomfortably like being put in my place and fostered a lasting aversion to goddesses.

Beatniks' views on sex might have been rough and ready on fidelity, but they held convictions about honesty and direct relating which were much more democratic and egalitarian than the conventions on offer. However, by that November I had abandoned hope of any beatnik sightings in Oxford, attaching myself instead to a group of students who also came from Yorkshire. We huddled together like expatriates over our Tetley's beers.

Among them was Barry Collins from Halifax. A politics student at Queen's, Barry was conducting a one-man cultural offensive against Oxford mores on behalf of the working class with all the heroic self-destructive fervour of a nineteen-year-old. He took the piss out of the chiselled upper-class voices with those precise angles which somehow gave them the power to make banality seem incontestable. Barry saw it as a con and Oxford was part of the plot.

We went out to the pictures and he made me laugh and laugh. His Halifax accent was reassuringly familiar, but he carved out meanings with words so that unexpected implications and irony were suddenly everywhere. Barry had the black hair and white skin of his Irish ancestry and a way of hunching himself against the cold in his donkey jacket and screwing up his eyes. He told me he was going to be a poet.

And, well, what could I do but fall in love with Barry Collins – which meant, of course, that sex came up again. Through Barry I was to discover how passion takes hold of your body as well as your soul. Great gobs of longing and shaking paroxysms would sweep me away on the back row of the pictures, outside the gates of St Hilda's, by the light of his gas fire. But I remained afraid. Like me, Barry's outlook on sex had been formed by D. H. Lawrence. Skin must meet skin. Barry had thus concluded that sheaths were un-Lawrentian.

Neither of us knew about any other form of contraception. We had reached an impasse. By this time I was able to envisage the terrible consequences of pregnancy more clearly. Not only would I be chucked out of Oxford: much worse, I would never, *ever* leave Roundhay. I could not imagine either an abortion or what having a baby would entail, but an abyss of dread would open before me, a terror even stronger than my desire. This fear of pleasure was meant to make us moral and I loathed it. I still loathe it.

At the end of February Barry gave me a copy of Jacques Prévert's poems for my birthday and told me it was over. He gave up Oxford, returned to Halifax, married his real girlfriend from school, Anne, and worked as a journalist before becoming a playwright. Nearly two decades later we were to meet again briefly. 'Nowadays nobody would be as ignorant as we were about sex,' he said.

*

By the end of the second term I had decided I had had enough of this falling in love with vanishing men. Numb and devastated I might be, but I was just nineteen and it was dawning on me that there was a frivolous fun in discovering you were attractive to men. It was spring and I set out to have a normal, nice time with a normal, nice and handsome young man. I bought an elegant shift dress, we sipped sherry at parties on Oxford lawns and I discovered that being driven over cobbles on his scooter aroused a vaguely pleasant sensation between my thighs. He did use sheaths but they seemed not to quite go on or to burst and my anxiety did not abate. Eventually, exasperated by my evasive sexuality, he told me angrily that I must be frigid. And that was that.

I was not the only one steering without a compass between the dreaded Scylla of frigidity and the humiliating Charybdis branded 'nymphomania'. A troupe of St Hilda's women in my year, investing me with an undeserved wise-woman status because I was not a virgin, were coming to my door, asking for advice. Should they sleep with their boyfriends? I found counselling a heavy responsibility. Of course, I believed all the fuss about virginity was absurd. But what if anything happened? Not only were we all ignorant about contraception, but we had no idea who we could ask for advice. We felt terrified of asking the college doctor about contraception in case we would be exposed to the dons. Abortion, an inconceivable horror of gin and screams, was still illegal. We couldn't be expected to see round the corners of time, to realize that it felt so uncomfortable because we were living through a turning point when sexual attitudes were changing quickly and old ideas of propriety were in the process of being junked. Change seemed so painfully slow. Even in my last year at Oxford, one friend who did become pregnant concealed her bulging stomach in flowing shifts and sat her finals without telling a soul, giving birth shortly after.

By the end of my first year I had grasped that beneath the superficial resemblances between Methodist Hunmanby and life in an Oxford women's college there were very significant differences. Methodist Hunmanby, preparing us for a life of moral witness, had instilled the virtues of honesty: regardless of the consequences, you answered to your inner conscience. Ruling-class Oxford, in contrast, was based on getting round the rules; the crime was to be found out – especially if you were female.

St Hilda's was replete with regulations which seemed to me and my dissident friends to be archaic. For instance, every evening we had to sign out and report in by twelve. You could easily evade this by going out earlier in the day. However, when you returned late, you then had to climb in. This involved dodging the porter's prodding torch and making your way over spiked railings, across a roof, through a window, out of the building, across the lawn, to scale up a fire-escape ladder flat on the wall for three storeys before clambering to safety. Games of commandos and cricket at Hunmanby fortunately enabled me to accomplish this cross between an outward-bound course and the *Gladiators* dressed in my customary tight skirts, stockings and stilettos without mishap. One St Hilda's student was not so lucky. I found her in the morning desperately staunching an open wound between her breasts with a bloody towel. She had slipped and impaled herself on a point of the railings but was too terrified to ask for a doctor during the night. Even that morning she wouldn't go to the college doctor. The rules were callous, not just absurd.

Not only did the Oxford regime induce hypocrisy and fear, it was also manifestly unfair. The penalties we faced in the women's colleges were much more severe than those governing male sexuality. In my first year Cathy, a wiry, small, dark-haired girl whom I knew slightly, was found in bed with her boyfriend in St Hilda's by a don. She was kicked out of college, lost her grant and could not get into any other university. He was sent away from his college for two weeks, 'rusticated'. The institutional injustice was blatant and the issue was personal behaviour not some distant cause. This could so easily have been me. Politics had landed in my lap. The sexual dissidents in the college cohered and a group of us indignantly signed a petition in protest. Whereupon the principal assembled us for a stern talking to. 'What will the gardeners think?' she demanded. It was a rhetorical question; she wasn't inviting debate. But my mind wandered back to the sexy Pete at Hunmanby and the succession of fifth-years in the stables. Was the principal worried that the gardeners would get ideas and, shades of Lady Chatterley, fuck furiously between the flower beds or was she concerned to protect their moral scruples in case they might revolt like the serfs of yore against the decadence of gentlefolk? As far as I was concerned, this was another piece of evidence that principals, like headmistresses, were completely batty.

The incident within St Hilda's escalated into an issue when our college principal found an ally in an English lecturer called David Holbrook. Though known for his radical views on education, Holbrook argued in an article in the university magazine, *Isis*, that sex should be confined to the act of reproduction. Judith Okely, along with a group of other students, wrote a critical reply. The university authorities responded by heavy-handedly putting a ban on any discussion of sex in *Isis*. The St Hilda's dons then interrogated Judith about whether she was arguing her case from personal experience. Cannily, she responded by pointing out that she had to write essays on many subjects outside her personal knowledge. They left it at that. However, the case had hit the headlines. Sex and women at Oxford had become newsworthy. Ridicule, the unwelcome publicity and our rebellion were to have an effect on the college authorities, who had misjudged the subterranean shift in attitudes which had been occurring. Slowly Oxford was to be forced to change during the course of the sixties.

Judith embarked next on a campaign to get women into the Oxford Union – we were still not allowed to be members. The *Daily Express* arrived to take pictures and Judith recruited me as the voice of the grass roots. I said rhubarb, rhubarb to oblige her, but I felt like a charlatan. I had mobilized out of a genuine sense of outrage at Cathy's treatment, but the demand to enter the Oxford Union was another matter. While I supported Judith's cause in principle, the truth was that I had no desire to go into the place personally. I was similarly lukewarm about the subsequent struggle for the right to get married at St Hilda's. I voted for it, grumbling that I didn't believe in marriage anyway.

I still hankered after the existential extremism which was increasingly beginning to look like my lost youth. Towards the end of my first year, my reputation from *Mesopotamia* distribution led to selling tickets for a performance of Jack Gelber's play about a junkie, *The Connection*. The Oxford cobbles had not been laid with high-heeled stilettos in mind and I clattered awkwardly between the bumps as I headed towards two tall, striking-looking men. Both were dressed in the dark-blue donkey jackets which, inspired by Marlon Brando in *On The Waterfront*, were replacing duffel coats as alternative student fashion. The taller of the two had a dark fringe and a faintly clipped, slightly bashful manner. At the performance he was sitting next to Judith, who later informed me that he was called Bob Rowthorn and was a maths graduate from Newport in Wales. They were going out together. Hmm, I thought to myself.

During my first term, I had drifted towards the Oxford University Dramatic Society. Anne Henderson had started going out with Braham Murray – who was to become director at the Royal Exchange Theatre in Manchester – and Braham was auditioning for his first production, Brendan Behan's *The Hostage*. 'Be a whore,' he told me. All those Marseilles and Toulon bars stood me in good stead and to my delight I got the part of Bobo. Braham believed in Method acting and encouraged us to enter our characters as much as possible. After a lecture, I zealously tried out my whore walk. Rolling my hips, I stalked Bobo-like down the High Street, still wearing my short black student gown. I must have looked like an undulating oxymoron. There was a crunch and a bang. I glanced to the left. A man was staring at me out of his open car window, mouth agape. He had just collided with the bumper in front of him.

Along with the Method acting, I learned from Braham how to say 'fuckin' hell' in stage Irish and do the twist. After twisting vigorously we had to line up and sing 'The bells of hell go ting-a-ling-a-ling for you but not for me' with pathos. Most nights genuine tears were pouring down my face because I would invariably be elbowed on the nose by taller people. I played my modest part to the full. It could not be seen as exactly demanding: on the other hand, I was convinced that it was going to take me towards greater things. With the bright lights beckoning, clad in a towel, I delivered my single line, was hauled off the stage by one of the punters and necked with the wistful 'hostage', a blond-haired Michael Johnson (later to be known as Michael York). I was feeling pretty chuffed with myself. My photo in fishnet stockings was displayed outside the Oxford Playhouse and I received a special mention in *Isis*. I had found my métier.

The St Hilda's dons had quite a different take on this. I was summoned before the principal and told that I had been seen looking 'conspicuously untidy' around college – which rankled, because the woman had no idea whatever of style. They had decided that my work was suffering and I was banned from acting for a term. A term was the equivalent to eternity. Anything could happen in a term.

They were right about my work; it wasn't good at all. But this was not just because of the acting. My whole frame of mind was the problem. Whereas I had thrived on Olga's social and intellectual history at school, I couldn't take to the works of Gibbon or Macaulay, which we had to read for our 'prelims' in the first term as texts rather than in the context of the history of history. I could just about get into the eighth-century monastic chronicles of the Venerable Bede through my beatnik interest in a spiritual vision of the world – though the big disadvantage was that Bede wrote in medieval Latin. Only the French aristocratic historian Alexis de Tocqueville, with his probing social eye, had really aroused my interest. An added bonus was that our young tutor, Hugh Thomas, could be lured into conversations about Ruskin and other nineteenth-century organic conservatives who featured in his thesis, and I always enjoyed learning what I was not meant to be studying. Moreover, I felt attuned to his tutorials because we were both high from lack of sleep. He and his wife had recently had a baby, while I was doing so many other things in the day I could find time for my essays only at night. Despite Hugh Thomas's sports jacket with leather elbows, I thought exhaustion gave him a gaunt Byronic air.

My tutor for European history, Charles Stuart, was a Conservative without any romance or Ruskin about him. Devoted to Prime Minister Alec Douglas-Home, Charles Stuart was a stiff, grey-haired Christ Church don who recognized only diplomatic sources as having any validity. He would rasp with irritation about 'these chaps like Asa Briggs who look at newspapers'. I was quite unable to get the hang of diplomatic history, which seemed like an elaborate dance without defined steps. Charles Stuart, who couldn't say his 'R's, would commence with a brisk, 'Now, Miss Lobottom –' My heart would already be sinking. 'If Austria were to –' My face would go blank. I knew what was coming and I knew I had no answer. 'What would Plussia do?' Far away in the distance, old diplomatic exchanges rustled in anticipation of the recognition they felt was their due, but I remained in a silent, sound-proofed antechamber of incomprehension.

In those tutorials with Charles Stuart, all sensuous human existence turned into something fusty and dry. Liking acting, for instance, became 'your predilection for the boards', while one day, when I told him that I felt cheerful when the sun was shining, he responded with, 'Not a historian, but perhaps a philosopher, Miss Lobottom.' I simply did not know how to assert, 'I'm interested in social and intellectual history.' Partly because I did not know how to categorize and name aspects of knowledge, but also because before 1968 it was quite inconceivable that an undergraduate could have any say over what they studied.

It was the medieval historian Trevor Aston who was to remind me how much I liked history. I was sent off to him for four tutorials in the summer term with Hermione. He threw my first essay, cribbed from textbooks, on the table. 'We read too many books,' he announced. I blinked. The sunlight was beaming through the narrow windows of the old room in Merton and playing on the stone. He wanted to know if we'd seen a Japanese film that was showing – that was the way to understand feudalism. I looked back, delighted at the eccentric figure with his long, lugubrious face and thinning hair. Some shutter in my brain opened. I had lost my way in the peculiar legal terms and had had no conception of how to orientate myself to the early Middle Ages as a significantly different society from any I had experienced. The flash of understanding made me diligent. I came across a book by a Russian called Kosminsky. One thing that seemed to annoy all teachers was to quote Communists. To my amazement, Trevor Aston calmly made some critical observations – this, after all, was an editor of the radical social history journal *Past and Present*. When I asked him shyly if he had read Norman Cohn's *Pursuit of the Millennium* (on the beat reading list because it described the religious fervour of rebellious heretics), he replied, 'You should read a much better book by my friend Eric Hobsbawm, who writes jazz criticism in the *New Statesman* as Francis Newton.'

I'd read Francis Newton on jazz and eagerly hunted for *Primitive Rebels*, which was to be the first book I ever read about social movements from a Marxist perspective. It proved to be revelatory, not only because I was instinctively sympathetic to peasant rebels, anarchist subversives and outlaws, but because it introduced me to a thoughtful Marxist approach to history. This was a rare find. The radical movement in social history was still just beginning, while Marxism was not exactly high profile as an intellectual force in the late fifties and early sixties. Trevor Aston's tutorials, along with Eric Hobsbawm's book, awakened a desire to connect the stray bits of knowledge about Marxism which had accumulated by chance and hung around in my head like an annoying clutter of jigsaw pieces that didn't fit together.

'Monkeys could type the Bible,' the boy at the Student Christian Movement day school for sixth-formers in Filey had announced, declaring that he was a materialist. I bought *A Christian Guide to Communism* to try to understand materialism and how the monkeys could do it, but the author was mainly concerned to warn everyone against Reds. I was to discover that materialism had an attachment called dialectics in an unlikely place: A. L. Rowse's *The Uses of History*. Excited by thesis and antithesis, I ran down the corridor to tell Lindsay and Bar that there was this great theory about history. At Oxford, Marxism had not shown up much; however, a lecturer on religion in the Middle Ages, referring to a book by Gordon Leff on Bradwardine and the Pelagians, had sneered, 'If you want to read a *Marxist* on medieval heresy . . .' Of course, I had tried, but the Marxism was obscurely coded and I didn't know how to crack it. Eric Hobsbawm's 'primitive rebels' proved more companionable.

I still did not identify cultural rebellion or radical approaches to history with 'politics', which I believed was merely about power and ambition. However, I was beginning to shift away from an exclusive preoccupation with the personal and to consider broader social factors. This rearrangement of my mentality, combined with an inclination to revolt, disposed me to the left. It was not only to be books and ideas which exerted an influence, but the kindness of several older people towards me. In differing ways they communicated a socialism which was conscious of irony, critical and open to ideas.

'Flemish Renaissance,' Claire Brayshaw, the mother of a friend from St Hilda's, had declared when I was introduced to her. Why couldn't

I have been brought up with people who talked like that, looked at paintings and piled their houses high with books! Claire, a warm, round, grey-haired woman in her fifties, told me how she became a socialist when her father took her to see the slums of Manchester in the thirties. Not only had she joined the Communist Party, Claire had become an art student, dressed in a boiler suit and been painted by Modigliani. She approached life with a high-pitched chortle. When the Nazis invaded Czechoslovakia, she recounted being sent out slogan-painting by the Communist Party branch with a young man and told she should pretend he was her boyfriend if they were caught. What were they to do with the paint pot, I wondered? For speed they began their slogan at opposite ends. 'Try spelling Czechoslovakia backwards,' Claire challenged. I couldn't.

My allies among the dons at St Hilda's, Bridget Hill and Beryl Smalley, were both socialists too. I discovered later that they had combined to rescue me when I was in danger of being kicked out after doing badly in the prelims exams. Bridget Hill was refreshingly enthusiastic and straight-spoken in the donnish atmosphere, and I was later to learn that she had a long-standing interest in the emancipation of women. Though I admired Beryl Smalley, I was less comfortable with her because she seemed scholarly in a remote, rather monastic way. She was, in fact, a Catholic Marxist with deep radical convictions. Observing my wretched bewilderment with the history of diplomacy, she sent me off to the iconoclastic historian of the French Revolution Richard Cobb to study European social history. This act of perception had decisive consequences for me. The impish figure with subversive eyes and a complexion veined with drink was to introduce me to the exciting 'history from below', which was beginning to note the voices and opinions of the poor. Moreover, when I went to Balliol to discuss what I should read during the holidays, Cobb instructed me to visit some friends of his in Halifax. 'They write about Chartists,' he declared, waving his arms vaguely.

I rang Dorothy and Edward Thompson from Leeds and shyly mumbled about being a student of Richard's. I had no idea as I tramped up the steep hill to their house that I was about to meet two friends who would profoundly influence my approach to history and to left politics. Nor did I know that these were two formidable former

Communists who, along with 10,000 other dissidents, had left the party in 1956.

An attractive dark-haired woman in her thirties dressed in black slacks and a black polo-necked jumper greeted me warmly in the kitchen. I took to Dotty immediately and loved the house, with its stark old farm furniture and all those books again. After a while a tall man with a craggy face and uncoordinated limbs emerged from his study. He jutted out into the surrounding space of the room at unexpected angles. Not only was Edward striking in appearance, there was a suppressed energy about all his movements. He repeatedly ran his fingers through a shock of hair which refused to stay flat. When he spoke, enthusiasm mixed with earnestness and jokes spluttered out.

That night, Dorothy and Edward took me in a Land Rover which Dorothy said reminded Edward of the tank he drove in the Second World War to see the Halifax Thespians perform Harold Pinter's play *The Caretaker*. When he bumped into a pillar in the car park I could see what she meant, though it was hard for me to imagine this man as a soldier. It was never to be easy for me to envisage the war. The forties as a decade still loomed too close to be distinguished as history, while hovering just outside my conscious memory. This blankness always exasperated Edward. 'Your generation has so many choices,' he observed once.

When I came to know them better, Dorothy and Edward laughed about my arrival. A cowardly Edward had been in hiding because they had decided my nervous voice on the phone must be that of a student, abandoned, possibly pregnant, from the nefarious Richard's time at Leeds University. He had emerged only when Dorothy had hissed into the study, 'It's all right.'

Around the same time I came across a socialist closer to my own age, the poet Ken Smith, who was then working on Jon Silkin's literary magazine *Stand*. When we bumped into one another in Leeds reference library, Ken was swathed in a long second-hand tweed overcoat – Leeds market pioneered retro chic – and he had just had his front teeth out. The amalgam resulted in an endearing appearance, part small boy and part tramp.

I used to visit Ken and his wife, Ann, who were the first couple I knew with small children, in a tiny one-up, one-down house in Pudsey and later in their Chapeltown flat in Leeds. Ken's accounts of his working-class childhood in Hull and the painful sense of separation which came from going to grammar school gave me a glimpse of the alienation Barry must have experienced at Oxford. He enthused about the First World War poets Wilfred Owen and Isaac Rosenberg, and berated the contemporary establishment of academic, sophisticated poetry as middle class and removed from everyday experience. Ken was associated with a rebellious group of Northern poets, which included Ted Hughes, and they were intent on defying the London ethos of middle-class gentility. Ken introduced me not only to the fierce class struggles of contemporary poets but also to his friend from childhood, a young intellectual shop steward on Hull docks called Dave Godman. Through Dave's angry class consciousness, I began to comprehend the meaning of class in the context of collective resistance, not simply as a sense of individual dislocation.

In July, Judith Okely and I set off for a holiday in Paris. She and Bob Rowthorn had split up, while I had concluded that I might as well settle for being frigid, rather than the more interesting option of nymphomania. Consequently we had resolved that this trip would be a period of contemplation, a rediscovery of the mind. We would spend our time quietly reading and thinking in our old haunts. Things started according to plan. I read our text book introduction to political thought by Sabine on the ferry. On the Left Bank we browsed contentedly through bookshops, perused books in cafés and wandered like female *flâneurs*.

Then, unexpectedly, Bob Rowthorn came striding towards us down the street – a coincidence which transformed the cerebral holiday and my future. When Bob wondered if we would like to go to see *Jules et Jim*, François Truffaut's film about a love affair between two men and a woman, played by Jeanne Moreau, Judith's serious face broke into a mischievous smile, which made her cheekbones even more Bardot-esque. Judith knew, though I did not, that Bob fancied me.

Bob was then twenty-three, which seemed to me at nineteen to be immensely old. From a lower-middle-class family in Newport, he had gained a Welsh scholarship to Jesus College and then a brilliant maths degree. Between 1960 and 1961 he had studied the history of science at Berkeley, California, which was just beginning to stir with the first signs of student radicalism. Through the left-wing friends he met there, Bob, who had gone a moderate supporter of CND, had returned a committed socialist.

I have a photograph of him taken in a booth in Paris, looking wild-eyed and existential, but this was most untypical. While Bob was philosophically intense about ideas and possessed a mathematical tendency towards dreaminess, he was not at all interested in bohemianism. Instead he approached ordinary life with ebullience and vigour. He brought a matter-of-fact manner – his parents were originally from Yorkshire – to the kind of abstruse theories which would intimidate most people.

I never saw him afraid of thinking, or afraid to admit ignorance. I admired his intellectual courage and was fascinated by his appetite for learning. Bob would grip concepts that I drifted around within, and create ordered patterns amidst my habitual chaos. He was doing some maths thesis about tying up the loose ends of bits of string which I could not understand at all. Appalled by my maths – he declared I had a maths age of seven – he set about teaching me Pythagoras's theorem, which had passed me by at Hunmanby.

The big mathematical breakthrough for me, though, was Bob's capacity to calculate safe periods and his scientific approach to female anatomy. He had methodically read the American sexologist Alfred Charles Kinsey's *Sexual Behaviour in the Human Female*, which promoted the clitoris. This was typical of Bob's approach to knowledge, which was in a straight and logical line. Need to know about sex? Read Kinsey. Want to learn to cook? Study a cookbook. When we got to know each other better, he decided to find out about nineteenth-century British history, so he went to the library and borrowed an economic-history textbook. 'You need to read Mill and Coleridge, Mrs Gaskell and George Eliot,' I wailed. But he didn't like roundabout routes and couldn't get used to nineteenth-century English.

Back in London, the rational Bob proceeded to organize me into birth control. He found out about Mary Adams, an unusually enlightened Fabian socialist doctor who would fit diaphragms for young, unmarried women. I was so nervous when I arrived for my appointment that they thought I must be pregnant. A brisk, posh-voiced Mary Adams reassured me by chatting away as she demonstrated how to squirt the jelly into the brown rubber diaphragm. Her mother had been a militant suffragette and she had once waited in trepidation because, like Guy Fawkes, her mother had planned to blow up Parliament. Unlike Guy Fawkes, however, she had never been caught. 'You remind me of my friend Ellen Wilkinson,' declared Mary Adams, shaking her head and washing her hands. I had not heard of the red-haired, left-wing MP who led hunger marches then. But the idea of a long legacy of rebel women arrived with my diaphragm. Freedom from sexual fear combined with political subversion. 'Always take it with you,' Mary Adams admonished me as I turned to go. 'Even if you just go for a walk in the woods.'

Bob was not only a source of information on politics and birth control, he was a believer in the emancipation of women – an unusual outlook in the early sixties. His mother, a hairdresser, had always worked and at school he had been impressed by Plato; Simone de Beauvoir's *The Second Sex* had done the rest. The result was to be a reassuringly systematic approach to sexual relationships, which he insisted should be based on reason and honesty.

Bob's views were a welcome liberation from the guilt and ignorance I had previously encountered. I consequently endorsed his conviction that I must be emancipated, while occasionally finding its application too severe. When Bob took me to visit his friend Robin Blackburn, who was involved in the *New Left Review*, I started chatting to Robin's younger sister Lindy, then a glamorous London sixteen-year-old. She gave me valuable advice about putting on mascara. 'If you do your whole lashes it looks common,' she explained. (I did my whole lashes.) 'You put it on lightly on the tips.' I marvelled how Lindy Blackburn could know stuff already which I hadn't even learned at nineteen. Bob, however, simply could not understand the importance of such knowingness, and became very upset and bothered that I was going to become 'all sophisticated and London'. My mascara remained a bone of contention. To my fury, he once threw it out of the window in an argument. Simone de Beauvoir might not wear mascara, but Simone de Beauvoir didn't have ginger eyelashes.

Bob also equated emancipation with women being athletic and independent. This meant they would accompany him up mountains and on canoe trips, but never make demands on him which would interrupt his work. Never very athletic, I failed dismally on the climbing and Eskimo rolls, but the last thing I wanted was to be dependent and I was happy with Bob's habit of hard work. That August we went to stay with Tony in a rather chaotic house in Cambridge. Every day Bob and I left the domestic confusion of an erratic geyser and flooded drains to head off to the reference library together. Thanks to Bob, I did most of the work I hadn't done in the year before. A woman living in the house was desperately trying to give herself an abortion with hot baths and gin. I shuddered to myself. Thank goodness for that diaphragm.

Back in Leeds, I went groggily off to meet Bar in York after having my wisdom teeth taken out by the dentist. I was bewildered by her absence at the station, but recognized an art student I'd met with her in the coffee bar we frequented in the Shambles. He'd found out that I was coming and persuaded her to let him meet me. I laughed so much at his cheek I let myself be seduced.

Dutifully abiding by the policy of honesty, I told Bob, who was furious – particularly because he had not got off with a friend in Newport because of me. 'It just happened,' I said in my defence, with an added mumble about wisdom teeth. This made Bob even crosser. Sartre had said you should be responsible for your actions; things didn't just *happen*. We were in the London underground, having our first row, and I stared across at the adverts feeling antagonistic to existentialist philosophers and wishing I was somewhere else. Bob's arguments were always incredibly convincing but I had a tug of resistance. Some things *did* just happen in my opinion and sometimes emotions didn't fit the theories.

I had acquired a pessimistic conviction that any man I *really* liked was destined to disappear. But Bob surprised me by being emphatic that he wanted us to stay together. Gradually I came to accept that this time it was going to go on. Through Bob I moved into a new circle of friends which included Robin Blackburn, his younger brother Richard and Gareth Stedman Jones.

I had already encountered Gareth in my first week at St Hilda's, when Anne Henderson had organized a blind date at the pictures. He had surprised me then by saying that he had been chalking in Paris – he had a more scholarly air than the typical pavement artist. When I asked him what he had chalked, 'Victory to the FLN,' came the committed reply – he had supported the Algerian anti-colonial movement. Whereupon conversation had stopped. Like Bob, these young left-wing intellectuals all possessed much clearer maps of intellectual terrains than my laborious and messy collages, and they set about arguing me into socialism. Gareth informed me it was definitely Sartre not Camus who was politically committed. But what about the individual's inner conscience, I worried? Gareth let out an exasperated, 'Pouf!' I then announced that I didn't think I could be a socialist because I didn't love the working class. Gareth replied rather testily that socialism was nothing to do with love. I realized I had said something that sounded silly. Of course you couldn't love a class. What I had wanted to say was that being a socialist must involve different ways of relating and feeling towards people.

On reflection I decided that a lot of my problems with the working class came from my being an outsider. 'You're a rough-looking twot,' said a Leeds voice as I marched through Briggate in my beatnik outfit. I decided I would try and modify my clothes a bit. I couldn't just be an impersonal socialist.

My other difficulty was that socialists were not interested in mysticism. One day when Richie Blackburn was visiting Gareth, we became embroiled in a long rambling argument about Marx and Blake. Richie, despite being ill with flu, defended dialectical materialism, while I maintained you had to be able to see the world in a grain of sand. I went away deciding I could be a Marxist after all and Richie told me later he was converted to the mysticism of Blake.

Just after I met Bob, I had come across a biography of the American anarchist Emma Goldman by Richard Drinnon displayed in the Leeds reference library. Attracted by the title, *Rebel in Paradise*, and the connection between her anarchism and personal life, I was delighted by the lesbian writer Margaret Anderson's comment, 'In 1916 Emma Goldman was sent to prison for advocating that women need not always keep their mouths shut and their wombs open.' I had found a political justification for being a chatterbox.

Sex, however, proved to be less straightforward than I had thought. I was getting worried as the months went by – no orgasms. Perhaps I *was* frigid after all. My brain kept monitoring for orgasms; tick-tock.

Bob began talking about giving up mathematics, becoming a development economist, doing something useful, going to India. Going to India. I panicked – which meant I became dependent. Things were not going well.

Early in the icy winter of 1963 we went to visit Bar in Bristol. When her outraged landlord discovered we were staying, he threatened to turn us out in the snow. Eventually he relented and let us use a sleeping bag downstairs. All the upheaval made me too flustered to bother about orgasms, when wham! I solemnly recorded this event in a letter to Tony about orange lights.

In the bath back at St Hilda's, I was horrified to discover a creature on me. The college doctor told me I had crabs – that sleeping bag had been lousy. 'You don't look the type to be going with GIs,' he remarked jocularly. I had to apply a yellow liquid called Suleo, put my clothes in a suitcase and cover them with the lethal disinfectant, DDT, and boil my underwear. That year I had been put in the St Hilda's hostel, which was more tightly regulated than college. I managed to sneak down into the basement late at night to boil in secret. But the DDT was spotted and I was interrogated. 'I thought I saw a moth,' I muttered. 'It's not the season for moths,' boomed my donnish persecutor.

During the crabs scare, the social historian Raphael Samuel, who was teaching at Ruskin College, gave a lecture on the Irish potato famine of the 1840s at the historical Stubbs Society. The small, skinny, dark figure with a lock of black hair falling persistently over his nose had a hypnotic aspect. Raphael kept shifting papers from one great pile to another across the table and, like spectators at Wimbledon, we watched them go faster and faster as his time ran out. His talk was a devastating *tour de force* in which he described how belief in free trade and opportunism had combined. In the Keynesian ethos of 1963, it seemed incredible to me that ideas of *laissez-faire* could have been maintained amidst so much suffering. Occasionally, however, my mind would wander into awful speculation. What kind of penalties would there be if you passed on your crabs to a don?

Sitting at the Stubbs Society meeting, I was unaware that I had found the hidden connection between Bob's socialist circle and my friends from the Monaco. Raphael had established the Partisan coffee bar as a cultural centre for the non-aligned New Left which had developed after Khrushchev's speech about Stalin's atrocities in 1956. More cautious members of the New Left had opposed the idea. But Raphael, who was prone to breeding creative but not necessarily democratic bees in his bonnet, had disregarded their advice. Predictably the Partisan had proved to be an economic disaster, even though rebel youths, bums, drifters and folk singers had a very good time there.

After the break with the Communist Party in 1956, it had seemed that a new kind of radical movement was going to emerge and New Left clubs were set up in many towns and cities. The journal the *New Reasoner*, edited by Edward Thompson and the historian John Saville, provided an important focus. In December 1959 it had merged with the Oxford-based *Universities and Left Review*, in which Raphael and Stuart Hall were involved, to form the *New Left Review*. By 1962, however, the *New Left Review* was fraught with practical and theoretical tensions and its relationship with the left clubs, scattered about the land, had become tenuous and uncomfortable.

One's point of entry into a body of ideas exerts an important influence, though this is far from obvious at the time. My socialist consciousness was to be crucially affected by the New Left, but in a period when it was being rent by divisions. The people I was meeting, Edward and Dorothy, Raphael and Robin, were in opposing camps and nursing painful wounds. However, the New Left was officially unsectarian, so I would pick up only vague rumbles of schisms and bitterness. For years afterwards I would come across various fragments from the New Left and would slowly reconstruct with whom they had connected or conflicted.

One consequence of being politicized during the break-up of a social movement rather than in a triumphalist moment like 1968 was that, deep in my bones, I never expected the glory days to last. I also learned how to survive amidst disintegration. Newly discovered landmarks would suddenly dissolve without any clear explanation. Bob and Gareth took me to some meetings of the magazine *New University*, which was a kind of student wing of the New Left. I was no sooner beginning to feel involved than it had gone, followed shortly afterwards by the less glossy paper, the *Messenger*.

My political awareness was thus to be formed amidst an implicit sense of disappointment about the New Left which I only partially understood. Lawrence Daly, the Scottish miners' leader, called at the Thompsons' house in Halifax when I was there one day. He had stood as an independent socialist candidate in his native West Fife and the New Left (the activist bits of it) had campaigned for him. Aged twenty, I found myself in the front room listening to these two extraordinary men talking, only half understanding the implications of what they were saying. Lawrence Daly, dark, burly and balding, sat heavy and still in the armchair, a powerful, purposeful man. Edward, in contrast, spoke and moved quickly, jabbing the air as if he was trying to break through some invisible barrier. They were talking about a break in the New Left, about how they had wanted a very different, much broader movement. Their lives had gone separate ways; Lawrence was preoccupied with the union now. Edward looked down, his head on one side, and said that a chance had been missed. I was too shy to ask what he meant. 'We failed,' he remarked to the floor, and then turned and looked at me as if they were including me in the conversation. Did he think I could do something? What could I possibly do? But that annoying little Jiminy Cricket voice said, 'You'll just have to try.' 'Methodism,' Edward said to me three decades later, 'gives you this terrible sense of responsibility.'

A persistent intimation of having arrived just a little too late remained with me. One day when I was visiting the Thompsons Edward gathered a bundle of *New Reasoners* from the late fifties and gave them to me. The feel of *New Reasoner*, engaged and enthusiastic, was very different from that of the *New Left Review*, which inclined towards cool overviews, not the creation of a new politics. 'What will distinguish the New Left will be its rupture with the tradition of factionalism, and its renewal of the tradition of open association, socialist education and activity,' Edward had written in May 1959. But where had the damn thing gone? I was to spend the rest of my life on the look-out for a socialist journal like the *New Reasoner*, where Karl Marx and William Blake could meet between two covers.

For someone my age, 1956 seemed a very long time ago indeed. Khrushchev's revelations about Stalinism and the Hungarian uprising were to me memories from childhood. I had watched refugees walking with their bundles to escape 'the Iron Curtain' on our new television. Their poverty and uprootedness had affected me in a purely human way, and I had posted off my pocket money to a charity collecting money for the Hungarians who came to Britain. In return they had sent me a picture of a woman with a baby.

The event had made a significant impression upon me, but in terms of the displacement of human beings, not the politics I was now hearing debated around me about the Soviet suppression of the rebellion. The closeness of Hungary was to make joining the Communist Party inconceivable. On the other hand, I didn't feel the personal sense of betrayal of former Communists. It just seemed self-evident that Communism was a dead end. Moreover, despite the splintering of the New Left, because of what Edward Thompson and the others had done, I took for granted that a non-aligned socialism was a possible political option. The year 1956 was a significant marker. Before then this political reflex would not have been possible.

I might have arrived a little too late for the New Left, but I was there just in time for the Trotskyists. At this time the Trotskyist groups which had survived the Cold War and Stalinism in terrible isolation had split and split again into tiny sects eaten up by spleen. My first take on Trotskyism was at a dull meeting of the Oxford Labour Club when the editor of the *Daily Worker*, George Matthews, was speaking on the freedom of the press. A dreadful hissing turned into uproar at the back. Venom shot across the room. 'That's the Trots,' smiled Bob with a shrug. My next encounter was with a know-all type in the International Socialist Group who declared, 'Bob's in the FI,' speaking in initials like a member of the elect. 'I don't know what you're talking about,' I snapped. To which he replied, 'You ought to inform yourself about your man's politics.' That was it with Trots as far as I was concerned. And Bob was no more a member of the Fourth International than I was.

Though there were no visible socialist institutions to which you could attach yourself, CND provided a vast umbrella – a social movement which was both political and cultural. It assumed an urgent relevance in October 1962, when President Kennedy ordered a blockade of Cuba until the Soviet Union withdrew its nuclear missiles. Tension had been building up since Khrushchev's declaration of Soviet support for national liberation struggles in 1961, when Kennedy had supported the disastrous Bay of Pigs attempt to invade Cuba. Filled with doom and trepidation, I went to Blackwell's and bought a book by the medieval historian Maurice Keen on the legend of Robin Hood, thinking, 'This could be the last book I ever read.' It seemed a rather incongruous way to go. Hazy images of Bulwer-Lytton's *The Last Days of Pompeii*, which I'd read at school, floated about in my head as I went to a call box and rang my mother. I had to warn her we were in imminent danger. My eve-of-destruction mood brought reassurances not to worry. My mother's view on politics was ignore it and it won't happen; in the event she was right. At the last moment Kennedy drew back from military intervention. We survived. However, with hindsight knowledge of the internal discussions of the American politicians makes it clear that the danger of nuclear war was very real in 1962.

The Cuba crisis had revealed just how powerless we were. It confirmed Bob's exasperation with the moral-witnessing strand in CND. With his customary energetic rigour, he applied himself to studying the history of the Cold War and learning about military strategy with his friend Douglas Gill, who shared a house at 123 Kingston Road. Like Bob, Douglas was tall, but blond with a large, stubborn face that reminded me of a giant in his castle. Believing the left had to beard the enemy in its den, the two well-read young men would take themselves off in their jeans to argue against nuclear weapons with officers from the military who came to speak at Oxford. For Douglas, military history was to become a lifelong interest, though he approached it with a radical eye and was later to write a history of mutinies with Gloden Dallas. As they would practise their arguments in the Kingston Road kitchen in very loud, confident voices, even I was soon able to hold forth on the inadequacies of the 'domino theory', which regarded Communism as a contagious disease spread through geographical proximity.

Bob and Douglas had helped the impressive CND organizer Peggy Duff to produce a duplicated news sheet called *Focus* at the Labour Party conference. However, as 1962 drew to a close, serious rifts had appeared within CND over whether it was worthwhile continuing to pressurize for unilateral disarmament within the Labour Party. The Committee of 100, backed by Bertrand Russell, believed in non-violent direct action and from 1961 had initiated 'sit-downs'. They were prepared to be carried off, arrested and imprisoned for their beliefs.

Sitting down was more alluring than sitting around passing resolutions to me and to many of my friends – including Bar, who had already been dragged off by the police in Trafalgar Square. Direct action also appealed to the wider mood of contempt for the Conservative government and the sense of urgency which came from the Cuba crisis. In the autumn of 1962 Oxford households received absurd instructions from Civil Defence about putting out sandbags. Meanwhile, we had discovered that Regional Seats of Government had been created to preserve an élite of dons.

After holding out on CND for so long because of my outsider scruples, I threw myself into preparations for the 1963 Aldermaston march with excited conviction. This was an Aldermaston with a difference. Just before Easter a small group had secretly produced the 'Spies for Peace' document, which revealed there was a Regional Seat of Government outside Reading, conveniently near our route. All over the country people in Committee of 100 groups began spontaneously Roneoing copies of 'Spies for Peace' and distributing them to CND members.

I was alone one night in Bob and Douglas' house when there was a knock on the door. A man with short back and sides, wearing a grey suit, stood on the threshold. On guard and convinced this was a plain-clothes policeman, I was noncommittal when he asked for copies of 'Spies for Peace'. To my great chagrin, he turned out to be a left-wing trade unionist who wanted to give them out at the Cowley car plant, where he worked.

The 1963 Aldermaston march was a massive 70,000 strong. But the leaders of CND and Committee of 100 were locked in conflict over tactics and strategy. Peggy Duff stood with a loudspeaker as we approached some woods near Reading. 'Straight on for lunch,' bellowed the portly, grey-haired toughie, who was such an efficient organizer. This time, however, about 1,000 marchers weren't listening. Defiantly, we turned off to the left, down a path which led into the woods. Fancy her thinking we could be dissuaded by our stomachs! 'If music be the food of love play on,' sang a bearded anarchist from University College, London, strumming his guitar, as we headed down a path through the trees. It led us to a square brick building with a flat roof surrounded by barbed wire, whereupon everyone started arguing. A hardened Glaswegian contingent wanted to break down the doors and cursed the lily-livered middle class; one man threw a desultory stone down the wooded slope. Anarchists and pacifists sat themselves down outside the door. This symbolic moral protest infuriated Bob, who insisted that as we had found the Regional Seat of Government we should investigate it properly. A picture of him later appeared on the back of *Anarchy* magazine, standing with his hand on his duffel bag surrounded by seated demonstrators in the middle of the woods. Years later I heard that the organizers knew there were guards in the Regional Seat of Government who had been ordered to shoot if we went inside. It was just as well this was one logical argument Bob didn't win!

As we all trooped back to the road, flushed with excitement and still disagreeing about what we should have done, a car came speeding towards us down the track. Always nosy, I stared curiously at the driver, a man in plain clothes wearing a trilby hat and a mac. Gripping the wheel, he returned my gaze with a look of apoplectic fury. Then he wrenched the wheel and drove the car directly at me. I froze in shock and the car missed me only because a quick-thinking Bob dragged me to the side of the path, kicking the car in anger. Briefly we had placed ourselves outside the customary relation of the middle classes to the law. Rejoining the march, our contingent busied itself by plastering the secret telephone number of the Regional Seat of Government in pub lavatories for the information of London citizens.

Back in Leeds, I wore my CND badge, which was briefly to be a declaration of wild extremity, with pride. I had turned into a kind of collective outsider now; people fell away from me in W. H. Smith. We had touched a twitchy nerve of state security and were denounced as hoodlums in the newspapers. To my disgust, even the left Labour paper *Tribune* joined the disapproving chorus. My Tory father, on the other hand, responded with unexpected pride. He had heard that the military police had been called to disperse us and he hated them. He had no time for ban-the-bombers or pacifists, but he thought the invasion showed grit and moral courage. As he went around selling his pit motors, he boasted to colliery managers about his daughter marching to a Regional Seat of Government.

The appeal of adventure in the woods provided an attractive alternative to political meetings. Before long local CND groups were excitedly clambering through the countryside, scouting around for their local Regional Seats of Government. Signs were erected announcing their whereabouts and they had become a joke. As for me, this début in political activism was to ruin me for committee meetings and points of order for ever more. It was to be networks and movements which drew me rather than 'proper' politics.

Direct action was, however, having a fissiparous impact in 1963 upon the broad church of CND, which could survive only through a will for tolerance. I had become involved just as the broad 'Ban the Bomb' movement began to crack under pressure. Nonetheless, as with all significant social movements, the dissolution of CND was to leave shoots in many unexpected places, from which came all kinds of ideas about alternatives, political and cultural. The repercussions of these were to travel through the sixties and beyond. Like the New Left, CND and its ramifications were to shift the parameters of 'politics' and lay the basis for a radicalism outside the orbit of both parties and trade unions. One example was the Campaign Caravans, started by a Committee of 100 member, George Clark, which were to contribute to the community struggles around housing of the mid-sixties. They brought the ideas of similar anti-poverty projects in the United States into the British left. Colin Ward's magazine *Anarchy* was also influential, pioneering direct action against poor-law conditions in homeless hostels, advocating squatting and anti-authoritarian free schools and exposing conditions in prison. The combination of the Civil Rights movement in the United States and the opposition to nuclear weapons in Britain meant that direct action was no longer confined to the tiny anarchist groups.

Committee of 100 and CND were also to have significant consequences for civil liberties. In July 1963 Bob wrote from Newport, saying he was going to demonstrate against the Queen of Greece, who was visiting Britain. The Greek royal family's association with the vicious right wing in their homelands had made them extremely unpopular. After this demonstration, George Clark was charged with incitement (for unlawfully obstructing the highway) and conspiracy. Historically the use of the notoriously vague offence of 'conspiring' has always been a sure sign that the British state was in one of its spasms of insecure authoritarianism.

Indeed, the Tory government that summer was in the throes of the sex and security scandal involving the Minister of Defence, John Profumo, and Christine Keeler. Her involvement with a Soviet diplomat and the osteopath Stephen Ward, who had links to MI5, made the revelations not only morally embarrassing but politically damaging. Harold Wilson pressed home the point. Macmillan's government was being assailed in the press as effete and ineffective and the forces of law and order were decidedly twitchy.

Though George Clark was to be released on appeal, other demonstrators were treated severely and it was to be the tenacious, dissenting spirit of CND which came to their support. It transpired that Detective Sergeant Challoner and other police officers had planted bricks on the demonstrators, whom they had also assaulted. CND bred a scepticism about the law among sections of the radical middle class which was to feed into the growing disenchantment with the police among the young during the sixties. A generation learned from experience that the law could be unjust.

A minor civil liberties battle flared up in Oxford, when Richard Wallis, an Anarchist who lived with Bob and Douglas, was stopped by the Oxford police from selling his copies of *Peace News* on the High Street. CND started a broad campaign for the freedom to sell on the street, so broad indeed that the budding Tory politician Jonathan Aitken was recruited to defend Richard.

Richard, a cheerful enthusiast with a brown beard, introduced me to the writings of Kropotkin and to health food. This consisted of lots of wholemeal flour and dark-brown sugar, bought in sacks for reasons of economy, though Bob queried sugar's classification as healthy. Richard, a carpenter, was also a staunch believer in the merits of wood: pottery, being vaguely associated with civilization, was tainted with modernity and therefore suspect. Accordingly, I would sit like one of the three bears, eating porridge from a wooden bowl and breaking up hard lumps of dark-brown sugar which had coagulated in the sack. Richard later went to live in a strange household in the Cotswolds belonging to a woman who received and typed spirit messages from Oscar Wilde and George Bernard Shaw, who, she maintained, were still trying to write in the afterlife. I sympathized with their frustration, but when I perused the typed volumes felt puzzled – something disastrous had occurred to their writing styles.

After CND dwindled, people like Richard who belonged to the movement's back-to-nature wing continued its unconventional lifestyle traditions, constituting a 'missing link' between the beats and the hippies of the late sixties. This anarchical strand in English radical culture was to prove extremely resilient, interacting with peace and green politics in the eighties and the direct action of the nineties.

Other offshoots from 'bomb culture' spread into folk clubs, which stimulated the folk and blues revival. They unfurled in jazz and poetry readings which aimed to make poetry more accessible and relevant, and were to become early gathering points for the hippie underground. Sometimes the margins affected the mainstream. Some blues and rock musicians had close links with CND and the success of the Beatles meant blues became big-time. A friend from St Hilda's took me round to 4A St Clement's, a CND house in Oxford where avant-garde art, poetry and music brewed amidst the banners. The singer, Paul Pond (later Paul Jones), was still living there with his partner, the writer Sheila MacLeod, but was soon to join Manfred Mann. By 1964 we were humming their hits '5-4-3-2-1' and 'Do Wah Diddy Diddy'.

CND enlarged the space to be weird. As the Aldermaston march approached London in 1964, I saw a peculiar figure standing by the side of the road holding a placard on which there was simply a question mark. He had a completely green face and strange insect-like antennae. 'That's Hoppy,' said someone, as if this was explanation enough. It was indeed John Hopkins, who later started the underground paper *IT*. He had just taken LSD.

A minority on the Aldermaston marches always tried to keep up standards: the sombre, older men in long grey macs, for instance, or Ken Smith's friend from Hull docks, Dave Godman, in his carefully polished winkle-picker shoes. 'You'll get blisters, Dave,' I warned. He was staggering in pain by the last day, but still insisting he wasn't having any of the middle-class crap. They could keep their boots and their carrot sandwiches. He was going to look normal.

Only a Tibetan inner eye could have seen that the scruffy horde chanting 'Hiroshima, Nagasaki, Slough decide now' were the advance guard of a future boom in British fashion. But the CND marches inadvertently provided a mass display of what had formerly been art-school styles. Copying Bardot, by 1963 we were not only cutting the inner seams out of our jeans and sewing them tighter but sitting in the bath to make them shrink. Bob Scheer, the left-wing American journalist who had helped radicalize Bob in Berkeley, was to be bowled over by this custom, which he insisted was peculiar to Britain, when he went to Aldermaston during a visit that year.

Bob Scheer sat on the sofa in Kingston Road that Easter, telling tales of corruption and dirty tricks about John F. Kennedy which profoundly shocked our English ears. When Kennedy was assassinated in November, he was to be instantly sanctified by the media. Because of Bob Scheer, Bob, Douglas and I refused to mourn. On reflection Bob Scheer was right about Kennedy's ruthless managing of the political machine; on the other hand, though lukewarm on Civil Rights when he took office, his support for desegregation in 1963 was to be crucial in America's internal politics of race. That November any criticism was profoundly heretical; we found ourselves in uncomfortable isolation and I was forced to modify my opinion of the handful of Trotskyists who then belonged to the International Socialist Group in Oxford. We gathered in the bedroom where they held their meetings, defiant, extreme and convinced that the rest of the world had wool over its eyes.

Belonging to anything remained a real dilemma for me. Rejecting the Labour Club, which I considered to be full of career politicians, I decided to branch out on my own. The dockers' leader Jack Dash, who was a Communist, gave an impressive speech. Despite Bob's scoffing, I took myself off to the Communist Club, resolved to hear what they had to say at least. Communism in this period at Oxford was certainly not the in thing and their meetings were tiny. An extremely dull talk on philosophy nearly finished me off, but I decided to give it one more try and went to hear a speaker on the persecution of the Kurds, struggling for national independence in the Middle East. It was there that I met a first-year student from Pakistan wearing a white woollen hat. 'Where did you get that hat?' I asked curiously. 'This is a Pakistani workers' hat,' he replied with pride, and invited me round to tea. I quickly lapsed from the Communist Club but had made a new friend in Tariq Ali.

I had become aggressively intransigent in my recently forged political views. During our second year my former débutante friend Hermione Harris suffered the full brunt of my abrasive Northernness mixed with Marxism because she happened to have a gas ring in her room. Never out of the St Hilda's hostel in time for breakfast, I would drop in for a coffee. On this ad hoc basis we grew to like each other against the odds of our dissimilar backgrounds and despite my obnoxious behaviour. I upset a horsy member of the Clarks Shoes family by denouncing hunting, waving *Capital* and delivering a lecture on the labour theory of value when she tried to explain that Clarks' policy was not to exploit their workers. I denounced Hermione when she went off to lunch with Alec Douglas-Home's son for collaborating with an enemy of the working class and in a long rambling row insisted that under socialism cars would be abolished because they were irrational. Hermione, a woman of grace and granite, was later to be radicalized by going to South Africa after we left Oxford.

I was talking to Hermione one evening at a party given by Christopher Hill in Balliol when a young man butted in. Deciding he had assumed that women talking together was of no importance, I started to berate him. Overheard by a chuckling Christopher Hill, he and Richard Cobb instantly nicknamed me Tiger Tim, after a comic-book marmalade cat. The name caught on with Dorothy and Edward Thompson and I was Tiger from then.

My exaggerated fierceness was my way of resisting being mopped up by the crafty Oxford upper-class way of putting you down by being polite. But I soon realized it was a trap; as you blustered away, you became a quaint caricature. The truth was, though, that, thanks to Bob and socialism, in my second year I was much happier in Oxford. I had found a way of being in and against Oxford. I had made friends, I was excited by my work and I felt I could make some sense of the world.

'Read Marx, not people on Marx,' advised my tutor Beryl Smalley wisely. I read him voraciously – so much better than A. L. Rowse. With dialectics bursting my brain, I was dismayed to find that I was quite unable to squash him into the one essay we were allowed on Marx. My fascination with political ideas was always in relation to their context and I pursued them historically from several angles at the same time. I thought this would eventually enable me to understand the contemporary arguments among socialists. I liked G. D. H. Cole's histories of socialism because they were clear and easy for me to follow. From him I gleaned a more sympathetic account of the early socialists than from Marx and was particularly taken by Flora Tristan, the French utopian, who developed the idea of a workers' international before Marx. I added her to my favourite women: Mary Wollstonecraft, Olive Schreiner and Emma Goldman. Unlike the starchy-looking Miss Buss and Miss Beale, the founders of St Hilda's, whose portraits looked down on us from above high table, my rebel women all had passionate love lives.

On visits to the Thompsons during the holidays I began to work my way through the books about socialism in Britain which Edward had accumulated while writing *William Morris: Romantic to Revolutionary*. Among these was a little book of verse written by a socialist in Leeds called Tom Maguire in the 1880s and 1890s. Some were ironic and affectionate poems about the young women workers in the Leeds factories whom he and other local socialists had tried so hard to organize. Tom Maguire, a handsome man in the photograph at the front of the book, had died in poverty in 1895, aged twenty-five. I was intrigued by him and by a comment in the essay Edward wrote about how socialism took root in Leeds, 'Homage to Tom Maguire', in *Essays in Labour History*. In passing, Edward remarked how Tom Maguire and other members of the Independent Labour Party had fought not only capital but 'Mrs Grundy' – the sexual hypocrisy of middle-class Victorian society. I could identify now as a person in a long line of Leeds socialists.

Edward was working on the manuscript of *The Making of the English Working Class* when I turned up in Halifax. Published in 1963, it was to demonstrate a new way of writing labour history which looked at relationships and processes, rather than simply focusing on institutions. As I read the first part in manuscript, I delighted not only in the drama but also in discovering early women radicals. Years later Edward told me he had groaned to himself when I had said how good it was to find so many women, knowing there were fewer in the latter part. Subsequently the book was to be criticized in the light of the women's movement for not looking at women enough. But this is hindsight. *The Making of the English Working Class* was actually far more aware of women's participation in radical politics than was customary at the time. Although an earlier generation of women historians had written about women, in the early sixties very few historians even mentioned them.

The Making of the English Working Class broke new ground by presenting class dynamically, by combining the political with the social and by linking work with community – all ways of seeing which were to be crucial for the emergence of what later came to be called 'women's history'. In 1963, despite the imaginative portrayal of living relationships of class in books, plays and films, from *A Taste of Honey* to *Billy Liar*, the prevailing sociological approach to class was a static affair which sliced it up in occupational surveys. In contrast, *The Making of the English Working Class* restored individuals making choices in their workplaces and communities, becoming aware of themselves in new ways through ideas and action. Edward was not alone; the French historians who had influenced Richard Cobb were engaged in a similar project. This moment in social history was to leave me with a continuing fascination for that most tantalizing of endeavours – catching an emergent awareness in movement.

Edward's book had an impact far beyond history. Existing ways of theorizing class clearly did not fit the changes which had occurred during Harold Macmillan's 'You've Never Had It So Good' years. A cultural sensibility about class as a relationship had been appearing through the writing of the men (and a few women) who created the 'angry' novels and plays. Richard Hoggart's *The Uses of Literacy* had similarly delineated the cultural parameters of a particular kind of class experience. There was, however, a strong counter-current. When I was a student, even radical sociologists such as Tom Bottomore were suggesting that class was no longer a useful category of analysis on the grounds that in the South-East the stark divisions were more blurred. Instead the fact that deference was beginning to decline, especially among the young, was seen as much more significant.

I was exasperated by the denial of class, which to my newly class-conscious eyes was everywhere evident. Though full employment under the Tories had led to greater prosperity by the early sixties, basic kinds of poverty persisted. This was particularly evident in the old housing in poor parts of the big cities – the inadequacies of which were being documented in the recently started journal *New Society*. Dave Godman took me to Hull to see his mother, who had brought up a large family in a house which still had no running water inside. I watched in horror as she had to go outside to a tap, fill a kettle and boil the water before she could wash up – so much extra work. On a holiday near Aberdeen, I saw a line of beaten men and was shocked to realize the dole queue continued to be present in Scotland.

My socialism made me observe the world around me more closely and learn from people I would have previously dismissed. Returning on the train from the 1963 Labour Party conference in Scarborough, where Bob was doing *Focus* with Peggy Duff, I became embroiled in an argument with a working-class Scottish delegate. He was a right-winger who loathed CNDers. By the time we got to York, however, the man had softened, having discovered I had been ill with gingivitis, sipping milky porridge through swollen gums. He had suffered from 'trench mouth' during the war. The St Hilda's diet must have been akin to the British Army's. He proceeded to reveal a burning hatred of the big landlords and described to me the humiliating power they still exercised over agricultural labourers through the system of tied cottages.

I was discovering that I liked *not* being an outsider. Labour was doing well in the polls, Harold Wilson was leader of the opposition and the Tories were going to have to call an election. Change was imminent. As I marched through the streets of Leeds brandishing Maurice Dobb's *Studies in the Development of Capitalism*, I got a friendly twinkle. 'We'll get the buggers out yet, love,' declared the man walking across the road towards me. Comradeship! When a Welsh bus conductor in Oxford began chatting to me about the historical studies in E. H. Carr's *Studies in Revolution* and gave me a free ride, I was chuffed to find a revolutionary proletarian. There was, however, a snag. He began to complain to me about the Oxford students – so scruffy. 'In Aberystwyth the students look ever so nice and tidy, see. They wear their college scarves.' I looked up at him from my seat in mute anguish. Wear a St Hilda's scarf – that was just too much to ask!

Fortunately for me young working-class styles were in the process of metamorphosing. In March 1963 I saw a band with fringe haircuts on TV. 'College-boy haircuts,' said an apprentice from Wakefield I met on the train coming back from our 'Spies for Peace' Aldermaston. The Beatles had arrived and we were soon dancing to 'Twist and Shout' at Oxford parties. Music and style crossed and recrossed class boundaries.

Thanks to Braham Murray's training for *The Hostage*, I could do the twist, though my swotty youth left me unable to do any other dance. In the summer of 1963 Bob and I went on a Progressive Tours holiday, spending part of our time building the foundations for a library at the University of Lublin in Poland. (My father took out a passport so he could rescue me from behind the Iron Curtain. 'They want us to go,' I expostulated.) It was in Lublin that, for the first and only time in my life, I became a dance star. Bob and I performed the twist to admiring Poles who wanted to buy his bell-bottom jeans.

I was not very good, however, at the digging and was always the slowest on the line shovelling earth. An obstreperous Irishman who had been in a Jesuit seminary in Dublin gave me a hard time. Pink and dizzy in the sun, baking in my allocated navy boiler suit and lacerated by his taunts, I was close to humiliating tears. There was no way I could keep up. Incredibly Bob, who despised chivalry, came to my rescue. Standing between us, he began digging like a madman. Bob had rowed for his college and the arm muscles went into his shovelling. My tormentor was left way behind and had to admit defeat. After that I was left in peace. When I was in Belfast in the eighties, I met Michael Farrell and finally made the connection between the sardonic, argumentative ex-Jesuit with a beard and the man who became one of the leaders of the 1968 Civil Rights movement in Northern Ireland. At last I could gloat, 'Bob dug faster than you.'

During our stay in Lublin I was often sad, because Bob fancied a young working-class Frenchwoman (who had no trouble digging). Even worse, the romantic Poles kept pitying me because Bob was flirting with her. I hated being pitied, though the archaic chivalry they displayed in order to cheer me up made me smile. Young Polish men still clicked their heels when they asked you to dance – particularly odd for the twist to Trini Lopez's 'If I had a hammer, I'd hammer out freedom'. Once a student ran round a corner when we were on an outing and returned with a bunch of flowers. 'Hopelessly unemancipated,' Bob grumbled.

We spent a few days in the beautiful old town of Kraków, where I fell for a dissident art student whom we met in a jazz club decorated with Nescafé labels. He asked me to dance and announced he was an Anarchist Communist. As we danced, I decided this must be what I was and the reason that I never fitted in. I was too Anarchist to be a Marxist and too Marxist to be an Anarchist. I had no sooner discovered our common hybridity, and was beginning to float into romantic union, when an official came across the dance floor and rebuked us for the abandoned style of our dancing – I'd taken my shoes off.

These holiday flirtations were geographical non-starters but they were emotional watersheds. We had both found that our relationship did not preclude being attracted to other people – but that we still wanted to stay together. We had not explicitly called it an 'open relationship', but the idea was around already on the left. This was to work all right in practice, but sometimes the emotions got more bumpy than our rational calculations had assumed that they would. On balance it was to be Bob, the sexual rationalist, who was more emotionally distressed by infidelity than me with my existential assumptions of freedom and promiscuous curiosity.

It is easy to be dismissive of the application of reason to sex. Yet in contrast to the muffled confusion I had known before Bob came along, his approach was liberatory. Officially I enthusiastically endorsed his outlook. Yet some contradictory impulse which would not quite settle for reason continued to twist and turn and wriggle and jiggle. Something that made no apparent sense, for which I had no words, rose out of the deep.

I had nothing in common with Paul, a scaffolder with an already passé Tony Curtis quiff hairstyle. I failed to get the punch lines of the jokes he related in an Oxford town burr. We did not converse much about life and politics, though once he screwed up his penetrative blue eyes at the gates of St Hilda's and, looking down the road at Magdalen College, remarked apropos of nothing in particular, 'They need people like me when they have their wars.' I wanted to say, 'That's not true,' but stayed silent, for I knew he was absolutely right. The eyes had hooked and aroused me and made me tumble into a brief affair. But, in 1964, I had no terms to countenance powerful physical arousal which could not be categorized as either a romance or a relationship. It flared, burnt quickly and died. And would have been simply a memory, except for Paul's friend Jess, who had introduced me to Paul.

Jess had chatted to me when we were waiting at a bus stop on a foggy winter night. He had dyed blond hair and wore a leather jacket and came from a mining village in the North-East. A few years younger than Paul, he hung around with the rockers who rode motorbikes and were under the protection of an amiable gay professor who used to defend them when they appeared in court. The teenage girls Bob and I were to meet through Jess still had backbrushed bouffant hair and rejected my rationalist admonishments about contraception. Pregnancy meant the boy might marry you and they wanted to get married more than anything. Jess developed a longer-term relationship with a friend from St Hilda's and my chance encounter with him at the bus stop was to set off a series of repercussions which were to play their way out in my life over the next few years.

While I was sitting with Jess and his rocker friends drinking beer in the pubs that students avoided, marijuana was hitting Oxford. That clear divide between beatniks, who smoked pot, and the rest of the world, who drank alcohol, was breaking down. The mods had emerged as a visible antithesis to the rockers, with their fringe haircuts and art-school styles, and they were into speed. Denim protest clothes and the protest songs were no longer confined to CND. Bob Dylan and Joan Baez had appeared at the Monterey Folk Festival in May 1963; by 1964 they were bringing an American stardust to beat styles. As the denim skirts we bought in the market became shorter, suspender belts were discarded for tights. I scuttled around Oxford in my denim outfits with a short black belted shiny mac – though still in the Leeds stilettos. In some barely perceptible ways, cultural assumptions were shifting. There was nothing definitive you could put your finger upon, just an anticipation of modernity.

Instead of watching flickering black and white films like Jean Vigo's *L'Atalante*, Howard Hawks was the thing; Hollywood was being rehabilitated. That celebration of the popular in art which laid the basis for the design explosion of 'Swinging London' was already in the air. The avant-garde and mass popular culture were beginning to discover the pleasure of one another's company.

I must have tuned in to this mood somehow, for I adopted a position of extreme cultural relativism in one of my finals papers, arguing against hierarchical value judgements which placed Beethoven above the rhythm and blues singer Howlin' Wolf. If I had possessed an ounce of strategic gump I would have kept my opinions to myself. Even I should have known that the examiner, Hugh Trevor-Roper, would not be on this wavelength.

I was not in a strategic state at all during my finals, being consumed by thwarted longing for a student at Balliol called Arnold Cragg. Arnold, who was in the year below me, belonged to a new species of floppy masculinity which had started to appear there. Displaying no interest in revolutionizing the world, they just listened to Bob Dylan and watched the world go by.

I first saw Arnold at a party, sitting like a crumpled doll in a corner, looking as if life was just too much for him. It was a characteristic pose – a passivity which had an irresistible pull for women. The reason was simple. As he was always inert, it left a delightful space for pursuit. In the sexual mores of 1964 this was novel and went to my head.

I had veered from one extreme of masculinity to the other. The only thing Paul and Arnold shared was that they were utterly unlike Bob in every respect. I was not able to explain at the time why I was so intent on unsettling the sexual order. One interpretation might have been pique. Bob, being much better than me at reasoning, held all the aces as long as you stuck with the rules. Another rendering would reveal an absence – some kind of connection that eluded me in relation to him.

Arnold, who was troubled by terrible angsts of every description, seemed quite unaware of my smitten response to him. I used to go round to tea with him and listen to his woes like a celibate and concerned maiden aunt. Bob, who was happily going up mountains with an athletic young woman who fancied him, mocked mercilessly. After a prelude which resembled the buried sexual tensions of a Victorian novel, Arnold and I did eventually make love in a sleazy London hotel. In a dazed glow as we hitched back to Oxford next day, I noted the name of the tube, Arnos Grove. Through the years this unlikely place on the tube map continued to evoke memories of a sweet and daffy romance.

Because of a distraught Bob, I agreed to end my sexual affair with Arnold. When I looked at my life steadily, I knew I wanted to stay with Bob; indeed I could not imagine existing apart from him. The result, though, was that Arnold became a repressed romantic ideal who lived on in my imagination, a might-have-been love who was to boomerang back.

In the autumn of 1964 life was changing too fast for musing. I was going to do a thesis at Chelsea College, London, on the history of an adult education movement called University Extension, and Bob was leaving Nuffield, where he had been studying economics, for Churchill College, Cambridge. He insisted that he had no desire to be in an academic ivory tower; he was going to live in London during the holidays and at weekends. Logical as ever, he took out a compass and drew an arc round Liverpool Street station and King's Cross, marking the areas from where he could get a train easily to Cambridge. How could I have known that my geographical location for the next thirty-two years was being determined?

It was a landlord's market. We were staying at Gareth Stedman Jones's parents' house far over to the west in Twickenham. Thus by the time we reached Whitechapel tube, the flats would all have gone. Exasperated by my slow-moving morning sloth, eventually Bob set out alone and came back victorious. He had found somewhere called 8 Junction Place in Hackney. I'd never heard of Hackney and, as we took the little train from Liverpool Street station, I looked out in apprehension at a grey, tumble-down, dingy London I had never seen before. I noticed a strange, sweet smell of vanilla which was soon to become a familiar sign of the approach of home. It arose from a sweet factory which used to be at London Fields, and hung thick and sticky in the polluted air. On that first journey it seemed as if London went on for ever and that we were heading for the end of the known world. But it wasn't even the end of the line, just Hackney Downs and a two-room flat, with kitchen and box room, at the junction of Amhurst Road and Dalston Lane.

CHAPTER 3

1964–6

Tired and hungry after carrying our belongings up to the flat on the second floor at 8 Junction Place, Bob and I went out to find some food. I remember wandering for about half a hour until we finally came across a solitary fish and chip shop down on Mare Street. It appeared that no one in Hackney ate out.

When I said I lived in Hackney, friends looked blank. 'Hackney. Where's that?' At that time the dissident young middle class tended to settle in Earls Court or Notting Hill, so our choice of borough was regarded as eccentric. Islington was just being 'discovered' but it was half an hour away on the 38 bus. Our isolation was heightened by the absence of any underground station and lack of a telephone. Living in Hackney was well off the known map – no conforming nonconformity for us.

The flat was above a Do-it-Yourself shop. Its rooms, being on the corner, were strange triangular shapes, and the whole building would rattle when the trains came into Hackney Downs station opposite. Our rent seemed high at £6 a week, but three of us would be paying as a friend from St Hilda's, Mary Costain, who was studying history of art at the Courtauld Institute, was to join us. Bob and I had to make a down payment for the furniture: a blue plywood kitchen cabinet with frosted glass, a Formica-covered kitchen table, beds and tall wooden chairs. These household possessions were to be gradually discarded or disintegrate over the next three decades of my life in Hackney. The chairs lasted the longest: painted and then sanded, they were eventually to be borne off by a second-hand furniture dealer in the early nineties, proving that the not-at-all-desirable of one era can be valued in the next.

Bob constructed a desk of orange boxes and I piled them on top of one another to make bookcases. As new books moved in, I would trek off to the nearby market in Ridley Road and collect more boxes. The bath was in the kitchen, making bathing a chatty and sociable event. It was covered by a useful wooden lid, painted in the ubiquitous cream, upon which visitors would sit in a row, discussing politics or gossiping.

Hackney in 1964 had the air of a borough which had seen better days. Settled by Romans and Vikings, it had been a thriving medieval community and then a place where puritans of the better sort had built their houses. Solid blocks of 'improved dwellings' had been erected for the nineteenth-century deserving poor, followed by the utilitarian modernity of the council flats constructed between the wars. Older housing had been flattened yet again for the disastrous sixties replicas of Corbusier tower blocks on the cheap. Nonetheless, the elegant architectural traces of the eighteenth-century dissenting villages in Clapton and Stoke Newington, where radicals like Mary Wollstone-craft, Joseph Priestley and Tom Paine had greeted the French Revolution, were still discernible. The 253 bus route took you from the worn-down urban wastes of Whitechapel, along Cambridge Heath Road, to pass by the refreshing oases of Victoria Park and London Fields, where handsome 1840s houses threaded between new council flats. The big houses in Hackney were multi-occupied by the sixties and the greenery was dirty and dishevelled, but you could still imagine how the move from the East End had seemed like a real step up for the Jewish working-class socialists whom Arnold Wesker was to portray sipping their chicken soup with barley in the trilogy of plays which began with *Roots* in 1959.

Even as he had been writing about them, however, they had been leaving, moving westwards to Golders Green or out east to Chingford. In 1964 you could still sometimes hear the very old speaking Yiddish on the 253 as it headed down Cambridge Heath Road to Bethnal Green. But in aspiring Hackney, the precarious second generation of the Jewish middle-aged who had remained regarded the changes they saw around them with displeasure. They complained that the borough was going down. Their eyes had a look of disappointment and their lips were set with a resolve to maintain standards come what may. On Sandringham Road a genteel elderly lady resolutely sold cream cheese, pickled cucumbers and smoked salmon in a fastidious shop which had survived the changing composition of the borough. At weekends, when the weather was sunny, this middle-aged aristocracy within the Hackney working class, clerical and skilled craft workers, could be found relaxing and reading in deck chairs on the steep slopes of Springfield Park, by the River Lea. Looking at them, I could visualize life in Vienna before fascism.

My neighbour in the flat downstairs, a Jewish woman in her fifties who worked in a betting shop and described herself as 'in business', would return each day to survey my unbrushed stairs. Obsessed by the impinging dangers of the urban slum, Cassandra-like she would screech up the staircase, reproaching me for inviting rats and mice. I would try to creep up to avoid her, bitterly resenting the fact that Bob was not held similarly responsible.

The woman upstairs was, in contrast, a friendly ally. Margaret and her partner, John, came from Dagenham, where he worked at the Ford plant. They had been forced into Hackney because the planners who had established a council estate there for Ford had not taken the housing needs of a new generation into account. Margaret, who at twenty-five was a few years older than John, had a child from another relationship, Eddy, a little blond boy who was about five when we moved in. Margaret had dark, short, curly hair; her face was still pretty, though unglamorized. She was beginning to put on weight and padded around in a heavy quilted dressing-gown, hoovering and mopping every day. 'Women,' my mother had warned, 'often give up and let themselves go.' Sometimes Margaret would come downstairs for a chat, looking out at the busy crossroads as if she were a prisoner.

There were only a few years between us but Margaret's air of resignation made her seem like a grown-up to me. I used to worry that twenty-five was a kind of dividing line: when you reached it you were definitely 'young' no more. I liked Margaret's warmth and respected her wisdom about children and men, but her fatalism terrified me. By some arbitrary throw of fate I had been granted a degree, my freedom and another destiny. But I couldn't leave it at that, for I knew that Margaret had many similar aspirations. She would observe our visitors with interest, cheekily sizing up the men. Yet her life had already become enclosed, not only because of external circumstances but because she was filled with fears of unfamiliarity which I found nonsensical, refusing to venture into Ridley Road because of 'the darkies'.

The diverse cultures of Hackney touched shoulders in Ridley Road. The cockney greengrocers were ensconced up at the top near Kingsland Road. Further down, Kossoff's Jewish bakery bustled with elderly women buying fresh white loaves topped with sesame seeds. Near Dalston Lane, around the dodgy but friendly butcher who everyone knew received stolen goods, new stalls had sprouted, selling yams and other West Indian vegetables. The Caribbean rhythms of ska records on the Blue Beat record label blasted out from a stall where young black people congregated.

In 1964 there were still many more West Indian men than women in Hackney. They congregated in the pubs, the older men still in suits with wide trouser legs and broad trilby hats. Many retained the slow, considered calm of country dwellers. Once, late and panicking on my way to teach a class, I asked a man in Ridley Road market the time and he gazed upwards at the sun before replying laconically, 'It must be around noon.'

Drawn by the British government's job-recruitment programmes' promises of prosperity, they had brought their histories and hopes from Jamaica, Trinidad, Antigua and the smaller islands like St Lucia across the Atlantic, to the damp and crumbling multi-occupied late-nineteenth-century houses around Ridley Road market which white families were vacating. When I recognized French words in patois the children in the streets would look at me wide-eyed. 'How can you speak our language?'

I took to Hackney, perhaps because I came from Leeds, a city accustomed to cultural mixtures. Because there was no single defining way of being, I could attain a fine balance in relation to my surroundings, treading a thin line of tension between separation and connection. Having arrived there by chance, I was to stay, and the place affected me as deeply as the Yorkshire in which I had grown up.

Two bronzed and skinny American friends of Bob's came to stay when we first moved in to Junction Place. Like Bob Scheer, Frank and Nancy Bardacke were part of the emerging Berkeley student movement which was to influence the British student protests of the late sixties. They were my introduction to the new American radicalism, the first friends to connect me to an international left politics. In 1967 Frank was to be arrested after an anti-draft demonstration, becoming one of the 'Oakland Seven' charged with conspiracy. He was an activist-theorist from a left background, with an energetic appetite for ideas and irony in equal part. Irony ran in the family: his grandfather had adopted the name 'Bardacke', which meant 'whorehouse', when he arrived at the immigration point on Ellis Island in New York. The tiny Nancy Bardacke had long black hair and a most impressive tattoo – a butterfly on her buttock. She showed it to me with pride, saying it had been hard to find a man in San Diego who would do it; they had all said, 'Nice girls don't get tattooed.' Before Nancy's butterfly, my own efforts at not being a nice girl paled into insignificance. I formed a mental picture of San Diego as a wild place filled with tattoo parlours. California, already an accretion of myths about beatnik life in Berkeley and Emma Goldman's tumultuous lecture tours, had gained yet another notch.

Frank and Nancy, for their part, found Hackney a romantic neighbourhood, with its recognizable working class. Eagerly they set out looking for class consciousness, to return chastened. An old Jewish man, recognizing fellow Jews from across the Atlantic, had waved towards a huge, ugly block of flats in Amhurst Road, declaring with pride, 'We own all these.' Despite this disappointment, a hopeful Nancy spotted a new proletariat arriving at Hackney Further Education College, opposite our flat, on their scooters. Their floppy-fringed mod hairstyles and green parka jackets with furry collars were unknown in Berkeley and she gazed at them with delight.

East London was in the midst of a style revolution. Working-class women of my age still sported elaborate beehive hairdos as they pushed their prams from the housing estates and flats to the small shops on Amhurst Road. But the teenage girls' hair was now straight and they wore the dark-coloured three-quarter-length leather jackets made in the local East End sweat shops. The east Londoners' legacy of deprivation had left them small; at five feet three I loomed over everyone, a giantess in my new short black coat which tied at the front. When Mary Costain arrived, she could just about pass as a local because she was smaller than me. Our long straight hair and pale make-up meant that both Mary and I were generally assumed to be in our teens.

Mary came from a lower-middle-class background in Lincolnshire. An undiagnosed spine injury when she was a child had caused her pain and unhappiness which still marked her face. The resulting combination of suffering, resolve and stoicism prevented Mary from being simply pretty and blonde and gave her a tragic, waif-like look. Part of the group of dissident friends who had clustered together at St Hilda's, Mary was to be the woman friend with whom I shared thoughts and musings on life for the next few years. I would borrow her art history books, while she read the novels from the late nineteenth and early twentieth centuries I was working my way through as background to my thesis.

Mary was also my cover. Bob was not meant to be living in the flat as far as my father was concerned, though I confided in my mother, who, being a natural underground operator, could be trusted with everybody's secrets. I was nearly always able to be frank with her, censoring only information which I thought would worry her too much – like cannabis, which she associated with the moral panics about Chinese opium dens of her youth in the twenties. She had been impressed at Bob's discovery of Dr Mary Adams and pleased to hear about the diaphragm, but she never really took to him as she had to Mel and Barry. 'He's too like your father,' she insisted. I could see no resemblance – apart from their liking of maths. 'He's domineering.' I didn't think this was fair. Bob was forceful but always democratic, while my father's approach was encapsulated by the Lancashire saying, 'I'm not arguing, I'm telling tha'.'

My parents came down to London shortly after I moved to Junction Place. My father was visiting an engineering firm he represented and my mother was having some medical tests done. Everything seemed to be fine when they arrived in a taxi to inspect the flat: the stairs were brushed, the orange boxes in place and all signs of Bob well hidden. Only later was I to discover to my chagrin that my father, who had popped out to buy some fruit, had tipped the greengrocer on Amhurst Road to keep an eye on his daughter!

They were staying in the Cumberland Hotel at Marble Arch and when Bob and I visited them with Douglas Gill for tea my father grumbled indignantly about the disgraceful presence of elegant call girls stalking the lounge. 'It shouldn't be allowed.' When he left the table to telephone, my mother, always sympathetic to women on the make, arched her brows and remarked, 'Men like your father are frightened by women like that, because they can make comparisons.' Douglas looked profoundly shocked. I smiled to myself with pride, thanking my lucky stars that I had a mother on the side of vice.

After my father returned to Leeds, she stayed on for a while at the Cumberland, in order to continue the medical tests. One day when I was visiting her there was a great din outside, and I looked out of the hotel window to see a demonstration weaving around Hyde Park. Enormous banners of Marx, Engels, Lenin and Trotsky were being borne aloft. The revolution, it seemed, had reached the Cumberland Hotel. Obviously this was not to be missed. 'I'll be back soon,' I said, putting down my teacup and hurrying out to join a great host of black-leather-jacketed boys from the North-East. Being all dressed up in a turquoise patterned straight-skirted summer dress and high heels, I received a warm welcome. The demonstrators had been scooped up by the Socialist Labour League, the hard-line Trotskyist group which had recently been expelled from the Labour Party for tucking themselves in as a 'deep entryist' faction.

The SLL had stuffed them all into buses early in the morning, promising a cheap good time in London. There was consequently a powerful odour of smelly socks as we marched through the West End. Amidst the enormous icons of Communist leaders, the boys had improvised their own. 'Up the Revolution' nestled with 'Girls wanted. Cockers only.' This march was not at all like Aldermaston. On the other hand, they were undeniably proletarian and some of them were socialists. 'You should join the Young Socialists, love,' they told me.

I decided that they were right. I didn't think it was enough to just talk about ideas like the *New Left Review*. Socialists should do things – proper working-class things. I looked 'Young Socialists' up in the phone book and found the Hackney branch met in Graham Road. I was thus probably the only person to be recruited into the Labour Party Young Socialists via an expelled Trotskyist sect. Moreover, I had landed by chance in one of the most intensely political Young

Socialist branches in the country, where I was to learn about left politics in a very different way from Oxford.

The burly Liverpudlian who gave me a membership form looked very worried indeed when I explained how I had got there. 'You should stay away from them,' Brian Smith warned me. Brian was a member of Militant, another Trotskyist group secretly burrowing away in the Labour Party. They hated the expelled Socialist Labour League, but Brian must have weighed me up and concluded that I was a complete dumbo rather than an infiltrator sent by the SLL's stern father figure, Gerry Healy. Never one for small talk, he decided to waste no time with my political education. As I filled in my membership form, I was puzzled to hear the kindly but uncompromising figure in a brown suedette jacket with a furry collar intoning like a nineteenth-century schoolmaster, 'United Front, yes; Popular Front, no.' I blinked, trying to concentrate. It would be easy to get this the wrong way round, and his tone suggested the consequences could be dire. Whatever did it mean?

Brian was from a Liverpool working-class family with a long memory of resistance. He had been brought up with stories of riots against the police and tenants' rebellions, as well as with tales of the 'Blue Union', the breakaway dockers. This ingrained class-consciousness proved stronger in the end than his adherence to any sectarian form of Trotskyism. But when I met him he was a great admirer of J. P. Cannon, the American Trotskyist leader, and lent me a well-thumbed cheap edition of the didactic Cannon's collected essays. I was never to share this enthusiasm, though Brian did awaken my interest in the international history of Trotskyist groups. It was also Brian who persuaded me, along with Bob and Mary, who both proceeded to join the Young Socialists, to read Robert Tressell's proletarian novel *The Ragged Trousered Philanthropist*. Like Wajda's films, Tressell contrived to dramatize Marx's labour theory of value – though I groused to Mary about the women characters, who were far too virtuous for my liking.

Every Friday all three of us would trail from 8 Junction Place to the Young Socialist meetings in the dingy Labour Party rooms. There, under the stark, fluorescent lights, in our serried rows, we endured the solemn rituals of sectarian combat, while Militant battled it out with their opponents in the International Socialists, about whether the Soviet

Union was a degenerate workers' state which required reforming or a state capitalist regime which necessitated revolution. Even then the models seemed to me schematic and the disputes scholastic. Indeed, these meetings were never enjoyable, nor were the weekly talks intellectually stimulating. Indirectly, though, I came to apprehend something of the dramatic tragedy of Trotsky's life and was soon well versed in the complex lineages of the tiny sects. I admired the tenacity and resolution of Trotskyism, though I found its emotional make-up alienating. Based on betrayal, forged in the bitterness of failure, Trotskyism subordinated all individuality to the calling of the professional revolutionary. For the Trotskyist, personal joy could be expected only as the faintest glimmer of sunlight on grass.

Periodically we would go out on recruitment drives, knocking on estate doors or bellowing through a loudspeaker in Ridley Road. It was a labour of Sisyphus: we would lure some normal, inquiring Hackney youth into our midst, only to repulse them by the byzantine disputes in our meetings about the pros and cons of 'minimum programmes' or 'revolutionary defeatism' during the Second World War.

The memory of Hitler and the Holocaust was relatively close when I arrived in Hackney. Anti-fascism still permeated the local labour movement and meant the Hackney left was politically sympathetic to anti-racism, though the Jewish experience of discrimination remained the main point of reference. Culturally the two communities of Jews and West Indians remained distinct and a new politics of race had yet to emerge locally. I was nonetheless regaled with stories of contemptuous Ridley Road stall-holders pelting the fascists when they tried to renew their agitation and whip up hostility towards black immigrants in the late fifties.

On one occasion, when the rumour reached the Young Socialists that the fascists were about to return to Ridley Road, a rota was hastily drawn up. Told that the local police tacitly agreed that whoever was there first had the right to speak, Mary and I were given the early morning shift. Off we went in trepidation at the crack of dawn, wondering how we would safeguard the speaking pitch. To my pusillanimous relief, the fascists stayed in their beds. Bob, who was at Cambridge during the week, could escape such duties because he came and went like the Scarlet Pimpernel, but Mary and I were easily organizable. In fact we were even promoted to chairman and vice-chairman – which meant I cooked a meal for the executive meeting.

Despite our best efforts to prove our seriousness, we never managed to *look* right in our King's Road hipster skirts, our Op Art dresses and the ragged old fur coats which we began retrieving from the mothballed cupboards of mothers or other relatives around 1965. Brian Smith would sadly shake his head about our 'petit-bourgeois' clothes. To this day I hear the term repeating in my head in regretful Liverpudlian tones, 'petty boogewah'.

Elected to the social committee, Mary and I decided to use our new bureaucratic power to branch out from the customary jumble sales. We started to hold dances in a pub room, playing recent hits by the Beatles, the Rolling Stones, the Animals, the Kinks. All kinds of people came: south London Young Communist League members, snappy dressers in bell-bottom trousers, Robin Blackburn representing the *New Left Review* in a fashionable pale-blue linen jacket and briefcase, International Socialist men in donkey jackets. It rankled that Hackney Young Socialists never really appreciated the London-wide fame of those socials, which in my opinion constituted the pinnacle of our organizational achievement in office. Despite the fact that people travelled from faraway places like West Norwood, Mary and I had to be content with being prophetesses recognized only in distant boroughs.

The Militant types, in the grey shiny suits which they mistakenly believed made them look proletarian, behaved like real wet blankets at the socials by refusing to dance to the Beatles on the grounds that they were 'petty boogewah' and demanding Jerry Lee Lewis's 'Great Balls of Fire' instead. I had nothing against 'Great Balls of Fire', I just wanted our Hackney Young Socialist socials to be *à la mode*. What was it about socialists, I wondered? Why did they approve only of music from times gone by?

Belonging to Hackney Young Socialists taught me how there was no such thing as a homogeneous working class. The Northern members of Militant were utterly different from the fun-loving skilled workers who joined the Young Communist League, for instance, and both were remote from the details of working-class daily life surrounding me at Junction Place. When my neighbour upstairs, Margaret, became pregnant, terror of her unfamiliar surroundings in Hackney intensified and she started keeping Eddy at home for company on the pretext that he had a cold. Opening the door one day to the school attendance officer, I was excessively polite and apologetic. Filled with dread of the state, I nervously told John and Margaret that the school attendance man had been round asking why Eddy wasn't at school. 'Tell him I'll thump his head if he comes again,' was John's response. I was aghast. Anxious about Eddy's academic future, I took him to join Hackney library, which was near my bank. 'Are you going to the bank?' he would inquire tactfully, his squeaky cockney voice pronouncing the new word 'bank' with my short Yorkshire 'a'. I watched him gradually stretch into imagining other worlds as we read the stories. While his parents had already taught Eddy many practical skills, fancy was a luxury and already circumscribed.

Before Margaret went off to the maternity hospital in Plaistow for two weeks, she made me promise to wake John up in the mornings so he wouldn't miss work. She explained he was a very heavy sleeper and that I would have to hit him with a pillow. I didn't believe her, but set the alarm clock at five and headed dutifully upstairs. The double bed took up most of the room; Eddy normally lived in the rest behind a sheet in the corner, but he was staying with Margaret's relations. John, square, muscular and blond, was fast asleep, lying in a vest on the bed. I tried shouting, but he did not even stir. Margaret was right after all. I picked up the pillow and hit him, but John slept on. I had to belabour him about the chest and head with the pillow before I was able to wake him. Every morning this became a regular routine and I concluded that to sleep in such a coma must indicate a profound psychological dread of Ford.

I had promised to visit Margaret and her new baby in hospital. Ignorant, I asked for Plaistow as if it were connected to 'plaice'. The ticket collector at Liverpool Street station looked blank and then translated, 'You mean *Plar*stow.' At the maternity hospital, we visitors sat on a wooden bench outside until it was time to go in. There I found Margaret looking contented and relaxed in a pink woolly bed-jacket on her own – the babies at that time were all kept separately from the mothers. She was worried about how John was managing. Everything, I assured her, was fine. Exhausted by rising at five, I was exceedingly relieved when she returned home.

The personal existence and relationships of Margaret, John and Eddy might be shaped by the circumstances of class, but they were outside the scope of the politics I encountered in Hackney Young Socialists. The members of the Trotskyist groups saw themselves as professional revolutionaries and thus apart. Despite rebelling against their approach to socialism, I could acknowledge at source it was driven by a romantic rejection of the narrow restrictions capitalism imposed on the human spirit. It was just unbearably closed in the meantime.

Sectarianism buried the hatchet briefly during election time in October 1964. The Conservatives, much ridiculed on the TV satirical programme *That Was the Week That Was* and in *Private Eye*, had started to look not so much a government as a grouse-moor comedy routine. Labour, in contrast, under Harold Wilson's leadership, was presenting itself as the party of brass tacks and streamlined efficiency. Officially the left line was that Harold Wilson was an opportunist who could be pushed towards radical politics. Rationally we had no illusions, but the Tories had been in power all our conscious lives and thus, despite our theories, we sat on the edge of the leather seats in Hackney's thirties town hall and cheered as London, defying the sociologists' prognostications of embourgeoisement, swung to Labour. The excitement of a Labour victory was irresistible, even though at the final count they had won only by a narrow majority. At last those rusty old establishment Tories like Alec Douglas-Home had been ejected from power.

Our ardour was to cool over the next few months as we studied the bland pamphlets issued by Labour Party headquarters about the need to increase productivity and embrace modern technology. We Hackney Young Socialists would diligently comb their opaque pages for hidden traces of exploitation and class struggle. Without realizing it, we were practising semiotics well before the cultural theorists popularized the search for signs and meanings.

The Labour Party central office, for their part, regarded us askance and, by error or intention, crucial documents would reach Hackney Young Socialists late. The older socialists in Hackney were generally tolerant, for they inclined to the left on the whole themselves. One member had been blacklisted for trade union organizing, another was a revolutionary syndicalist, others were close to Militant. Some were odd and some artistic. One older Militant sympathizer, for instance, was a member of the Flat Earth Society – an organization which denied the world was round. Art was upheld in the Hackney Labour Party by Alderman Bert Cohen, a supporter of Arnold Wesker's attempt to take art to the people, Centre 42. Thanks to Bert Cohen, we had not only the Hackney Arts Festival but also the sensual joys of saunas in our municipal swimming baths, because he had been inspired by a Progressive Tours holiday in Finland. Though he liked culture – especially the Jewish all-male choir which always performed at the festival – Alderman Cohen was wary of the artistic temperament. 'You should never allow artists to organize anything,' he told an embarrassed young speaker from Centre 42. Bert Cohen was an active member of the Hackney Debating Society and Bob and I went to hear him speak against the motion 'England is a Philistine Nation'. His Irish opponent wearily pointed out that the English were indeed such philistines that they could not even defend themselves, but had to have an Irishman opposing them and a Jew defending them.

They all seemed far too patient and trusting to us. Bob's influence and the experience of CND had convinced me that a combination of direct action from extra-parliamentary movements and pressure from within the Labour Party was needed. Inside the Labour Party a much more passive view of politics persisted. When a right-wing local labour MP came to speak, an old cab driver inquired of him, 'When are you going to bring us socialism? Is it to be five years, ten years? Just give me a date. I'm an old man and I want to know.' At twenty-one I was convinced that Parliament would never *give* socialism to you. But when the taxi driver went on to describe how he saw the class system all too starkly as he drove through London, I knew exactly what he meant. I too read the city like a social document on my long bus journey from Hackney to Chelsea College on the King's Road.

I had been given some teaching by the head of the Liberal Studies Department at Chelsea to supplement my grant. Chelsea was one of the Colleges of Advanced Technology set up by the Tories during a burst of enthusiasm for science and technical instruction. Someone had decided that the scientists needed 'Liberal Studies', which involved a mix of history, sociology, philosophy and what later became known as cultural studies. The students, bored scientists training to be pharmacists or teachers, were only a few years younger than I was and called me Kinky Boots, which troubled my dignity. In my first lecture a cocky young man crossed his leg over his thigh, compelling me to deliver my lecture on time and work discipline in the Industrial Revolution with a yellow sock directly in front of my nose. I knew if I wobbled I was lost, but couldn't help noticing that he was fanciable. I joked about the sock in a letter to the Thompsons and in reply Edward sent one of his many letters back admonishing me affectionately about personal and political responses. Dorothy, he said, had felt that I was letting down the side. The side was that of women's emancipation. I felt exasperated at the older generation's strictness about how women could be in the public world. It seemed so restricting. Surely you could be a teacher and feel sexy, I thought to myself. Why should 'emancipation' restrict whimsical desire?

I needed more teaching and at this time it was possible to collect a few hours by ringing round the principals of further education colleges. I took my list of numbers to the call box in Hackney Downs station, glancing out nervously as a queue began forming outside. After a rejection from Hackney College, I tried one in Bethnal Green. 'I've got a history degree from Oxford, and I'm looking for some teaching in liberal studies.' 'Have you heard of Blanqui?' demanded the cockney voice on the phone. Of course I had, and Babeuf, the earlier advocate of conspiratorial groups, to boot. This odd interview was my introduction to Bill Fishman, anarchist, historian and principal of Bethnal Green College of Further Education. Bill had winkled his day-release students off local employers like Charrington's brewery and the Port of London Authority by spiel and gift of the gab. He was a veteran of Hackney Labour League of Youth, had studied while in the army in India and was to go off to Balliol while I worked at Bethnal Green College (renamed Tower Hamlets when the boroughs were reorganized). Later he wrote on the history of Jewish anarchism and became a professor at St Mary's College, remaining indefatigably outrageous regardless of eminence.

When I started teaching secretarial girls for two hours a week, Bill Fishman translated Rowbotham into Yiddish as Rowtuchas – a sobriquet I regarded as preferable to Kinky Boots. My pay was £2 12s. and I researched my first class on housing as if it was an Oxford seminar. The East End girls, who were aged around eighteen and nineteen and already accommodated to adulthood in their brightly coloured sling-back coats and perms, patiently set about teaching me to teach. They held decided opinions. Either you had a job or you had kids and that was it. They didn't hold with talking about sex. 'There's them that do and them that talks about it,' declared the spokeswoman for the class. They were in favour of capital punishment. 'Rich people's daughters don't get murdered, it's working-class people's,' an otherwise mouse-like girl remonstrated. They hated the sociological studies of kinship in east London which I showed them. 'It's not like that down here, miss.'

They often surprised me. For instance, they belied the 'embourgeoisement' theories about the working classes current at the time. My Bethnal Green typists had no desire at all to be counted among the middle classes. Indeed, a lesson on imagery compared their fellow office workers to 'lovely white wedding cake, icing on top and inside nasty, gooey marzipan'. They wanted to marry dockers or lorry drivers – real men. 'He ain't half tasty, miss,' was the metaphor that really made me laugh. In a series of classes on crime and the law, I read them the ballad of 'Van Diemen's Land' about transportation to Australia during the eighteenth century and asked them why they thought people had risked such harsh punishments. As we talked about poaching off the land, the pale face of a tall, dark-haired girl lit up and she answered with animation, 'Perhaps they thought they had a right to it, miss.'

At least I taught them history sitting down. This was not the case with an old socialist teacher, a friend of Bill Fishman's who loved local history. He conducted his classes about the Stepney Parliament and the route of the 1381 Peasants' Revolt at a great pace through the East End streets. When our group joined his I was just able to keep up because I had abandoned high heels for the fashionable stubby Cuban heels. But in Bethnal Green stilettos still prevailed and my students tottered along far behind. 'They never taught us about all this history at Oxford,' I told the enthusiastic local historian breathlessly. He gave me a conspiratorial look and nodded sagely. 'There's a lot they don't teach you there.'

Under Bill Fishman's benign rule, Tower Hamlets College of Further Education on Jubilee Street, near to the site of the old Jewish Anarchist Club, provided a historical home for Wat Tyler and revolting peasants, Blanqui and nineteenth-century revolutionaries, along with sundry species of east London Anarchists. From Bill I learned about Rudolf Rocker, the Anarcho-Syndicalist who had organized Jewish clothing workers in the early twentieth century, and about Guy Aldred and Rose Witcop, Anarchist-Communist advocates of birth control who had lived together in a free union. Bill invited Mary and me to meet an old anarchist woman in her eighties who had known Emma Goldman. She explained with pride that she had never married because she did not believe that love was the concern of the state. I inclined more to her version of 'emancipation' than the kind I associated with feminism.

My visits to Bob in Cambridge would be stark culture shocks after east London. Its architectural beauty and the intellectual peace of its libraries were undeniable but I was uncomfortable amidst the cool superiority of many of the academics, for whom a clear demarcation line divided dons from the rest of humanity. Aware of being tolerated simply as Bob's appendage, it was a relief to escape into the sawdust-floored Criterion pub, the hang-out of a marginalized Cambridge where leather-jacketed bikers, American GIs and alienated town druggies met students taking a walk on the wild side – a harmonious conjuncture of 'beer heads' and 'tea heads'.

I was to realize from Cambridge that being on the left was not a guarantee of approachability. Joan Robinson, the distinguished Keynesian economist, liked Bob, but remained a forbidding figure to me, grumbling about the materialism of the West, which she contrasted with China. 'I bet you don't do all your own washing by hand,' I thought, silent and resentful as she dismissed the need for washing machines. However, thanks to Joan Robinson, Bob and I went to the rather bizarre Sword Edge Society, where Cambridge China enthusiasts converged, including the inspiring, white-haired expert on Chinese science and technology Joseph Needham.

Bob's Sikh friend the economist Ajit Singh became my friend too. Ajit was sympathetic to China and active in the Cambridge movement against the Vietnam War. The hostility towards him in the local Chinese restaurant puzzled me until Ajit explained that the British had used the Sikhs to police the Chinese and I understood how the legacy of imperialism continued to divide long after political dominion had ended.

Ajit's descriptions of his village in India, which had collectively enabled him to continue his education, gave me another perspective on India to put beside my mother's stories. We used to argue furiously about the position of women, for Ajit, rather like my father, combined an admiration for women of spirit with a patriarchal outlook. Unlike my father, however, he was a man of reason and if I could make a convincing case for equality he would concede the argument. Ajit would explain how the Sikh religion put a high value on organization and told me about the Asian left groups in Britain.

Ajit's rationalism and his machiavellian preoccupation with strategy presented a very different take on politics from the anger of the American Black Power movement which was beginning to be discussed in Britain. Interest in the American debates was stimulated by the visit of Malcolm X in 1964. He was in the process of breaking with the Black Muslims to develop a left-wing black politics which combined race, class and anti-colonialism, speaking at several meetings including one at the Oxford Union which was filmed. The black and white footage catches a youthful Judith Okely in the audience, her head raised in attentive concentration, and a boyish Tariq Ali, who had become President of the Union that year, gripping Malcolm X by the arm as he descended from the podium.

Malcolm X was to be assassinated the following year. Though he died so young, the publicity surrounding him in the mid-sixties revealed not only racism but the endemic poverty existing within the richest country in the world. Sociological studies of race current in Britain in the first half of the sixties tended to focus on attitudes, but Malcolm X's approach, along with an influential 1962 book by a white American socialist, Michael Harrington's *The Other America*, connected the sources of material injustice with cultural domination. I seized on these insights from across the Atlantic because they illuminated the daily evidence of race and class inequality surrounding me in Hackney much better than concepts of a 'prejudice'.

This revival of radicalism in the United States after the Cold War made me wonder what had happened to the American left in the past. Bob Rowthorn used to talk in awe about Bob Scheer's mother, who had been a militant in the International Ladies' Garment Workers' Union. He also introduced me to the labour songs of Woody Guthrie and Pete Seeger. It was to be these, together with plays at Unity, the left theatre at Mornington Crescent, and novels, which revealed to me that 'other' hidden America of hoboes and labour organizers, of immigrants and poor farmers. I read everything I could find: Jack London, Upton Sinclair, John Dos Passos, Frank Norris and many more. Without realizing it, I was retracing my steps back through the documentary tradition to naturalism. I did not see any connection at the time, but a fascination with the 'real' was in focus more generally. There was a grainy interest in actuality in the Wednesday Plays on television, in Joan Littlewood's drama based on oral history at her Stratford East theatre, in the folk and blues revival encouraged by Alexis Korner.

A favourite haunt in my search for old novels was a second-hand bookshop near the Narrow Way in Clapton, run by a very old man and a woman who told me how she had caused a scandal by wearing her skirts to her calf during the First World War. Happy amidst the random muddle of the shop, I was also looking for even more obscure works by or about the long-forgotten, dusty characters who had gone to lecture in the University Extension Movement in the late nineteenth and early twentieth centuries.

Day after day I caught the 38 bus from Hackney to the British Museum reading room. Crab-like, I was teaching myself not simply about working-class education between 1870 and 1910 but about the social and intellectual background of the period. I ranged from church history to the history of economic thought, from the Independent Labour Party to social imperialism, from the emergence of economic history to arts and crafts. This apparently aimless process, though the antithesis of modern-day thesis-writing, was to serve me in good stead later in life.

Edward Thompson had warned me that the University Extension movement would be dull and he was right, though when you research any topic with intensity it acquires a certain fascination. Fortunately for me there were some eccentrics among the lecturers who went off to teach the workers. These included Edward Carpenter, the socialist and sex reformer who settled in a cottage outside Sheffield and wrote on homosexuality, and Charles Ashbee, the arts and crafts architect and designer, influenced by William Morris. After working at Toynbee Hall, the Whitechapel social settlement established in 1885 by anxious upper-middle-class reformers to encourage social harmony, and lecturing in University Extension, Ashbee formed a Guild of Handicraft, taking the cockney silver-workers out to the Gloucestershire village of Chipping Campden.

With great excitement I discovered that I could track down some of the working-class students who had attended University Extension courses through scraps of autobiographical material in the *University Extension Journal* or in local papers from the small towns, such as Todmorden in Yorkshire, which reported Extension lectures. The *Toynbee Record*, still tucked away in the leafy Oxbridge oasis of Toynbee Hall, contained amusing accounts of troublesome Russian Jewish Anarchists disrupting the University 'settlers'' meetings.

I was deep in the *Toynbee Record* one day early in 1965 when I was startled by a voice inquiring, 'And who are you?' I twisted round from my desk to see, sitting in an armchair, a dark, balding man. The most arresting things about him were his eyes, which carried a challenge, and the extreme whiteness of his laundered shirts. Shirts in east London were just not that kind of white. I told him my name and, responding to the look in his eyes, asked him bluntly who he was. 'I'm John Profumo,' came the reply. I kicked myself under the table. Of course, I'd heard that the Conservative minister involved in the sex and spying scandal with Christine Keeler was doing good works in east London – ostensibly penance for lying to the House of Commons but really for being found out.

We all sat round at teatime with the warden, who was Labour but still somewhat in awe of his notorious visitor. The Tory Party had just decided to elect their leaders in future rather than appointing them. 'Democracy,' declared John Profumo with a twinkle, 'doesn't suit the Conservatives. They prefer that all the old animals in the herd get together and make a decision.' As I sipped my tea, I couldn't help my mind wandering off in the direction of Christine Keeler, though I tried to banish the images which kept flickering around the stiff white collar of his shirt. It was unfair on the man to be defined for ever by the disclosure of scandal.

The archive of the London School of Economics library was in Houghton Street, off the Strand, which meant I was also spending time there. The LSE had not yet turned into a synonym for revolutionary students, though there was a small group of socialists there and some sympathetic staff. Among them was Peter Jenner, then a young lecturer in social administration, whom I used to tease for being a reformist. Peter was soon to leave academia and, as a manager in the music industry, remained a resolute left figure behind all kinds of radical cultural happenings from Pink Floyd to Billy Bragg.

The LSE as an institution has a mixed tradition, being at once the intellectual centre of both social imperialism and anti-colonialism. One day Fei Ling Blackburn, Robin's Chinese wife, took me off with the LSE sociologist Ruth Glass to meet a minister from Tanzania called Babu who was visiting London. I'd never met a government minister before and was amazed that such a young, jokey man could be part of a government. I was equally surprised to hear Ruth Glass, who had been his teacher, tell him off for adding Coca-Cola to brandy. 'You mustn't do that when you go to Paris,' she admonished. Babu just grinned. Until this meeting, my idea of government ministers had been restricted to the stiff-backed, white-moustached Anthony Eden model.

Labour in office meant that even in Britain ministers were changing and were increasingly hanging out with academics. Barbara Castle now headed a new department, the Ministry of Overseas Development, marking the shift which was occurring from anti-colonial politics to economic growth. In 1965, another of Bob's friends from Berkeley, Brian Van Arkadie, a development economist, went to work for this new ministry and, on a visit to 8 Junction Place, recounted how Barbara Castle used to hang her evening clothes up in the office. Ministers might be distant figures, but it dawned on me listening to Brian how difficult it must be for Barbara Castle as a *woman* in an official position. People always judged women by their appearance.

Brian Van Arkadie, a jovial Londoner with an Asian father and white working-class mother, who was to become an economic consultant for the World Bank, characterized himself as an extreme supporter of moderate causes, unlike the organizationally elusive Bob, whom Brian teased for being a moderate supporter of extreme causes. I reckoned this must make me an extreme supporter of extreme causes. Reared in Yorkshire intransigence, I went in head over heels.

Brian's new boss, Barbara Castle, had been one of the many bones of contention which had disrupted our Roundhay teas in Leeds. She had made her way on to my father's list of most hated socialists during the fifties, when she criticized British soldiers defending the base in Cyprus – a treasonable offence in my father's eyes. My habit of disagreeing with him about the Empire and foreign policy, from Suez onwards, had personal roots which pre-dated any knowledge of anti-imperialist politics. When we first moved from Harehills to middle-class Round-hay, I had played alone. Children were kept away because I was too 'rough', until I made friends with a little girl called Janina, whose father, a Polish Jewish refugee, owned a button factory in India. I must have been eight when he returned with a servant called Ram, who used to looked after Janina. We were badly behaved girls but Ram was the kindest, most patient adult I had ever known. When I was about nine or ten he came round to say goodbye: he was returning to India. Strangely my father left him at the door. Sad that he was going so far away, I went out to the porch and hugged Ram goodbye. My father was furious. I could not understand his reaction and was upset and hurt that Ram was being treated differently from other adults. My mother explained it was because of my father's attitude to Indians. The shame of the inhospitable reception which Ram had received became something wider as she spoke. In my distress, the conviction formed that my father's outlook was wrong.

From this childish refusal, and encouraged by my mother's attitudes, I was to question other barriers and divisions. This desire to cross over, to go beyond the place you happened to be, crystallized when I read E. M. Forster at school. Eventually this personal sensibility transmuted into a political resistance to the hierarchies and appropriations which prevented people from being regarded fully as human beings, making me a socialist and a feminist.

The rejection of my father's views of the world was so intense that our moments of real contact were few and far between, occurring on the rare occasions when he ceased to be an infallible authority. My mother subverted one of his lectures on morality when I was in my teens with the query, 'What about that woman with the fish-tail dress?' She then recounted how, on one of their voyages to India, my father had enticed a woman with whom he played bridge up on to the deck. Unfortunately for the illicit lovers, she was wearing one of those tight twenties layered evening dresses. When she finally descended into the dance room, her ruffles were sticking out horizontally like a fish's tail in shock for the whole boat to see. Exposed, my father had grinned sheepishly and shut up. He had a similar look on his face when I had walked out of St Hilda's one day and, to my amazement, bumped into him sneaking out through the porter's lodge dressed up in a new trilby hat he had bought in London. It was my last year at Oxford and he had given £500, a vast sum which he could not afford easily, to the college building fund because he thought the principal would then give me a good reference for a job when I left. I tried to convince him that principals of Oxford colleges could not be bought so directly, unlike the colliery managers he bribed to take pit motors, but gave up and laughed at his secretive, protective generosity.

When he asked me one autumn day in 1964 to meet him at King's Cross station, I felt pleased. At last, now that I was living in my own flat and economically independent, I might be able to encounter him on a more equal, less conflictual footing. Just before we reached my mother at the Cumberland Hotel, sitting in the taxi, he told me that her medical tests had revealed a lump. She had throat cancer and would die in a few months. As yet she did not know this herself. I stumbled out numb. How was I to behave when we reached her room? I think he did not know how else to tell me.

My mother went back to Leeds, to the Brotherton Hospital. When I took Dorothy and Edward Thompson to visit her during the Christmas holidays, she perked herself up, putting on her lipstick, her bright social face and her posh 'telephone voice' to greet them. I could see that these people I loved so deeply had little to say to one another; they were glancing off one another without really meeting. But I felt glad that momentarily my different worlds had at least been present together. Dorothy and Edward sustained me through the grim months that followed; they provided an alternative socialist family, including a twenty-first birthday cake cooked by Edward.

Few friends of my age had any experience of illness and dying, and they found it hard to comprehend grief and loss, including Bob. One surprise was the silent sympathy which came from the seemingly stolid and impervious John, the Dagenham worker who lived upstairs. His wordless perceptivity communicated directly with my raw grief. I returned after a bleak Christmas in Leeds to find Margaret had left him, taking Eddy and the baby to her mother's. John had vanished too, along with my old transistor radio. I assumed that with no one to wield the pillow he had finally lost his job.

It had never occurred to us to put internal locks on our doors. Those were trusting times; danger simply did not occur to us. Mary and I would amble off without fear for a walk on Hackney Downs at night and one evening I invited eight young mods high on pills whom I met at Liverpool Street station back to our flat to keep them out of harm's way. They chatted out the speed to Mary and me through the night, trotting off amicably at dawn. Violence was something confined to gangs like the Kray twins, or it was far away in other countries. Travelling up North one weekend to see my mother, I was drawn into an argument about British imperialism with some servicemen on the train. The man next to me, with a bitter expression, indicated under the table. He had lost his leg fighting to defend the British base in Aden.

Throughout the winter of 1964–5 I seemed to be permanently on trains, one weekend to Leeds and the next to Cambridge. On one of my visits to Bob, Mary rang from London. In a frightened, shaking voice she said there had been a fire in our flat. Fire was inconceivable, something that happened to other people. I returned to find that the top flat, where the fire had begun, had been destroyed. The ceiling of Mary's bedroom was open to the sky and some of her books were charred by the heat. We had no electricity, but our gas cooker still worked and the room I shared with Bob was luckily unscathed.

Mary and I searched for another flat but, discouraged by a succession of bleak rooms in Amhurst Road filled with plastic settees, decided to stay. She moved into my room while we waited for the ceiling to be fixed. Months went by as we huddled over candles through a freezing winter, marking essays from Tower Hamlets College, where Mary was now also teaching. Her long hair touched a candleflame one evening and began to burn. Remembering an Enid Blyton story, I grabbed a rug and extinguished her.

The delay in repairing the damage was caused by the landlord's attempt to blame the fire on the television of the new tenant upstairs; the insurance company maintained the wiring was faulty. The fire left me no longer simply theoretically against landlords; I loathed ours personally. Even after the memory of cold and discomfort had faded, the acrid, burnt smell, mingled with paraffin from the stove, would return. A brown hole right through the middle of my copy of Asa Briggs's *The Age of Improvement*, which had been in Mary's room, remained an incongruous memento of the miseries of the private housing market. After the fire, Bob, the Marxist economist, began to say we should move. It was irrational to pay rent. Buying somewhere would make more sense.

But throughout 1965 I was able only to take each day as it came. Every time I went back to visit my mother she had become weaker. She had defied all the predictions of a quick death. By that Easter it was evident she was surviving through her incredible inner will alone. I knew this powerful spirituality, mystical rather than religious, from the unspoken, umbilical closeness of childhood. It was simply part of my mother's being, a private awareness which had no means of expression in her everyday public persona.

In her last months the morphine she was given for the pain altered her perceptions. She began talking about people having coloured haloes, becoming exasperated because I could not see them. In the face of death, a psychological change occurred and the anger and resentment she had suppressed with such discipline broke out. Being much younger than my father, she had always imagined having a few years of freedom and now this was being snatched away. In her frustration she turned on my father, refusing to allow him into her bedroom. After dominating her for so long with his bombast and humiliating her with a succession of affairs, he collapsed into abject misery, his hurt, hopeless adoration of her still locked within his stocky Yorkshire chest. As the end of my mother's life drew near, her passive resistance exploded into combative rage.

I was heavy with the guilt of being young, healthy and wanting life.

On one visit I dug out the black and gold silk pyjamas bought on one of her voyages to India, which I had played with as a child. Could I take them back to London with me? The floppy trousers were coming into fashion for parties. She looked straight at me, nodding. 'I won't be having much use for them any more.' My mother was speaking the truth. She could always use words to strike the core of meaning, but so much of this had been in fun. The truth of death was too terrible and it separated us.

Death and anger seemed everywhere. Apart from James Cameron and John Pilger, the press seemed to be uncritically pro-American. Photographs of the Vietnam War and its coverage on television were profoundly shocking to those of us who opposed it. Our eyes had not acquired that veil which was to come from prolonged subjection to images of pain and suffering. So many people were dying. I told myself I should feel the same grief for the unknown that I felt for the tiny, gaunt figure lying in her bed at Roundhay. But I didn't.

The generalized peace politics of CND were beginning to seem irrelevant. Bob and Ajit Singh were planning a Cambridge teach-in against the war in Vietnam, along the lines of those held in US universities. On 29 May there was an anti-Vietnam War demonstration in London and I went on it before going up to Leeds. Bob needed to talk to people about the teach-in and I wavered undecided, missing a train.

When I reached home my mother had gone into a coma and was no longer conscious. The nurse who was looking after her said she had thought I had come. But I feared she was saying this to assuage my remorse. My mother was breathing in great laboured gasps. She died the next day, aged sixty-four.

While the Anglican priest at her funeral intoned inappropriate platitudes, I sat remembering her zest and irreverence. A lifetime Conservative voter, yet anarchical in her personal outlook, my mother had been instinctively against the powers-that-be. 'It's old men who start wars and young men who die in them' was one of her many sayings. These proverbs about human existence accompanied the stories about her own life which she would relate as she sipped the brandy and dry ginger she kept in the kitchen cupboard or reclined for her afternoon nap in the double bed from which my father had long been banished.

I used to sit listening to them on a stool by the electric fire where she lit the cigarettes she chain-smoked.

Now there was only a coffin in an aloof Anglican church and all I could do was to go over them in my head, gathering up memories. Through her I had heard of my father's resolute courtship – how he had driven her other suitors away, running after a tram in Sheffield when she stormed off in a rage. I knew about the bungalow in India, my brother's ayah and my mother's delight in dancing with young officers at the club. When they returned to England in the depression during the early thirties, my father could find a job only as an electrician in a colliery. I could feel her humiliation, the former memsahib reduced to cadging Woodbines off the young miner in the family where she was living with my brother, Peter. Her voice would lift then with accounts of how my father had secured a sales job and they had settled in Leeds, living in lodgings in Harehills with a family called the Blacks. 'We've had our ups and downs.'

Life at the Blacks was one of her 'ups'; my undomestic mother clearly enjoyed being part of an extended family of lodgers. She would chuckle as she told me about young Graham Black, off on a date, singing about putting on his tuxedo as he Brylcreemed his hair in front of the mirror. 'Tuxedo' was a funny term, like the 'finishing kibosh' that an old major, also lodging at the Blacks', used to make my brother Peter put on all the shoes he polished for the household.

There were bits in these stories I did not understand, discontinuities that I could not piece together and parts I had forgotten. When I faltered in the midst of the narrative to myself, I would turn as if to ask her. Then there would be silence, blankness. She was dead.

I had to sort through her belongings. The clothes could be folded to give away. But her shoes stood in the bottom of the cupboard. As I crouched on the floor looking at them, they assumed a malevolent indestructibility. These objects I had never stopped to consider had outlasted the human being I had loved. I recalled the dreadful emptiness of the piles and piles of shoes I had seen in the Polish concentration camp near Lublin.

Among her papers I discovered a tiny visiting card from an army major. Along with a green army rug, she had kept this all those years, through her travels back and forth. She had told me about the older man who had talked to her about Indian art and music, making her question my father's assumption of British superiority. He had been a medical doctor but left the army after his wife ran off with another man. Addicted to morphine, he had delivered the rug with his card one day, gone home, taken an overdose and died. And she had kept them both.

I also found letters from my father and tried to imagine the young man whose tone reminded me of those socially mobile characters in H. G. Wells novels, a modern man without any frills, embarking on a brand-new century. He had met my mother towards the end of the First World War, when Jean Turner was eighteen and staying with friends of her family in a farm near his village of Aston. He was already in his early thirties, separated from the wife he had married at sixteen. My father had acquired a bad reputation with women and the village schoolmaster reported their courtship to my mother's parents in Sheffield. Lance had been banned, which of course greatly boosted his desirability to the defiant young Jean. One of the letters was apologetic, there was the suggestion of passion. I was moved by the ardent, unrespectable, awkward man they revealed – so unlike the father I knew. But feeling as if I were eavesdropping, I bundled them up to give him and never saw them again.

I stayed in Cambridge with Bob for a while after my mother died. The bustle of organizing for the teach-in about Vietnam came as a relief from the grim sadness of the house in Leeds. By chance one day we came across E. M. Forster in the quad of King's College. He was extremely frail and had been ill for a while. I had an accumulation of questions to ask him. I knew Edward Carpenter's working-class lover had inspired Forster's novel *Maurice* and that Forster had known Charles Ashbee and other unconventional lecturers who had gone to teach in the University Extension Movement. But a glance at the face of this fragile-looking man made me aware that such questions would have been intrusive. I could not even explain how the perceptions of personal relationships in his novels had shaped my own attitudes so profoundly. My mother's illness had made me sensitive to that delicate threshold of death, a pause in which it seems as if the inner being is already looking down on the physical form, when peacefulness is all-important. I was filled by a contentment at being in the presence of this old man, who strangely seemed to sense the unsaid. He smiled into my eyes and moved on.

Long after, when I had a baby, I re-entered that terrain of nuanced sensibility from the other side and found that I could recognize a vibrating intensity of minute happenings. For weeks after my mother died I wept in abandonment. Some random memory or incident, like reading the account of the death scene in Thomas Mann's *Buddenbrooks*, would trigger off an uncontrollable grief. Everything became heightened. External events like the teach-in seemed particularly vivid experiences now I knew that consciousness could be snatched away. I was relieved to be caught up in debates which did not return me to personal memories.

That summer I stayed with my father in the house, which now seemed hollowed out and emptied. Leeds reference library became my haven and I found a fellow spirit in a friend of Ken Smith's called Danny Padmore. Danny, who was training to be a teacher, played modern jazz in a pub. He had been brought up in an orphanage in Whitley Bay, the son of a black seaman and a white working-class mother. Danny had a tacit understanding of loneliness.

Bob and I went for a holiday to Hungary that year, again with Progressive Tours but no work camps this time. I was longing to be carefree in the sun and swim in Lake Balaton. But Progressive Tours were never that simple. In Budapest we found ourselves in an apprentices' hostel with eight bunks to a room. We middle-class puritans from the Labour Party accepted the privations of state socialism – not so the Young Communist League members who were our leaders. They might be Communists but they were young, mid-sixties London workers who went on holiday for sex and a good time. They deserted us for a man our Hungarian guide archaically depicted as a 'spiv'. 'Spivs' to me belonged to the war years, had moustaches and were dressed in long check jackets. This Hungarian simply had a flat and a good record collection.

Our guide seemed to be the Communist equivalent to a Young Conservative. In contrast to the anarchical Poles, who had been left-wing critics, she blanked out on every question. Bullet holes in buildings? Oh, they were from the Second World War. Bob became increasingly exasperated. We had both become friendly with a seventeen-year-old boy from Castleford who was bewildered by the obvious class divisions in Hungary. He had gone on the holiday through an old Communist in the cycling club in his home town who had told him he was going to a land of working-class milk and honey. Bob said we had to demonstrate that there were critical socialists, otherwise the youthful cyclist would go back to Castleford completely disillusioned. So he bombarded our guide with questions about agricultural policy. She must have thought she had got the Progressive Tour from hell.

We had not been back in London long when, very early one morning, there was a knock on the door downstairs. I descended bleary-eyed to find a boy of fourteen with a bag over his shoulder. This was Brian, the younger brother of Jess, whom I had met at the Oxford bus stop. He had hitched all the way from his home in Chester-le-Street, near Durham, and he had come to stay.

A year before Bob and I had met Brian while visiting Jess in an Earls Court flat belonging to a friend called Felix de Mendelssohn. 'You could come and live with us,' Bob had declared upon hearing that Brian wanted to remain at school. Now here he was, without any warning, keen to live with us in Hackney. What could we do but take him in? Neither of us gave much thought to the implications of our new responsibility. Brian's life had been troubled. His mother had left his father for a lorry driver and lived in Ramsgate. His father, a miner, had married again and, while still a child, Brian had taken £5 from his stepbrothers and run away to stay with his mother. Whereupon his stepbrothers had called the police and Brian had been sent to a remand home, where he had begun to wet the bed. He felt unwanted by both parents and the unreliable Jess was his only ally.

I took him to see the head of Stepney Green comprehensive school, who clearly thought it somewhat odd, but agreed to take him. Bob wrote while I was visiting my father that September to say he thought the science teaching at Stepney Green seemed good and Brian was learning chess. I taught Brian to cook and became accustomed to having a clean school shirt ready for him every day, along with his dinner money. Bob and I had become parents but were doing it backwards by starting with a teenager from a broken home. Our flat suddenly seemed to have grown smaller; Brian clearly couldn't live in our tiny box room for ever.

My father's health deteriorated during the winter. That Christmas his favourite sister, Aunty Glad, with her short cropped twenties hair, large bosom and swinging long beads, came to keep him company and we ate a lugubrious dinner. She was in her eighties, my father was seventy-nine. We had little to say to one another. I escaped to Danny Padmore, seeking him out in the smoky Leeds pub where he was playing. His girlfriend was away and we began a low-key affair in his freezing back-to-back heated only by a coal fire.

When the new term began at Chelsea College, all the students and staff had our fingerprints taken. A porter had been given arsenic in his tea and had died on New Year's Eve. We were asked for our alibis. I looked around. The boys I was teaching were standing by me. I couldn't say I'd been with a man all night, so I mumbled that I'd been at home in Leeds. It seemed close enough to the truth. I certainly hadn't been murdering porters.

I had reckoned without Aunty Glad. When the police drew up at Ladywood Road she assumed my brother, Peter, had committed some driving offence. 'No, we're looking for Miss Rowbotham,' the policeman at the door told her. 'It's in relation to a murder inquiry.' Aunty Glad was appalled and when she was appalled, indeed when she was making even a moderately emphatic point, her eyebrows – she had large black bushy eyebrows, flecked with grey – shot right up to her short cropped hair. 'Our Sheila may be a Communist,' she told the West Yorkshire constable, 'but she's no murderer and we hope she's going to grow out of it.' 'So do we,' replied the policeman with sympathy. Aunty Glad, who had a good memory, told them I had not been at home on New Year's Eve.

My brother sent me a telegram. I was to come back to Leeds, my father had had a stroke. The pugnacious, dogmatic man I had contested so often was lying downstairs on a bed in the dining room, which he used as his office. He had lost all the flesh under his jaw and the skin was stretched over his bones. He looked small and skeletal and vulnerable. The bone structure which had been suddenly revealed made him resemble the old yellow photographs of his father – the man who had sired fourteen children. He was dying. The blonde frowzy nurse who had looked after my mother was back. My father had flirted with her, pinching her bottom, before he lost consciousness. She and my brother sat in the lounge drinking whisky. I tried to find some composure in my bedroom, rolling joints and reading Alexander Trocchi.

In these grim circumstances the arrival of the police gave things an edge of farce. This time my sister-in-law came into the lounge to support me. Again I was trapped. I was still not officially living with Bob. A violent row with my brother when I had gone to stay with Bob in Cambridge in 1962 had made me determined to keep my sex life to myself. Desperately, I invented an all-night party with Bar. Poor Bar had just begun teaching in a school in Harehills. Called from a lesson to meet the police, she confessed and sent them to Danny – now back with his girlfriend. Luckily for me he nobly confirmed my alibi.

My father's death left only a dull numbness; none of that tearing grief which had accompanied my mother's death. All emotion seemed to have drained out of me. But in the long run it was the troubling non-relationship with my father which was to continue to affect me in unexpected ways. It was as if we had never met and yet I was ineradicably shaped by him, regardless of the force of my rebellion against him. Unity Theatre put on Arthur Miller's *Death of a Salesman* in 1966 and I thought I could recognize him in the salesman, cultivating his colliery managers – a bottle at Christmas for the men and chocolates for their wives.

Soon after my father's death my brother Peter had been disturbed by a telephone caller whose voice closely resembled Lance's. In his new house in affluent Burn Bridge, a commuter village between Leeds and Harrogate, Peter, obviously discomforted, offered me a double whisky. I hated whisky and declined. He then announced to me that our father and mother had not been married. We had two half brothers and a sister and we were bastards. How absurd, I thought sadly, that our parents had thought it necessary to deceive us. Peter, pushed into engineering instead of art by our father, in contrast felt betrayed.

Dave Godman wrote from Hull to express sympathy at my father's death. Dave had been treated with antagonism by him on a visit to Ladywood Road, I suspect because his gruff Yorkshire voice made him a recognizable male. Alien Southerners were never convincingly male in my father's eyes and if he saw anything of himself in another man he suspected danger for his daughter.

Dave, who had started studying at Workers' Educational Association classes, was experiencing a political isolation I could recognize. He was arguing with all and sundry, and was completely at loggerheads with his brother, a right-wing Labour supporter, over Vietnam. His distressed mother had told him he would end up alone because no woman would put up with all his politics. And to top it all, he was upset because he had clashed with Edward Thompson at a meeting.

Edward had been in Hull to support the journalist Richard Gott, who was standing as an independent radical candidate to raise the issue of Labour's support for Vietnam. Dave, like many other left-wing trade unionists, was disenchanted with the Labour Party, but believed you must continue to support it as the party of the working class. These arguments were to be wearily repeated over the next few years and I was unsure where I stood. I had, however, learned from reading the history of attempts to create socialist groups that it was easier to criticize the Labour Party than to replace it.

Dave did report some brighter news: the fishermen on the Hull trawlers were in a militant mood. They were to go on strike that March. This forgotten fishermen's strike signalled the seamen's dispute in May 1966, which was to be the industrial watershed for the left in relation to the Labour government. The seamen were asking for a forty-hour week and a 12s. 6d. a month increase. Wilson denounced them as 'a closely knit group of politically motivated men', immediately making this more than a wage dispute.

Labour had just been re-elected for a second term with a majority of ninety-eight. It could no longer be said that opposition would bring the Tories back. Left support for the seamen's strike coalesced regardless of sectarianism; about 2,000 of us marched in protest on a demonstration called by the Socialist Labour League. The ad hoc coalition ranged very widely. When the Hull Strike Committee produced a pamphlet, 'Not Wanted on Voyage', listing the groups who gave support, they included Dave Godman's Hull Dockers' Unofficial Port Workers' Committee, alongside the Oxford University Liberal Club. (Young Liberals infected by direct action were beginning to transmogrify into Anarcho-Syndicalists.)

Hackney Young Socialists were among the scattered organizations which united in solidarity with the seamen. Our commitment had a personal warmth, for, at last, we had new recruits, seamen whom I called Sailor John and Sailor Bob. We held a public meeting in Hackney Trades Council hall, chaired, rather formally, by an old cabinet-maker. The young seaman who spoke impressed me by his informality and the modest directness of his manner. A new generation of trade union-ists was emerging, much closer in style and culture to the left radicalized by CND. But some traditional attitudes persisted. He was bewildered to see so many women at the meeting.

The seamen's strike was the first time I became conscious of a labour *movement* as distinct from the Labour *Party*. The government imposed a wages freeze that July. Pay increases had to be vetted by the new Prices and Incomes Board and a four-month cooling-off period was instituted before a settlement could be reached. The left union leader Frank Cousins resigned from the Cabinet and trade union agitation against Wilson's policies intensified. On the intellectual left an aware-ness of the need for alternative socialist structures contributed to a short-lived attempt to set up Centres for Socialist Education, and Bob began going to the discussions of the May Day Manifesto, a New Left grouping which included the Thompsons and Raymond Williams.

The Americans were bombing Hanoi that summer and our anti-Vietnam War demonstration outside the embassy in Grosvenor Square became angry, ending in violence and arrests. I was the delegate from Hackney Young Socialists to a new Trotskyist-inspired organization, the Vietnam Solidarity Committee, formed to campaign for victory to the Vietcong rather than peace. Our first demonstration attracted only a few hundred people, but VSC was to become the main force in the anti-war movement as the mood changed.

During the lunch break at the founding meeting of the VSC, I was drawn into a protracted argument with two leading men in the International Socialists, Chris Harman, a member also of Hackney Young Socialists, and John Palmer, who was later to become a well-known journalist. I maintained that in socialist households men and women shared the housework. My conviction that this was self-evident and fair was based on my observation of the Thompsons and on my relationship with Bob. When Chris Harman and John Palmer pooh-poohed such an assumption as utopian I grew exceedingly irate.

I had no idea that rows about changing personal behaviour in the here and now were to be shades of things to come. No connection was evident then between democratizing daily life and 'feminism', which meant to me simply professional women getting into well-paid jobs.

A new feminism was, however, beginning to stir in 1966. Juliet Mitchell's pioneering article 'Women: The Longest Revolution' had just appeared in *New Left Review* when I met Jean McCrindle. A former member of the New Left, Jean had left the Communist Party in 1956. She and Juliet Mitchell had been discussing the position of women before Juliet wrote the 'The Longest Revolution' and Jean took me along to a meeting to debate the article. Juliet was ill and didn't show up, so Robin Blackburn spoke instead. An American woman who was a member of the International Marxist Group stood up and talked about the importance of women controlling their own bodies – an idea which had persisted from the feminist-influenced socialism of the twenties. Of course I knew she meant contraception and abortion, which was still illegal, but thought mischievously to myself that what I wanted was more chance for my body to be out of control. The atmosphere was somewhat stuffy, so I kept my joke to myself. I came away considering that emancipation was too prim and proper for me.

Neither the meeting nor Juliet's article touched the exposed nubs of anger which kept making me question how women were expected to act. My awareness of women's subordination arose from the sexual humiliation still evident in terms like 'promiscuity', 'nymphomaniac' and 'slags'. The subtle constraints I encountered when expressing certain thoughts and feelings and the implicit assumptions of women's place among many men on the left niggled away at my consciousness. I was troubled too by class differences; the narrow aspirations of the girls I taught and Margaret's isolation in that upstairs flat. When David Godman wrote with the good news that his mother had finally been rehoused, I reflected on the waste of her life's energy carting all that water. And this awareness of women's thwarted potential merged with the sharp pain of my mother's bitterness, with death upon her before she had known freedom.

Dorothy Thompson's conversations about the working-class women she had met through the Halifax labour movement had also made me aware of the personal meanings of class inequality. Dorothy always related abstract theories to people and to actual human relationships and I preferred this to the theoretical structuralism then fashionable in the *New Left Review*. I was later to discover that Dorothy had written an article which the editor, Perry Anderson, had rejected well before Juliet Mitchell's. It was still the case in those days that differing viewpoints on the position of women were rarely debated on the left. A remark of Dorothy's about Simone de Beauvoir registered: the existential freedom of living in two hotel rooms might be all very well for adults but it didn't solve the really big question about women's emancipation, which was how did you bring up children and retain your autonomy? I resolved I would somehow contrive both – but not quite yet.

I did not apply any theorizing about emancipation to my own circumstances, assuming I was an independent woman purely by individual choice. However, I was learning from the responsibility of caring for Brian that while Bob and I shared the commitment and the cost, the practical reality was that Bob was in Cambridge during the week and the main brunt was on me. I'd always assumed we would have children after I finished my thesis, but how and where? Bob talked constantly of leaving Cambridge. But its intellectual pull was undeniable and its élitism pervasive. One don told him he should stop wasting his time with second-rate minds in London, like his Trotskyite mistress in Hackney. Me a Trot? Me a mistress?

Our geographical toing and froing put considerable strain on our relationship. On the other hand, it gave us a degree of autonomy and we both also had relationships with other people. I did not feel jealous, but I did want to understand more about men and women's responses to sexuality. Little cultural space existed at this time for expressing the sexual feelings emerging among young women of my generation. We were beginning to want relationships with men on quite new terms, yet were barely conscious of these needs. I was fascinated by the discussions of sex which appeared in Nell Dunn's collection of interviews, *Talking to Women*. For the first time I was seeing in print perceptions I recognized from intimate conversations with women friends. But Bob dismissed it as frivolous and not political.

Involvement in left politics remained quite separate from my personal experience as a middle-class woman. My thoughts about women remained fragmentary, embedded in specific discordant moments and clustering around specific incidents. An apprehension of discontent would come and go depending on circumstances, to be cast off when my interest engaged with something else. Even though we talked about 'revolution', cultural behaviour appeared as immutable. Powerless, I would resort to guerrilla outrages. In a restaurant with Bob, Perry Anderson and a group of other men from the *New Left Review*, I was, as usual, out of the conversation. Irritated and bored, I noticed a man's silhouette through a lighted upstairs window. He was getting changed. I began a monologue on his state of undress. It took a while for the table to notice, they were so preoccupied with their intellectual debate. Perry regarded me with distaste. According to hearsay, he referred to me henceforth as 'that girl'.

We were definitely going to move. I had been left £4,000 after my father died, and Mary and I roamed estate agents in east London. 'We want to buy a house,' we declared. 'Have you got any money?' they inquired sarcastically. Stray young women simply did not purchase houses in Whitechapel or Hackney at that time. In Islington things were different and they were more polite, but property prices were too high there and a woman couldn't get a mortgage. At last we found somewhere near Ridley Road that looked likely. I returned on the bus from an estate agent with the key, reading Mayakovsky's *The Bed Bug* and feeling light-hearted and hopeful. The best thing about the house, 12 Montague Road, was a grey tumble-down shed which backed on to the garden wall which reminded me of those faded-out shacks on my blues records. I knew I wanted to live there.

London seemed suddenly to be brimming with bright sunny colours and a new feckless stripy style that summer. A mysterious shift seemed to be occurring. Initially there were these little signals. Just before we moved, Peter Jenner, from the LSE, had come round to visit us in Junction Place. 'I've just put £2,000 in a pop group,' he announced, grinning. This enormous sum now meant half a house to me. I gasped. 'You're mad,' opined Bob, the Marxist economist. Not so mad as it turned out. The band, Pink Floyd, were to produce a distinctive tangled sound heralding the inside-out sensations and criss-crossing lights of psychedelia.

Pete Jenner's other alternative venture, the Notting Hill Free School, started with Felix de Mendelssohn and John Hopkins (Hoppy) in a basement flat owned by the reformed hustler turned Black Power militant Michael X, was to prove much madder than leaving the LSE to manage a pop group. This effort at libertarian education was to founder, though it contributed to the Notting Hill Carnival. One thing seemed to lead irresistibly to another in an unexpected tumble of creativity in the summer of 1966 and music was the barometer of consciousness. Freedom and movement sang to you everywhere – the Troggs' 'Wild Thing' and the Spencer Davis Group's 'Keep on Running' – while the playfulness was caught by the Beatles in 'Yellow Submarine' and 'Good Day Sunshine'. The clearcut throbbing sexuality of the blues bands inspired by the left-wing Alexis Korner was giving way to complex lyrics and mystical echoes. Eric Clapton typified the trend. He had been sleeping on the Covent Garden floor of a friend from St Hilda's but hit the big time and moved out. He played first with John Mayall's Bluesbreakers and then with Cream, joining Jack Bruce and Ginger Baker. The distinctive Pink Floyd zither sound was devised when Sid Barrett simply ran his Zippo lighter across his guitar strings. Much other weirdness in cultural innovation could be laid at the door of the increased consumption of LSD. The search for pure authenticity gave way to a delight in free expression. The result was to be that instead of borrowing the culture of black Americans, something original, energetic and confident was coming out of Britain.

'Swinging London' was the invention of an American journalist in *Time Magazine* that April. It was always an external definition and regarded as a joke. It did catch something that was happening, though, some process of interaction between music, art and fashion which Julian Palacios, in his book on Pink Floyd, *Lost in the Woods*, calls a 'feedback loop'. The creative mix resulted in an alternative way to be which was no longer simply marginal. A gangly young man I met in Collet's radical bookshop, David Ramsey, with whom I had a brief affair, recruited me for a German film on 'Swinging London'. We had to act ourselves, he said. I wore my favourite dress, which was short with bright-green and golden-orange 'V'-shaped stripes. Though I did not realize it at the time, my Hackney 'Chelsea Girl' dress exactly replicated the colours and stripes of a Venini glass vase designed by

Ludovico de Santillano in 1965. Art was being rapidly turned into mass fashion.

The pull of the market was evident everywhere. David Ramsey lived in a house full of folk musicians: Bert Jansch, John Renbourn and a group called the Young Tradition – Pete Bellamy, Heather and Royston Wood. They had all come out of that early-sixties quest for the 'authentic'. But this was splintering by 1966. Bert Jansch and John Renbourn adopted a finger-picking style which meant they could meet the more popular blues and rock halfway. In contrast, the Young Tradition, influenced by the Hull folk singing family the Waterstones, sang English rural folk music which most resolutely defied 'commercialism'.

The Young Tradition lived in extreme poverty on a peculiar diet of cornflakes and treacle, with beds divided by hanging bedspreads. Into this household, the well-known singer Donovan had introduced his big influence, a by now very wheezy Derroll Adams, the older folk musician influenced by Woody Guthrie whom Mel had admired. Things looked up when they produced their first album, *The Young Tradition*. However, they faced a dilemma. What exactly was this 'young tradition'? Royston Wood once said to me that they couldn't really occupy the same place as the Waterstones. They smoked grass and were based in London, playing in the Soho clubs which were the beginning of the metropolitan 'underground'. One bizarre and unforeseen outcome of the early-sixties folk revival, with its links to Woody Guthrie and the Communists who uncovered working-class protest songs, was its influence on the fantasy and whimsy folk songs of the hippies.

When I visited David Ramsey, Heather Wood would survey my 'Swinging London' Chelsea clothes contemptuously and call me 'the bird'. I turned up my nose but took note. Women on the folk scene were respected for their skills as musicians by the men. They were fiercely independent, wearing jeans and carrying their sleeping rolls like the men. But they seemed to relate more to men than to other women. It reminded me of a throwback to the beats or of CND without the politics. In defiance, I revelled in the fast-moving fashion of boutiques like Biba or Bazaar. The sharp zigzags of Op Art were being quickly superseded by the flowing lines inspired by Aubrey Beardsley and the vampish boas of the early silent movies. Young designers dived into the past like raiders searching for lost wrecks of spoil and their time-travelling motifs overlaid the early-sixties quest for an obscured bedrock of truth.

Richard Wallis's wooden bowls in the Kingston Road kitchen had defied commodity production by being made to last, but there was a shift towards the throw-away attitudes of the late sixties. A tiny anarchist with a bald head and a beard called Gustav Metzger kept popping up, busily making things he was going to annihilate. One of his former students, Pete Townshend, received rather more publicity when, following his teacher, he smashed up his guitars. Auto-destructive art was a joke, but it communicated something which was to have a deeper cultural resonance – a feeling that creativity should be cast upon the waters, not hoarded or exchanged as an art 'object'.

Ideas about spontaneous happenings – immediacy, fluidity, change – were in the air by the mid-sixties. There was talk of moving environments made out of startling new materials; the houses of the future need not stay in one place. This situationist approach to architecture appealed to me. Why should we be pinned down by our surroundings? Structures, I thought, should respond to human need instead of defining us between fixed barriers. From the vantage point of several decades of accumulation, I am doubtful. What about the clutter of daily life, the accession of knick-knacks and paper?

In 1966 my belongings still fitted into one room and I saw things differently. That summer Bob hired a van and we moved our orange boxes and books round the corner into 12 Montague Road – a structure which, despite a bulge at the back, to be much measured over the years with a spirit level, conventionally stayed put. We painted it white all over, like the interiors of David Mercer's film *Morgan – a Suitable Case for Treatment*, and Bob built long bookshelves down the corridor in the basement which he filled with sturdy tomes on economics.

Our communal household had grown to include a south Londoner called Kathie Humby. From a working-class family with an Irish mother, Kathie worked as a dentist's receptionist in Bethnal Green. Bob and I had met her in the Dolphin pub at King's Cross, where London Young Communist League members used to gather. Kathie was in Lambeth YCL, though by the time we started living in Montague Road she was inclining to the Mamas and the Papas' 'Dancing in the

Streets' rather than Marxist-Leninism. Kathie assumed a wise-woman role in the household and began reading everyone's tarot cards and astrology charts. The neighbours couldn't make us out at all. At first they thought that Brian and I were a young couple who had lodgers. This theory was exploded when they saw him going to school. So they then concluded that we all slept with one another. Visitors searching for our house would be immediately asked, 'Looking for the 'ippies?'

Like Bob, I considered rent irrational, so each week we all paid £1 into a common fund for bills and rates and £1 to a political fund of our choice. The economic flaw in this theory of rent was that we never covered the cost of repairs, and the house disintegrated gradually around us. Only Bob, who had done O-level carpentry, had any idea about how buildings hung together, and he worried persistently about this slow process of decay. The rest of us paid little heed to structural factors, regarding our living space in terms of purely surface aesthetics. I invested in fashionable dark-purple curtains. We covered up the marble fireplaces (restored by the eighties occupants) and installed 'modern' gas fires. Charlie Posner, a young academic at Essex University who was working with Bob on a document which aimed to alter Labour's economic policy of wage freeze, came round and helped pull out an ugly fifties fawn tile fireplace in Mary's room upstairs with truly auto-destructive zeal.

Bob and Charlie's document was published that September as a pamphlet, 'Beyond the Freeze: A Socialist Policy for Economic Growth'. It was a collaborative effort of left academics with MPs such as Ian Mikardo and Frank Allaun and advocated import and capital controls and a reduction in military spending, along with devaluation, as short-term solutions to inflation. More generally 'Beyond the Freeze' challenged the Wilson government's preoccupation with modernization, arguing that the Wilson model did not go far enough; there had to be a conscious shaping of society on human, as distinct from business, needs. Its authors added, 'In the formation of any socialist programme for economic growth this ultimate objective must be kept clearly in sight. Immediate programmes must be related to socialist objectives. If this is not done, socialist aims can become mere platitudes which are trotted out to still the conscience.'

It was a gallant effort, but the Labour leadership wasn't listening.

A political vacuum was opening up as left-wingers all over the country internalized the fact that we were not going to have any impact on the Wilson government. The result was to be that we began to look outwards towards the emerging left in the trade union movement and towards the new community politics, influenced by the American New Left. My first encounter with this direct, informal approach to politics was a bearded member of the Campaign Against Racial Discrimination who came to Hackney Young Socialists from Islington to talk about how they were resisting slum landlords' tactics of intimidation. When we started a similar private tenants campaign in Hackney, I responded with enthusiasm, keen to do something at last which connected with the problems of people in the borough rather than listening to sectarian wrangles.

Yet when it came to the crunch of knocking on people's doors and prying into their rent and housing, I felt an intruder rather than a deliverer. Only a handful of people wanted to come to meetings and make their landlords go to the rent tribunals established by Richard Crossman's Rent Act to assess whether rents were 'fair'. Our campaign required hours of work in making contacts and then advising tenants and following cases through; the positive results were small. Nonetheless, it was to be an eye-opener for me into the appalling conditions behind the exteriors of the old houses in Hackney. I would be invited in sometimes to listen to woes and found families living in one room with walls so wet that the wallpaper hung off them in great curling leaves. Cookers were out on the landing and lavatories and bathrooms were shared.

In one room a group of older black women with scarves wound round their heads sat in a circle sewing. I nodded in helpless sympathy as they listed complaints. A big, imposing woman spoke with authority. 'These black landlords are the worst,' she grumbled, leaving me wincing in white liberal embarrassment. But it was true that small landlords were harassing their tenants to make money. Next door to 12 Montague Road the Jamaican landlady was trying to get her tenants out with the help of her henchman, a pimp called Mr Archie. Bob and I became friendly with our neighbours, helping them to resist in court. They loathed Mr Archie. 'He pushes those white prostitutes' heads down the toilet,' announced a woman who was to become a close friend,

Barbara Marsh, indignantly. Indeed, one night I awoke to a terrible howling. A naked woman was lamenting in a strong Irish accent on the steps outside, ejected by Mr Archie.

That winter homelessness was exposed in the Loach/Garnett TV film *Cathy Come Home*, written by Jeremy Sandford. It was not Cathy's poverty but the indignity which accompanied it which made the film so compelling. By no means a victim, Cathy kept on struggling against an overwhelming combination of forces until her children were taken away by Social Services. The response to the film was an indication of changing attitudes. A new kind of housing activism was appearing which blended pragmatism with anti-authoritarianism, and the same spirit was evident in the spread of libertarian ideas about education. These were no longer limited to the progressive schools. At Risinghill, the comprehensive at the bottom of Chapel Market in Islington, Michael Duane was causing a furore as an anti-authoritarian head.

The debate around education was particularly relevant to me because of both my teaching and the subject matter of my thesis. When I had begun my research I had hoped to find outright rebels among the worker students, like those who had revolted at Ruskin College in 1909 to form the Marxist education group Plebs. Instead I found respectable Lib-Lab artisans and the occasional Independent Labour Party member, all too inclined to be dazzled by the beauty of Balliol and the kind consideration of the dons. Exasperated with them for not following my revolutionary script, I was nonetheless intrigued by the accounts I was uncovering about the personal contacts between men of differing classes. I had never seen this kind of material in any histories of education and was unsure how to write about it.

Dorothy Thompson encouraged me to pursue the individual biographies I was building up of worker-students and an enthusiastic Raphael Samuel suggested that I should give a talk at Ruskin on the 'Self-educated Working Man'. I quickly came to learn that Raphael-style historical productions grew in scale and occurred later than expected. In December 1966 a letter came from Raphael to say my talk had expanded into a day school. This was later to be postponed until the following autumn because he had another meeting coming up on Chartism early in 1967 – the first ever Ruskin History Workshop.

In retrospect, a synchronicity is apparent; my historical responsiveness to personal experience coincided with a new note sounding in popular culture. Recognition of subjective identity in Sartre's philosophical writing had mysteriously been relayed, via the art colleges, out into the world. I had been hearing it pounding over the airwaves. 'Help' sang the Beatles at the end of 1965, and the singer-songwriters of 1966 were habitually exploring the personal unease of the working-class hero. As yet this new sensibility had not cohered into any explicit orientation about how to be; it was still not a cultural way of seeing, but was simply a disconnected voice charged with an unconscious force.

The changes occurring beneath the surface of events were affecting me unawares. Those two years since I had left university were not only to see me an orphan; I was also gathering impressions and understandings about class, race, personal identity and what was later to be called 'sexual politics'. My outlook was being cast.

As 1966 drew to a close a counter-culture was emerging which was to run alongside the radical movement, sometimes interacting with it, sometimes diverging from it. A heady mix of music, drugs, art and underground papers was ready for take-off. The great congregation of people who showed up at the Roundhouse to launch *International Times* that October seemed to be the alternative manifest. The vast old round building, a former railway turning shed, in Chalk Farm, north London, belonged to Arnold Wesker's Centre 42. It was dank and freezing cold, and the lavatories flooded, but the spirit of excitement was so strong it didn't matter. Around 3,000 of us danced and wandered in the coloured lights while Pink Floyd, Soft Machine and a steel band played. In the middle of the Roundhouse a garish Pop Art fifties American car stood like a giant junk-shop joke about the hope of modernity. Its next stop was to be a cultural scrap heap, for on the cover of *IT* the kohl-rimmed black eyes of Theda Bara, the vamp, stared out – the designers had muddled her up with the original 'It' girl Clara Bow. Hippies didn't bother too much about accuracy and that retro-decadent look was to be quickly marketed by Biba in Kensington Church Street.

That night the Roundhouse was claimed as a space for spontaneity. *IT*'s launch was filled with an expectation that something was about to happen and this sense of 'happening' was one of the most attractive features of the underground. 'What's Happening' was to be the heading of *IT*'s listing section. However, while the underground was meant to be open-ended, in establishing its own space it also developed a self-engrossed 'in club' atmosphere. Julian Palacios quotes the painter Duggie Fields: 'There was definitely a group identity that was different. It wasn't that we were going to change the world, but it was that the world would change.' The emphasis on 'vibes' and on direct relating appealed, but I could never simply be part of the underground because of this abnegation of any attempt to change the external world.

In contrast to Britain, where older labour institutions of the left continued to retain more life, by 1966 in North America the counter-culture's utopianism had pervaded New Left politics. Unbeknown to me, Frank Bardacke was declaring 'the first mission of the American radical is to escape. The radical must present a counter-vision, he must create new values.' Though Frank was soon to be puzzling just how this transformatory vision could relate to the needs and aspirations of the mass of ordinary Americans, this stress on alternatives was to shape the emerging movements among blacks, women and gays in the United States.

Unlike me, Bob was never greatly affected by the shifts within popular culture or drawn to the anarchical ideas of alternatives and community politics heading east from Notting Hill. He maintained a strong commitment to the mainstream, which he still saw as working in the Labour Party. These differences were accentuated by tensions in our communal house. Kathie, whose day job at the Bethnal Green dentist's was from nine to five, came home to groove, while Mary was casting off the rigorous denial of her upbringing and beginning to relax into hippie culture. Bob, in contrast, wanted to study and, being still early-to-bed, early-to-rise, was repeatedly enraged by the Beach Boys and Bob Dylan playing upstairs far into the night. I was torn between my relationship with him and my close friendship with Mary, who was gently blossoming in her new pleasure-loving hippie milieu up on the top floor. Less able to be comfortable amidst the joss sticks, the personal conflict left me wrestling indecisively with my own ambiguities about left politics and counter-cultures.

These external pressures were not the only problem. Something had gone flat within the relationship between Bob and myself. We were no longer able to spark off one another. When we went out to visit friends, I would find myself feeling distant from Bob's responses. I was trying to locate my own bearings, no longer prepared to be in his orbit. But I did not know any language to express these inward rustlings of resistance. Overtly our relationship was egalitarian and democratic. I could find no reason for my growing unease. When I read the anti-psychiatrist R. D. Laing's *The Divided Self* I, along with many others, decided that here was a metaphor for my discontent. Split in two, it was as if one part of me had begun to observe the other. This new self-consciousness brought a paralysing sense of atrophy, accompanied by a fearful dread of being absorbed, of not existing.

I woke up from a nightmare panicking. I had dreamed there were translucent star-shaped fish, dark red, emerald green and turquoise, swimming towards me and they were grafting themselves on to the skin of my forearm, merging into my skin. I was desperately trying to tear them off me, screaming as they folded into my flesh.

1) Me, the sixth former, in the grounds of Hunmanby Hall, 1960

2) Me, aged 17, a new arrival in Paris, 1961

3) An existential-looking Bob Rowthorn in Paris, summer 1962

4) Hermione Harris in the mid-1960s

5) The communal household,
12 Montague Road

6) Mary Costain – the friend from St Hilda's
who lived with me in Hackney in 1967

7) John Hoyland in 1959, the radical bohemian in the Partisan Coffee Bar, which I never managed to get to

8) Wisty Hoyland in 1968 carrying her baby, Kate, at the Agit Prop Revolutionary Festival which John Hoyland was compering

9) Jean-Luc Godard filming 'British Sounds' in London 1969.

10) Playwright David Mercer in the late 1960s.

11) Me in my 'Chelsea Girl' Sergeant Pepper coat, holding the policeman from my puppet show against the Labour Government's White Paper on industrial relations, Victoria Park, East London, May Day, 1969

12) Tariq Ali with Stokely Carmichael and black power activists at the
Dialectics of Liberation Conference, 1967

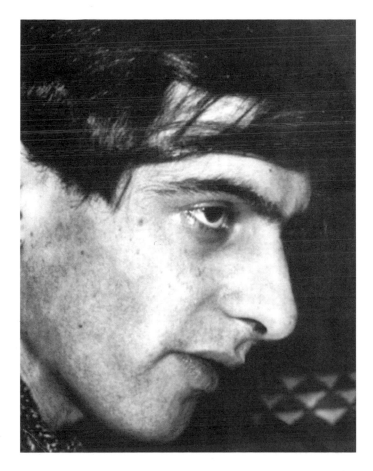

13) Raphael Samuel the social historian
who started the History Workshop
conferences at Ruskin College,
Oxford in 1967

14) Posters from the late 1960s

15) Protesting against the Vietnam War, 1968

16) Enoch Powell's 1968 'Rivers of Blood' speech gave racism a new legitimacy. British Fascists marching in support of Powell in the late 1960s

17) Anti-racist demonstration 1968

18) Putting Black Dwarf together in the office in Carlisle Street, 1968. (Top left & centre: Bob Rowthorn; Top right: Bob with Clive Goodwin; Bottom left: Clive and Bob with John Hoyland; Bottom centre: Clive Goodwin; Bottom right: John Hoyland and me)

19) Me and Roberta Hunter Henderson at the Sheffield Women's Liberation Conference, 1970

CHAPTER 4

1967

Not only had I turned into a divided self, I was leading a double life during the hippie revolution. I had embarked on a journey into the interior, covering scraps of paper with inchoate scribblings solemnly documenting the shifting nuances of my inner psyche. Meanwhile, with equal diligence, I was ploughing my way through my thesis, which had been extended into a PhD, supervised by Eric Hobsbawm.

Bob, long-suffering about reading the chapters on University Extension in my handwriting, was not at all interested in my obsessive analysing of emotions and relationships. His brain habitually worked on a level of abstraction which I could only glimpse in rare moments. I gathered impressions, anecdotes and stories, trying to piece them together, while he analysed, boiling life down to some essential element. Bemused by people who commented at length on literature, his approach was to say it in one line. His brain ran like a hare's, while mine struggled along like the proverbial tortoise. As I laboriously contemplated my splintering identity, seeking words that somehow glanced off my fingertips, clinging to an assortment of stray ends I couldn't fit together, Bob would breezily blow all this bother away, dismissing my half-formed psychological utterances with a puff of intellect. Winded and dismayed, I kept trying to communicate perceptions I could not articulate, wanting him to meet me halfway in a realm beyond reason. When I couldn't reach him, I would give up and become withdrawn, which made him upset and angry.

I continued to equivocate. Part of me did not want to abandon reason, the reason which was so crucial to Bob's personality and which had characterized our relationship together. On the other hand, the pull to float off once more into the irrational, where things just 'happened', was becoming irresistible. Some separate kind of me was developing, reaching around for footholds in memories I had put aside as irrelevant. I was tussling with myself. And, in some confused sense, I intimated that I could not become myself because I was always in Bob's shadow. Not only was he older than I was, he was a particularly brilliant and compelling individual. Over the four years in which we had been together we had fallen into that common habit of couples, we had parcelled life out. Through this division he had been allocated the economics and the theory, while I went off with the poetry and the emotion. Contrary now, I wanted to wander off emotionally and not be accounted for, while also laying claim to think theoretically in my own right.

This was my first long-term significant sexual relationship; I had been crucially formed by Bob's outlook and ideas. He was my closest friend and separation was barely conceivable to me. Yet I could not find an independent track while remaining connected to him. I was aware that the rush of feeling which was making me recoil in Bob's presence, leaving me scratchy and disconsolate, must be partly generated from the many unresolved struggles with my father, whose death had left simply absence. But reasoning to myself that I was dumping the thwarted rage of childhood and adolescence upon Bob did not make me feel happy with him.

Our relationship was also affected by our responsibility for Brian, who was gravitating decisively towards the hippie visitors. It was becoming increasingly difficult to get him off to school and the rows between him and Bob were starting to resemble those in my own family. Only a few years away from my own teens, I was terrified by this cycle of anger which had repeated itself in my life so quickly. Neither Bob nor I had anticipated how difficult it would be for Brian to move from a North-East pit village to a London commune. The result was that we found ourselves caring for a troubled and difficult adolescent in rebellion against us.

Meanwhile, the unrelenting music continued to blast away, while brightly decorated figures floated up the front steps, exchanging hippie in-talk. Sociably, these visitors would invite people they met round at random. I was awakened one night by a terrible crash: two fat drunks had fallen through the front window of my bedroom in the basement.

Someone had suggested at the tea stall in Ridley Road that they might like to drop in. Rather too literally, they had done just that. They stood disorientated and bemused, as I leapt out of bed and berated them with the self-righteous fury of an affronted property owner. Sheepishly they hung their heads and shuffled off, all meek and mild and dumbstruck. As they shut the back door, I calmed down and realized I had nothing on!

When Bob arrived from Cambridge at the weekends I would tense myself against his complaints. I could have asked Mary and Kathie to move out, but this would have been to act the landlady and violate my principled rejection of the economic power of ownership. It also seemed to me that this would have been disloyal to Mary, who had been a close friend through the terrible time of the fire and my parents' deaths. Disregarding the emotional and physical chaos which surrounded me, I continued resolutely to turn out chapters on University Extension.

So we drifted, with me hoping that things would somehow get better. They got worse.

One afternoon, coming home from the British Museum, I climbed up to the top of a 38 bus and bumped into Arnold, whom I had not seen for several years. This chance encounter acted as a catalyst. The distress and discomfort of the preceding months steamed to a head and, after months of evasion, everything appeared with a startling clarity. That was it. I'd always really been in love with Arnold. I'd taken the wrong decision. Bursting with a sudden romantic inflammation of certainty and an overwhelming desire to act, I announced to Bob that I had met Arnold on the bus and this had made me decide to leave him. Bob received my initial declaration in blank astonishment.

I had not consulted Arnold before deciding he was my lost true love. Three years were three years. Arnold's response when I announced I had now left Bob was to look aghast. The responsibility of an unattached me was clearly alarming. Well, that was that, the die was cast. I would be alone, I felt a mixture of relief and terror. But I was free.

In the room we shared together, I surveyed the familiar arrangements of Bob's pencils, the ruler, the two paintbrushes in a jam jar on his desk, the cupboard he had designed, with long tall drawers too high for me to see in at the top. Everything was the same and yet utterly different now, for I was seeing it through new eyes. These had become external objects, they were no longer part of that lived intimacy which means that your surroundings simply 'are'. I was distancing them, separating myself.

Needless to say, it was not so simple, this disentanglement. In the months that followed, Bob's unhappiness haunted me, though I continued to be driven by a decisiveness I did not understand. Breaking away from someone you have loved is always painful, and our excessive rationalism during the whole affair left the emotions of parting even more raw because they had been so soundly covered. It felt as if I had been with him all my conscious life. It was hard to adjust to encountering the world alone, rather than as a person in a couple. There was no longer Bob to waft away unease with his laughter. Now I was alone.

The truth was that, having put so much effort into becoming separate, I was unsure how to be apart and on my own. A diffuse anxiety assumed physical form one night when I was overwhelmed by a choking feeling which left me panting for breath. Kathie, with dental nurse aplomb, took my pulse and declared we should send for the emergency doctor. This made me gasp and puff even more. Twenty minutes passed, half an hour. By the time the young emergency doctor arrived, an hour had gone by which seemed like an eternity. But I had calmed down and was just weak and frightened. He patted me, took my pulse, listened to my chest and suggested that I take a Rennie – which of course left me feeling a terrible fool.

But I was still in a state of stress when I arrived at my own doctor's surgery in Bethnal Green next morning. With a chain of reasoning which I saw as irrefutable then, but later seemed clearly absurd, I decided he had forgotten I was in the waiting room and started banging on his door. Dr Michael Leibson, who had a profoundly conservative view of the human body as an inevitably disintegrating assembly of bits, took odd behaviour in his stride. He was sceptical about psychological theories and newfangled ailments, but he had watched a large section of Bethnal Green go by for twenty years and before then he had been an army doctor. This had left him with a *savoir-faire* about the vagaries of the human spirit. His face had a mask-like quality, lined with humour which could make most of my illnesses go down in size. His gruff irony usually did the rest.

I had been sent to Dr Leibson worrying about thrush the previous year by Bob's friend Charlie Posner. 'I know a doctor,' declared Charlie, 'who is never shocked.' In the mid-sixties thrush was still a catastrophe. Its cure was not a matter of buying a tube of effective Canesten ointment from the chemist's, but required a trip to Whitechapel VD clinic, where building workers leered at you as you went in. Once inside you were assumed to be either a prostitute or the wronged wife of a man who had caught the clap from prostitutes. 'Where did intercourse take place?' they would ask me, presumably to determine categorization. 'I don't see the relevance of the question,' I would reply, and get into a row. Then they needed the name and address of the 'contact'. 'No intercourse for a week,' declared the tight-lipped nurse, giving me another appointment and a cream that took for ever to work.

Michael Leibson lived up to his recommendation from Charlie Posner of being unshockable and uncensorious. His 'I've-seen-it-all' chuckle became familiar over the years. I went to him for about twenty-five years, until he retired. My usual ailments were of the sore throat and sinus type, and he always offered me a cigarette. 'I don't smoke.' 'Oh, no, of course you don't,' he would say regretfully, putting them back in his pocket. His questions were not easy to answer. 'Why do you think people go to doctors?' he wanted to know, as if we would get to the root of the matter together. 'What do you think is really important, ecstasy or security?' he inquired once in oracular tones as I snuffled, woeful and fluish, in the seat opposite him.

My panic attack he treated with time and a walk to Bethnal Green Hospital, where the white-haired consultant had a brisk, fatherly manner. 'I suggest you get married. Women need security, you know.' Enraged by this inapplicable advice, I started shouting at him furiously. Didn't he know these were completely reactionary attitudes? The pesky man wrote to Dr Leibson saying it had obviously done me good to get things off my chest.

I kept on going to the British Museum as a kind of habitual security that February, but I was too abstracted and agitated to concentrate on my research. As I gradually inched out of self-preoccupation that spring, I noticed that things were not quite as they had been. I was surrounded by people in a drifting, ambling daze, quietly absorbing the Beatles singing 'Strawberry Fields Forever'.

The ska stall in Ridley Road had turned into a record shop and the young black man behind the counter appointed himself as my musical adviser. 'Listen to this,' he said one day. It was the Jimi Hendrix Experience. David Ramsey, who had deserted the folk scene, took me to his concert at the Saville Theatre, where the wild energy of Hendrix on stage tearing up the American flag was accompanied by ear-bursting music exploding from the biggest speakers I had ever seen. Music throbbed through 1967: Cream, the Incredible String Band, the Beach Boys, the Mamas and the Papas. And music was no longer just for dancing; it signalled psychic discovery.

Peculiar and interesting places were sprouting. Tony Godwin had opened his alternative bookshop, Better Books, on Charing Cross Road, selling slim volumes of poetry. The hippie club UFO had started in Tottenham Court Road, and the underground entrepreneur Jim Haynes had set up his avant-garde Arts Lab with its café in Covent Garden.

The counter-culture extended options by creating a new kind of public space which was accessible to women. In a conventional club, as a young woman, you were there to be picked up and it was not easy to feel comfortable sitting in a pub on your own. As everything in the counter-culture was meant to be weird and mystical, you could take cover under the imperative on everyone to be a free spirit. You could hang around alone, bump into people you knew, pirouette in the light shows to music, hide in a corner or meet someone new. None of the old rules applied.

Moreover, the very topsy-turviness of the underground provided a way of being women which could bypass some of the restricting rules. It was the licence of misrule. We could all play the fool. The whimsy and nonsense rhymes were not only fun, they also provided a route into remembering direct responses, before the self-consciousness of puberty. This fascination with childhood was there in the music. We could be kind children, loving children, bad children, wayward children or awestruck children – and all these children could forget about being grown up.

Hippie London was pleasantly sociable; the dancing and the dressing up for special occasions constituted a round of engagements without any defined etiquette. At the fourteen-hour Technicolor Dream at Alexandra Palace, in north London, 10,000 of us wafted past one another, displaying our latest exotica like bizarre courtiers in a science fantasy court where there were no rules and everyone was young. Such mass gatherings confirmed the realization that there were more and more odd people in the world. They were multiplying so rapidly that it seemed as if large sections of the country would shortly become completely detached from that dull mainland where straight ruled OK, to create variegated and decorative cooperatives where the sun always shone and everyone did their own thing.

Hippies were more cheery and colourful and decorative than the beats in their austere minimalist black sweaters, but some of the attitudes were the same. The emphasis on direct relationships, on more natural ways of being, the introspection and the preoccupation with pushing experience to the psychological limits, were all familiar. I felt betwixt and between. I'd been a very junior beatnik; now at twenty-four I was a bit old for the hippies. I could go along with them but I wasn't quite of them.

Throughout 1967 I wavered. I enjoyed the prettiness, the display, the release, the conviviality of the hippies and their gatherings. I was affected emotionally by the great rush of creativity in music and in design which had been gathering momentum from 1966. At various times I was to be deeply moved too by the trust between strangers and the genuine mutuality of hippie settlement. The exploration of inner states of consciousness also made long-hidden private preoccupations surface as part of a communicable culture. It was a relief to be able to envision the knotted veins of my father's hand in my own or muse on the instability of meaning in a word. The membrane which separated the inner and outer worlds seemed to have become permeable. I sensed some shift in how men were too. Some of the unstated barriers between femininity and masculinity were down. The self-decorative aesthetic of the urban hippie and the unquiet serenity of cool augured a different kind of maleness.

But I could see the tribe-like underground possessed its own snob-beries and conceits like any other social world. In rejecting the ways of 'straight' culture, hippies surreptitiously introduced implicit conventions of their own. Exclusivity and hierarchy appeared and were policed with the sneeering snobbery of 'cool'. The hippie subcultures which formed, renouncing these hip aristocracies, were, in their turn, rapidly to be soured by that curse of those who would purify – sanctimony and pride.

At first glance hippie culture appeared androgynous. In fact, as certain assumed facets of masculine power were relinquished, others took on a greater significance. Real women could never live up to these sad-eyed ladies of the lowlands – the Belle Dames of legend who were the ideal heroines in John Lennon's, Bob Dylan's and Jimi Hendrix's songs. In *Revolution in the Head*, Ian Macdonald points out, 'In folk tradition, these love/death figures traditionally dwell in a twilight borderland of the male psyche where masculine identity dissolves.'

It was terror of annihilation perhaps which bred a particular kind of ruthlessness – the antithesis of chivalry. The divested trappings of masculinity could, as if to compensate, produce a more exaggerated desire to control women. It was to be this peculiar combination of a new spaciousness in gender identity and a tighter grip in unexpected places which laid the basis for women's rebellion.

My dithering and dathering about hippie culture related to a persistent indecisiveness in my character. While part of me hankered after some utopian harmony apart from the bustle of the everyday, an even stronger wish was to dive into a normality which was transformed by becoming so intensely real it ended up being more normal than normal.

When it really came down to it, I found the hippie camp too confining; it pinned you down and rolled you out like a gingerbread person with hair and beads. What I wanted was fluidity and being able to move between worlds. So I bought my bits of velvet and lace on the King's Road and then went off to Chelsea Girl on Dalston Lane and tried on mass-market compromises.

This oscillation was not just a matter of philosophy but a practical necessity. Despite personal upheavals and regardless of hippie flower power, I was still teaching at Tower Hamlets College, where I had graduated from typists to engineering apprentices. The majority were boys with short-cropped hair and pullovers, class conscious in a defensive trade union way, still linked to the world of their fathers and to the past of the labour movement. When I took them to a trade union exhibition in Stepney library they listened with earnest expressions to an old socialist, Walter Southgate, who believed in teaching labour history through memory-jogging objects. His exhibition 'Things' was to inspire the Labour History Museum (now the People's History Museum in Manchester). However, a minority, influenced by the mods, were listening to Cream and smoking marijuana. They were not particularly interested in unions or in being connected to a labour tradition, but, taking their cue from the music they liked, were more likely to be anti-racist.

Regardless of whether they identified with traditional working-class culture or were exploring the new values of popular culture, they were all very confused about girls. With sexual values exploding and colliding and miniskirts all around them, the boys were profoundly disturbed. 'What do they expect us to do?' The girls, for their part, were increasingly up in arms. In three years east London femininity had changed markedly. Those sober young matrons of eighteen with their perms had been replaced by forthright sixteen-year-olds with long straight hair and leather jackets. 'Every boy in this place is a raving sex maniac, and yet they say they want to marry a virgin.'

The mod boys' hairstyles had shifted from the fringe to two longish and rather becoming wings over the brow with a central parting when, to my dismay, they suddenly walked in with no hair. Working-class east London was proudly presenting the exaggerated hard-edged masculinity of the skinhead against the hippies' flowing locks. And, no doubt about it, the skinheads had declared war on hippies. A sixteen-year-old mod-turned-skinhead called Chris in one of my new classes gave me a terrible time. He was the undisputed leader of the group and I knew that, unless I could somehow deal with him, I hadn't a chance. In despair I decided to cop out of a lesson and show them a film. The film hired that week was *Alexander Nevsky*. I had recently wiggled my way through a film projection course by being good at the 'theory' and buttering up the ponderous trainer, but I couldn't work the actual projector. Somehow I got the film inside the machine and it began to whirr. We all settled down. I suspect they thought it was some kind of horror film. Then the subtitles appeared. An uprising was imminent when we came to the famous scene on the ice. 'Shut up,' said Chris to the grizzling apprentices. 'This is good.' Silence fell and from that day I had an efficient and draconian sergeant-major and no trouble at all with that class. Despite my resemblance to a hippie – Chris continued to hate them – thanks to Eisenstein I had passed some mysterious test.

We were on our way to the British Museum one day (the mummies were always a popular draw) when Chris came face to face with a hippie in a dark-grey duffel coat and long, black greasy hair and glasses. 'Fuckin' 'ippie,' snarled Chris, jowl to jowl. 'Come along, Chris,' I said briskly in a determined-teacher voice. But this was Chris's male honour and he stood there, glaring and provocative. I walked a few paces back, remaining protectively by the persecuted hippie being bullied by my skinhead. Chris's demeanour changed suddenly. Out from inside the duffel coat a knife was gleaming. The knife was at Chris's face. Oxbridge saved the day. 'Come along, Chris,' I said in ringing middle-class *loco parentis* tones, striding off down Great Russell Street. This time Chris obediently trotted after me. Only when we were at a safe distance did he begin cursing hippies again.

Far from being the stereotypical skinhead, Chris was well disposed to all other groups of humanity, apart from hippies. Passionately anti-racist, he argued with the rest of the class against any suspicion of racial prejudice. He was class-conscious too. But again this came from his own angry, individual perceptions, not simply in a handed-on collective manner. A Käthe Kollwitz exhibition was showing at Bethnal Green Museum. Before taking the class, I explained the historical context of her work and showed them some other German art, including drawings by Georg Grosz. Chris, who was fascinated by Grosz's satires, reacted ferociously against Käthe Kollwitz's portrayal of workers. I think it was her sympathy towards workers which he loathed. It felt patronizing in 1967, when young skilled workers were confident that life was going to be good. Images of the oppressed proletarian of the past just seemed insulting.

A woman from the radical theatre group the San Francisco Mime Troupe came with me to Tower Hamlets and talked to my class about their approach to theatre. When she suggested that we should try out some acting exercises, I felt a little worried. But to my surprise, they all wanted to have a go. It was me who was being the conservative one, fearful that my fragile teacher–pupil relationship was going to be overturned. One exercise involved standing in a circle with someone in the centre who relied on the others to catch them. When it was my turn I looked around at them all, meeting their eyes. They were smiling 'Trust us', communicating the certainty that I could fall without fear. Next week they shook their heads and smiled. 'That was a funny lesson,' one boy said. But we all knew that the games had revealed something we had not noticed happening. Liking and mutual respect had grown regardless of dissimilarity, without us even stopping to notice it.

My American actress friend told me after the class that she was recovering from a period of taking speed. Her account of how it had drained her confirmed my decision that speed was not for me. I'd tried it once in Paris and found the hollowing-out sensation in the come-down unpleasant. I was equally resolved never to take heroin. A small group of friends were completely dependent on getting their next fix. 'Hooked' was a good word for this subservience to the deal. Not only did it mean you had to live your life helplessly around heroin, but it also left you with a white, greasy, slightly luminous spotty skin and the sweating agony of the cold turkey. I was as unromantic about junk as I was about nicotine and now I added speed. My head had always tended to buzz too fast anyway and the dozy calm of marijuana suited me better.

There was suddenly a lot of acid around and I approached it with the cautious conservatism I had had towards marijuana, sitting around for a long while with friends who were taking trips before deciding it seemed not to cause them harm. Even then, I took the sugar cubes (later the blotting paper) warily and only occasionally, over a period of several years in the late sixties and early seventies. Each time brought some insights I valued. Acid stripped away many of the socially acquired buffers and reminded you of the wonder of the ordinary. It intensified for me the capacity to see beauty in details which my eye would normally have lazily passed over, and it deconstructed the customary: the taken-for-granted symbolism of money could suddenly appear so evidently artificial, while a snail could be revealed as a magical and majestic creature.

Acid also helped me to reflect upon childhood, which now seemed to be without obvious reference points because of my parents' death, enabling me to reconsider my relationship with them. It was to heighten my awareness too of the discordance in the personal exercise of power I could observe in the everyday relations between men and women. Ever the historian, I was anxious to record and trace how my perceptions were being altered. But this was chasing bubbles; the scraps of paper document banalities. Acid, like sex, defies the chronicler. The cascading insights of the moment won't sit still and allow themselves to be transplanted into words on the page. They are apt to lose the gleaming intensity of their moment, like pebbles which reveal startling colours in the water but look dried and dull when the tide goes out.

There was certainly risk involved in taking a drug which had such a powerful effect. However, in my twenties I was prepared to take risks which later would seem unnecessary. I had no faith at all in the blanket condemnation of all drugs by officialdom, which I dismissed as biased and inaccurate. Relying instead on observation, I had ascertained that the risks did not seem insuperable. We regarded 'trips' as solemn ceremonials rather than recreational highs and took acid only in very safe circumstances. Out of the many people I knew who took LSD, only a tiny minority ever suffered serious psychological distress. I could acknowledge that it would be better in an ideal world to see the world anew as an artist, a poet or a mystic. But the scrambling of customary reality and the vividness of the particular which usually passed unnoticed were, in the meantime, things which fascinated me.

I had no desire to make acid a way of life, or to become completely absorbed in the culture of the underground – where there were as many bores as you might find in the straight world of the Mr Jones they so despised. My occasional trips simply broke up the rhythm of the everyday. In the late sixties and seventies whole stretches of time seemed to be available for contemplation. And I contemplated.

Being on my own left me more open to making close friendships. I met Roberta Hunter Henderson, who was to play a vital role in the emergence of the Women's Liberation movement, through the

Thompsons when Edward went to work at Warwick University, where Roberta was studying philosophy. Her face had a dark classic beauty belied by her frequent change of expression. She would furrow her brow, arch her eyebrows ironically, toss back her long brown wavy hair with a look of dramatic insouciance, all in quick succession. Roberta, who possessed an exceptional gift for maths and logic, was sometimes so abstract and disconnected that she was more or less unintelligible. I used to joke that I could earth her. She coexisted with her intellect rather uncomfortably and was drawn emotionally to the hippies' aesthetic playfulness. The year before I met her Roberta had become very famous at Warwick, when John Lennon had come courting her in a sports car just before he met Yoko Ono.

Another friend who dipped into the counter-culture was John Hoyland, who came to teach at Tower Hamlets College. John was long, blond and skinny, just like his wife, Wisty. They reminded me of two lurchers. John came from a Quaker and Communist Party background, influences which had had a similar effect to my Methodist school. John had edited the Youth CND paper, then he and Wisty had been caught up in tumultuous student uprisings in Latin America. John lived out two opposing extremes: one part of him headed after pleasure and fun, while another was responsible and slightly puritanical. I recognized the dichotomy. In the late sixties we were involved in the same radical networks.

I came across Vinay Chand at the London School of Economics and he was to guide me through the explosive politics which were brewing there in the late sixties. When his family moved from India to Britain, Vinay had learned how to survive in a London comprehensive where an Indian boy was still a novelty. These were skills he was to adapt to student politics. Very much the politico, Vinay was unimpressed by hippiedom, though even he was wearing black crushed-velvet trousers and a bright-yellow shirt in 1967. He was my first friend from India who had negotiated the everyday racism of growing up in Britain and was a pioneer in what is now described as 'hybridity', which he carried off with a carefully disciplined light touch.

Like Roberta and John, Vinay shared an eclectic approach to left politics and made friends across boundaries. From a Hindu family, he had become a Buddhist and a vegetarian and introduced me to the

Indian restaurants behind Warren Street station. He also used to take me to the Marlborough pub, off Tottenham Court Road, where his student friends from southern Africa would gather: real exiles these, drinking beer and speculating about the overthrow of the last vestiges of white colonialism.

The anti-colonial tradition at the LSE was transmuting into a 'Third World' radicalism by 1967 and the left was growing. Various camps were appearing, arguing about whether the revolution was to begin with the working class in the West or in national liberation struggles in the 'Third World'. Vinay, the diplomat, maintained connections with everyone but formed his own group, the FLN Society (a reference back to Algeria), with Ronnie Kasrils (later to be deputy defence minister in South Africa). Along with the southern African exiles, they included Asian socialists, North American New Leftists and variegated Latin American revolutionaries.

Since 1966 radical students had been protesting against the choice of Walter Adams, a former principal of a university in white Rhodesia, to be the director of the LSE. In March 1967 they held a sit-in against his appointment. The very act of sitting-in itself became a learning process, not only because it enabled students to talk together continuously but because it broke the pattern of daily life and involved a bodily defiance, not just ideas and words.

During the late sixties the LSE was to become a clearing house for radical ideas from many countries, influencing people like myself who were only remotely connected to it. Like the counter-culture, this newly emergent radical student milieu related subjective experience to political action. George Sorel's writings on the educative nature of direct action were being revived and mixed with the work of Frantz Fanon on colonization, while the theories of the French situationists about claiming space combined with the participatory democracy of the student Free Speech Movement which had erupted in Berkeley in 1964. The little band of earnest American New Leftists at the LSE brought with them ideas of the personal as political, along with a nihilism which expressed the vehement, helpless anger of US ultra-radicalism in the late sixties. It was not that the ideas of the late sixties were in themselves new; it was to be the particular mix which proved so explosive.

The creative consequences from this political whirlpool would send ripples through to the social movements of the next decades and contribute to the long-term attempt to produce a radical alternative to Stalinism. Yet the preoccupation with the transformatory effect of action upon consciousness could also display a negative aspect, wrenching the subjective away from objective circumstances. Then the action, rather than the effect of action, turned into an end in itself. This loss of balance was accompanied by a rhetoric of violence and sustained by an apocalyptic sense of the inevitable degeneration and disintegration of capitalism. For a minority this was to spiral off tragically into real violence in small terrorist groups.

One of the confusing features of periods of intense cultural and political transformation is the coexistence of opposing attitudes. Both the student radicals and the underground were ostensibly indifferent to the past and assumed that a complete break had occurred with everything that had gone before. Less overtly, this was accompanied by an apparently quite contradictory impulse to discover roots. While the iconoclastic hippies cultivated their romantic medievalism, many of us on the left were finding our bearings through the 'history from below' which Raphael Samuel's Ruskin College History Workshop meetings helped to inspire.

The political impasse of the New Left had proved the proverbial ill wind that blows nobody any good; socialism's loss was, ironically, to be radical history's gain. Several of the leading participants in the New Left, among them Dorothy and Edward Thompson, had returned to writing history. Early in 1967, Raphael's historical schemes too had begun growing and multiplying at a great rate, as if a surfeit of political energy was steaming backwards. The meeting on working-class education to which he had asked me to contribute had now increased to eight speakers and was to be held the following autumn. The Chartist day school occurred in March. These meetings were soon to be called History Workshops – the name Raphael took from the radical participatory theatre of Joan Littlewood and community politics in the United States.

The gatherings Raphael organized, like his papers, were always 'in progress', defying conventional constraints and endings, and this quality gave History Workshops the feel of the happenings which were part of the underground and meant they were attuned to the emphasis on 'process' in libertarian left politics. In fact, underneath the apparent chaos of 1,000 flowers blooming, Raphael, the former Communist, always had a plan – even if the plan was tucked well up in his jacket sleeve and not at all evident.

The skinny figure with the already thinning hair falling over his face would peer at you intently as if you were a walking social document and appear to be open to suggestion. However, behind the gaze and under the charm ran a tough vein of rigour and zeal, even though this was so esoteric in its expression and so utterly peculiar to Raphael's idiosyncrasies that it took a while to spot.

While Raphael the organizer was a benign despot, his creative imaginative leaps and his interest in all and sundry made space: for people, for cultural insights and for original approaches to history. Generous with his time, he read my thesis, which was in handwriting and three times the required length, simply out of friendship, sending me page after page of handwritten notes suggesting more on this and more on that. And for this I felt ever in his debt.

Urged on by his enthusiasm, I had managed to track down the last living member of Charles Ashbee's arts and crafts Guild of Handicraft in Chipping Campden and when I went to Oxford for the Chartist day school in March, I visited George Hart, then in his eighties and still at work as a silversmith. Ashbee had been convinced that a rural life would keep the workers' minds on their craft and away from socialism and revolution. But George Hart told me that most of the men had hated living in a village and drifted away. He had originally come from the countryside and, unlike the cockneys, had been able to adapt to Chipping Campden. The old silversmith was still grumbling about Ashbee's art nouveau designs being very difficult to execute in silverware, which he put down to Ashbee's training as an architect rather than as a craftsman in silver. In his youth George Hart had lived for a while in Hackney, playing football on Hackney Downs in the 1890s, just like the boys I used to see kicking away on the scrubby turf – a continuity of ordinary life which intrigued me.

After the talks on Chartism, Raphael decided to take us to a Chartist land colony at Witney. And it was while he tramped us around amidst mud and pigs that I realized I was fancying a young man with black curly hair and a large luminous face. Fancying is no easier to define than falling in love, which I also did with Steve Balogh, then an undergraduate studying biology at Balliol. It had something to do with his intense, quizzical regard and the way he cocked his head on one side. A little voice in the corner of my head did point out that this might not be the easiest person to organize a love affair with. But then everything whirred rapidly out of hand and passion took hold and swept the warning away.

The passion struck deeper than lust and lingered because Steve possessed a perceptivity about the power relations of personal behaviour which I had not encountered before in a man. He saw things women comprehended but from the vantage point of a man. He was able to name things that floated around my consciousness in a miasma of confusion, pointing consciously to responses still enmeshed in whorls of unstated half-understood resentment. Recognition did not, however, affect how he acted.

Not long after we met he took me round to a meal with a friend of his. I felt sidelined as they talked after we had eaten, but this was familiar. Relieved to be alone but also feeling martyred by my self-exile, I did the washing-up. They were both sons of intellectual mothers: Steve's was a psychoanalyst and his friend's a writer and broadcaster. As the cutlery rattled angrily in the kitchen, Steve told me later they had looked guiltily at one another.

Steve's psychological awareness of the dynamics of male–female relations haunted him like a heavy shadow and he performed elaborate contortions to discard a mindfulness beyond his years. I was to be wrapped up and turned inside out trying to interpret his bewildering emotional moves like a hypnotized rabbit for the next three years until I finally cast off the attraction in a belated but emphatic recoil.

Destiny had landed Steve with a hard act to follow. His father was the well-known economist Thomas Balogh, who was an adviser to Harold Wilson and a living legend in Oxford for eccentricity. Like other friends whose parents were Oxford academics, Steve had a nonchalance about odd behaviour which I envied and resented because it was impossible for me to emulate. I also marvelled at his lack of awe for the intellectual world of Oxford, which I had entered as an outsider.

When I first met him, Steve's consciousness seemed in perpetual flux. Not only did this keep me guessing; it suited the temper of the times, as did his eve-of-destruction mentality. He declared with confident conviction that the world was going to end in ten years' time, expressing a chiliastic spirit which had been an element in 'Ban the Bomb' and was to find its way into the counter-culture and eventually into environmental politics. In Steve's personal case the sense of inevitable doom didn't help his tendency to be inattentive about details – like when he was going to show up, for instance. He arrived just often enough for me not to entirely lose patience, appearing suddenly outside my window with the mysterious air of someone who had landed from another planet and therefore could not be held to account for not telephoning.

Steve was living at 46 Paradise Square, already familiar from my brief stay in 1964. By 1967 Oxford was much more druggy than in my time as a student. A morose gay Canadian junky haunted Paradise Square, cursing me from the kitchen. Town hippies wandered in and out. Upstairs, Welsh and charming and butterscotchy, lived Howard Marks, who was later to be imprisoned for marijuana dealing and emerge to write the best-selling *Mr Nice*. There was much panic about police raids after Steve had been dragged off by the police and found to be carrying sugar lumps. This proved to be a farcical incident as Steve's sugar lumps were simply hoarded from Balliol meals for his tea and coffee, containing nothing more sinister than sugar. However, after this scare Paradise Square operated an austere regime of constantly washing ashtrays – a nervous tic I was to retain over the years.

In the first half of 1967, such paranoia was, however, not unreasonable. When Mick Jagger, Keith Richards, Brian Jones and John Hopkins (of the green face and antennae) were arrested and tried on drugs charges, their cases were widely publicized. The police repeatedly raided *International Times* and drug busts were frequent. Perhaps because the forces of the state did not know how to keep tabs on networks, as opposed to hierarchical organizations, they seemed to be peculiarly rattled by the anti-authoritarian counter-culture, which for its part mainly wished to go off and do its own thing. The meditative euphoria of large numbers of young people who were quite indifferent to the sectarian cadences of the Trotskyist sects was thus repeatedly being invaded by the screech of police sirens and Black Marias. Having gone through the doors of perception, only to be treated as outcasts, they were left feeling profoundly unappreciated. Their personal resentment against the police was to turn into an undirected rage against 'the system'.

A politics of anger was already sweeping through the North American New Left and that July it was to clash head on with the vision of inner change which inspired the British underground at an extraordinary series of discussions held at the Roundhouse in Chalk Farm called 'The Dialectics of Liberation'. I went off on the overground train from Hackney to hear Ronnie Laing talk about the 'institutionalized' violence of the asylum. Social control was being presented by antipsychiatry as embedded within the texture of daily life, an idea which the women's movement was later to adapt. But that night it was posed as the personal versus the politicos, and the long-haired supporters of Laing roamed restlessly around the back of the hall when it was the turn of Stokely Carmichael, the Civil Rights activist who was shifting from non-violence to Black Power, to speak. I can remember the crackling tension in the air and the scorn with which he dismissed a young white woman who questioned separatist politics from the audience. Without any conscious feminism, I recoiled angrily from his refusal to listen to her and his disdain of her political support.

This first troubling encounter with a separatist politics made me want to understand more about the new black consciousness which was beginning to form outside the existing organizations for racial 'understanding', marking a break from the early-sixties sociological discourses about 'colour' and 'race'. The next day I went to a follow-up meeting at the Roundhouse which was nearly all black. Among the handful of other white people there was Allen Ginsberg, who wandered down the aisle chanting a mantra. The meeting greeted him with a laugh and a clap.

Long after the meeting ended I sat listening to a small group of black intellectuals arguing. Some stressed the political link with anti-imperialism, others wanted to create an alternative culture, economically or aesthetically, while one man defiantly protested about the oppression of having his artistic work judged in terms of black art. He insisted he wanted to be regarded as an individual – race was irrelevant. 'Black power' acquired more nuanced meanings.

Nonetheless, it was a very different black politics from the perspectives of the southern Africans I had met through Vinay who discussed strategies against white colonialism as an actuality rather than talking about race in terms of subjectivity or culture. We shared a common perspective sitting together in the Marlborough pub because we were on the left; the defining difference between us was their exile from their own countries, not race.

I never learned the personal circumstances which had forced them to flee, nor did I hear about their daily lives in Britain. The universalism of our Marxism obscured the specifics from which individuals came and, possessing no language to describe the process of being, it papered over gulfs in experience. 'Black power' was a more uncomfortable approach to politics for a left-wing white sympathizer, because you were cast as 'the other', yet it expressed an awareness of an apprehension beyond the intellect which struck an emotional chord of recognition. This dimension of understanding which we called 'liberation' was to reorientate how I saw politics. Although I continued, like Vinay, to be aware of the strengths of the Marxist emphasis on reason, analysis and strategy, which avoided some of the self-punishing, destructive aspects of separatist identity politics.

The black radicals I had met through 'The Dialectics of Liberation' encouraged me to read more of the American literature on race and black power, and from these I turned to Sartre's *Black Orpheus*, the poetry of Aimé Cesaire and, of course, Frantz Fanon. On the back of my Grove Press copy of Fanon's *Black Skin, White Masks* in 1967 I scribbled the names of writers he critiqued: Jacques Lacan, Karl Jaspers, Octave Mannoni. Existentialism and psychoanalytic thought appeared to offer a means of interpreting the inner and outer worlds. I was groping towards a new language of politics.

'All You Need Is Love' sang the Beatles; Cream released 'Strange Brew'. Throughout the summer of 1967 floating, gyrating rhythms played all around us. When Steve acquired tickets for Pink Floyd's gig at Warwick University that June, I wore a wafty green-gauze dress and we waved our arms in the air to the hypnotic lights. When the Pink Floyd roadie offered me a lift home in the van, dropping me off near the 38 bus stop on New Oxford Street, I sailed back to Hackney feeling the cat's whiskers of cool.

My fixated longings for Steve had persisted, but we saw one another only spasmodically and I had no idea when or whether he would appear. As everything became a hopeless tangle, I tangled matters all the more by a series of transient affairs. I even broke my own rule, which was not to get involved sexually with someone living in my house. Mary and Kathie had departed to live the simple life in floppy trousers on the tiny Spanish island of Formentera, when a friend from Oxford called Adam Hart sent me a new tenant he had met at the London Film School. Lawrence arrived at the door of 12 Montague Road wearing an extraordinary pair of winged sunglasses which made him look like Robin in *Batman* – well, a Robin who had been hanging out with the Beach Boys. His blond hair was eccentrically short by 1967 London standards and he had that brown, lean, healthy sheen that no one in London possessed. He was a surfer from California.

Lawrence looked so much the all-American conventional boy he seemed like a send-up. He said odd things like 'gooky chicks' and 'gremmy chicks' and 'go crash' (when he went to bed). He couldn't adapt to our diet (in which fried yams figured largely) and kept buying himself steaks, which seemed like excessive luxury to English commune dwellers at the time. He suffered greatly when we teased him; mildly sardonic jokes were deadly barbs to Lawrence, who interpreted run-of-the-mill irony as cruel.

Another oddness about Lawrence was his approach to geography. He thought nothing of hitching down to Cornwall and back in a weekend to go surfing. Later, when I learned how he had surfed in Hawaii as well as California, wandered around sleeping rough in Mexico, dodged fighting in Vietnam and twice hitched across the Sahara, I came to see how Cornwall must have seemed a piffling little distance. When I accompanied him one warm summer day, I was surprised to find that it was indeed feasible and that, in Newquay, the Lawrence we teased was treated as a god-like figure because he had been in surfing films riding the enormous waves of Hawaii on acid. This was my first introduction to beach society and I noted that, like any other, under its free-and-easy exterior it was regulated by strict rules and marked by rigid status divisions. These were of course all male-determined. However, I wasn't too proud to bask a bit in his reflected glory.

Lawrence managed to persuade unphysical me that the sun and the sea could be sources of pleasure. I had regarded the sun as an enemy before, assuming that because I had ginger hair I would never be able to go brown. As for the sea, I liked swimming but was secretly frightened of monsters. Lawrence showed me I could swim for much longer than I imagined. To him the sea was something to read and to move within; understanding how to negotiate its currents, he could dive through big waves or ride them in triumph. His approach to nature was part physical, part mystical and part practical. His sunny demeanour was charged with a frisson of darkness, but he kept this in reserve. Surfers, like racing-car drivers and gliders, carry their death wish lightly.

He had been a lifeguard and I listened carefully to his advice. I have always worried that through lack of gump I would fail in some testing natural disaster. Consequently I store away information about what to do in unlikely circumstances. 'What to do if shipwrecked'; 'What to do if stranded on an island'; 'What to do if someone is drowning'. Lawrence was emphatic; never try to rescue a drowning person without being trained in life-saving because they would undoubtedly hit you on the head, knock you out and drag you under. I worried nonetheless how you could stand there and let them drown, mumbling apologetic-ally, 'Sorry, I never did a life-saving course.'

Lawrence was going off to surf in Spain and suggested that I went with him. The daily upkeep of the house, filled with decorative and unemployed musicians who were friends of friends, had foisted a landlady responsibility upon me which I hated. I was lonely and unhappy about Steve for long stretches of time. Travelling with the amiable, pleasant Lawrence would, I imagined, allow me to shake off all my troubles in the sun. The night before we left, like a telepathic homing pigeon, Steve appeared. Ecstatically happy because he was there, I didn't want to waste time being angry about the occasions he had not shown up. 'Why is my life such chaos?' I asked him. The question was rhetorical but he replied, 'Because you invite chaos into your home.' Part of me acknowledged responsibility, part of me still believed that things just happened.

The usually easygoing Lawrence was fuming next morning because of Steve's nocturnal arrival. 'I did tell you I was with Steve,' I protested. But Lawrence clearly considered being 'with' someone meant you actually saw them in person. As far as he was concerned Steve was some guy who had appeared out of nowhere. Nonetheless, we headed off to Bilboa to pick up his surfboard, lent to a surfer in Newquay. In Bilboa things began to go seriously wrong. It took us a long time to track down the place on the docks where the surfboard was to arrive. When we got there, we were told by a shrugging Spanish official that it had not been sent. Day after day we returned. Lawrence became more and more wretched. Eventually he was forced to admit that the Newquay surfer had betrayed him. We would go on without it. I was relieved because I was fed up of being stuck in Bilboa. We went first to Barcelona, where we would get a boat to Ibiza, which had become a hippie holiday place, and then cross to the secluded island of Formentera.

A lorry carried us through brown rocky countryside which I scanned in excitement. Spain felt very different from France; not only was the landscape starker, the heat made the air heavy. I was conscious of being in a country ruled by the fascist Franco and in my imagination it seemed as if oppression weighed physically on the land. I was telling myself that you can't sense a dictatorship in the air when an old peasant woman walking towards us on the dusty road in the middle of nowhere fixed her eyes on the lorry driver's in silent communication. Slowly and eloquently, she raised a finger to one eye. 'Police,' announced the driver, and promptly hid us in the cab.

General Franco retained his power over the Spanish state during the late sixties and early seventies, though the economic need to attract tourists, which left the coastline scarred with concrete ugliness, was to loosen the authoritarianism of his regime in everyday culture. However, in 1967 this commercialization had not reached Formentera and no tourist hotels existed on the island. There was just a tiny landing place, a cluster of houses and two small restaurants inland where the roads joined. Up on La Mola, the hill with its Roman track still leading down to the sea, another café was run by a laconic youth nicknamed 'the fat boy' and his severe mother, who had straight black eyebrows and a black shawl over her head. The rest of the island was flat, with a tawny bleak beauty dotted with green fig trees. Profoundly peaceful, Formentera had a long history as a place of retreat; the Carthaginians had fled there after the Romans sacked their city. The island people behaved distantly, though they were not unfriendly to the strange flocks of hairy visitors who were coming to their little settlement.

By the time Lawrence and I arrived, Mary and Kathie had already left the small white house with a well where they had been living for several months. But the transient community of hippies from Europe and the United States radiated a welcoming spirit of cooperative spontaneity, enhanced by apparently unlimited supplies of hash – great chunks of it, like Cheddar cheese portions in a supermarket. Nature, immediacy and love were the watchwords of this wandering society. Strangers were greeted and shown the isolated beach where everyone spread out their sleeping bags. Nobody bothered to wear clothes much – nakedness felt unaffected and comfortable. We played with lizards on the sand or swam amidst the shoals of tiny fish in the warm sea. I was to return again and again to Formentera and each time found a special serenity in its landscape. But that hippie moment of innocence, when freedom and security were held in harmonious balance, was to be unique to the untroubled summer of 1967.

Lawrence was not one to lounge around and announced we had to move on. I followed him, puffing and panting through Spanish towns, a rucksack on my back, going dizzy and swaying in the sun. 'Eat olives and salty things,' instructed a sun-wise Lawrence. I didn't like olives but ate them nonetheless. In Alicante we arrived in darkness and couldn't find anywhere to sleep. The clear patch of land hidden away where we finally collapsed turned out to be the town dump. I awoke in the early light of morning surrounded by rubbish, desperate for a coffee and extremely disgruntled. And Lawrence, grinning and good-natured, extracted his revenge for me not being in love with him by filming me stomping off bleary-eyed through piles of rubble. My mother had always warned me that with my attitude to life I would end up on the Mile End Road. Well, the Mile End Road was manageable, but a rubbish tip was too much. I demanded the luxury of a hotel the next night.

Lawrence was a firm believer in sleeping on beaches to avoid mosquitoes and one night on the south coast, heading in the direction of

Morocco, we put down our sleeping bags on the sand. Shortly after we had settled, two Spanish policemen appeared, towering over us in their intimidating regalia. They let us stay with an admonition to be off at dawn so we didn't upset the 'tourists'. Later that night I woke again and thought I was having a nightmare. A man was bending over me in the darkness. I could see a gun and holster lying on the ground. A face with a moustache was just above mine. One of the policemen had returned and had unzipped my sleeping bag. He had the cover folded back and was looking at me. The eyes that met mine were filled with a dangerous fear.

For a moment I froze, too terrified to speak. Lawrence stirred. The Guardia flicked back the cover of the sleeping-bag and grabbed his gun belt, standing up and abruptly resuming the authority of the law. Lawrence awoke and assumed that some arbitrary change of mind had brought him back. The policeman brusquely demanded our passports. We dug around in our bags and he solemnly inspected them, telling us to get going. Light was just beginning to break over the sea as we tramped across the sand with our bags. It took me a while to tell Lawrence what had happened. I felt embarrassed and ashamed, though rationally I knew these were incongruous responses. He listened in silence and I got the impression that he thought things could have been much worse. As dawn lit the sky I glanced at my watch to see the time. It had gone, stolen by the law – this was Franco's Spain.

As I staggered through the heat down the Spanish coast I tried to remember the history of the Civil War. Gerald Brennan's *The Spanish Labyrinth* had given me romantic expectations of Malaga, the city of heroic Anarchist defiance. I could not connect the city through which we were walking with the pictures in my mind. It was only about thirty years before but no traces of that other Spain were apparent. The revolutionary past had, it seemed, been entirely erased. Not until over a decade later, after Franco died, did Spanish socialist women tell me how a continuity had persisted – 'the historical memory'.

That summer of 1967 I wondered how on earth anyone could *fight* in such heat. The sun burned down on my head and I could barely walk with my bag on my back. As I talked to Lawrence about the Spanish Civil War I realized to my amazement that he had no idea what I was talking about. Lawrence would enthuse about Herman

Melville's *Moby-Dick* or Ambrose Bierce's stories, but history seemed to have passed him by. How could you be a radical kind of person with no knowledge of the history of revolutions, I asked him? Lawrence smiled his smile of the sun and the present. He was still hoping to surf. In the long dead periods between rides, I resolved to fill him in with lectures on the debates between Jacobins and Girondins, the differences between the left Communists and Trotsky in the Russian Revolution, and a few asides on the history of Anarchism. Lawrence was a patient man and listened with moderate interest. On a dusty Spanish road there was not much alternative entertainment.

Eventually we crossed the sea to Morocco and arrived in Tangier. The courtyards and variegated levels of flat-roofed houses linked by narrow criss-cross streets enclosed and confused, evoking those wandering dreams of being lost in an aimless maze. With my appalling sense of direction, I feared I could well disappear in the old part of the city for ever and stuck close to Lawrence and the boy carrying our bags. My miniskirt fascinated street urchins, who would surround me if I ever faltered, so I kept moving. At last we found a hotel, where I was startled to see myself in the mirror. Ginger or not, I had changed colour. My hair had lightened in the sun and my face looked like a freckled brown egg. I was delighted with this other 'me', and kept checking to see if I was still there. Lawrence was perplexed by my frequent scans in the mirror – like many effortlessly good-looking people, he was without petty vanity.

On our return journey we caught a plane to Madrid to avoid hitching through the centre of Spain and were befriended by a group of friendly elderly American tourists who loved Lawrence. His short surfer hair meant he could easily pass for the all-American boy and we were briefly treated as sweet young things. I was touched by their genuine warmth and liked being mopped up and fussed over by them, leaving me perplexed by the paradox that was North America, so kind to the familiar, yet so cruel to the Vietnamese far away.

Our last stop beyond the Pyrenees was Biarritz, where at last Lawrence could ride the surf. The old resort had gone out of fashion and its past grandeur was peeling. Undeterred by the pervasive feel of decay, indefatigable sixties surfers, attracted by the Atlantic breakers, had rediscovered its fading delights. A band of French and Australian surfers were camping in an abandoned hotel and we moved our sleeping bags into a room with bare wooden boards. Downstairs an enterprising Frenchman had established a grill which produced baked potatoes and steak.

When I saw how much the surfers ate, I realized why our Ridley Road diet had seemed so frugal to Lawrence. They were tall, craggy men, their skin darkened by the sun and their hair so bleached they looked as if they used peroxide. These global roamers had their own versions of the Marxist International: instead of exchanging information about workers' struggles, they discussed waves in various parts of the world. They had a ballerina grace on the waves, but out of the sea they were monosyllabic billy-goat-gruffs and they would never speak to me or even nod in acknowledgement of my presence. 'Why don't they talk to me?' I fumed to Lawrence. He would patiently explain that in surfer etiquette – especially in Australian surfer etiquette – if you spoke to a chick, it was assumed you were coming on to her and that would be to insult the man she was with. The Australians might seem like rough diamonds; in fact, they were being studiously polite. But I continued to grumble, because I felt like a non-person.

There seemed to be a pattern in this: first Bob's intellectual *New Left Review* friends, then the Oxford bikers, now these Australians. How could apparently dissimilar men have this peculiar behaviour in common? Why did being a woman make you invisible if they weren't going to chat you up? Lawrence just shrugged off these questions and got back on a surfboard. I didn't even have a captive audience to lecture on the French Revolution.

I tried body-surfing and Lawrence was encouraging, but I was an awkward novice in this world. The young French women, 'gremmy chicks', as Lawrence called them, were much more skilful. 'Women,' Lawrence declared, 'can never really be good surfers on big waves.' I began arguing with him furiously. He insisted that it was something about women's bodies which meant they couldn't balance. I refused to be convinced. The Biarritz beach was fostering feminist thoughts. What chance had the women in this male scene, I wondered to myself grumpily?

*

Leaving Lawrence to his waves, I returned to London, turfing an unknown hippie out of my bed before I wearily fell asleep. Lawrence was soon to leave London; he had decided that despite the danger of being drafted he needed his big waves. I resumed my occasional meetings with Steve, seeing him briefly at a party given by some of Adam Hart's innovative friends from Balliol, who were now making gliders and inflatables.

With Kathie and Mary back, the music and the visitors had recommenced at 12 Montague Road and a Hammond organ was now playing in the room next to my study. I felt lonely and isolated in the house and would lie in bed putting off complaining about the noise, then finally, unable to sleep, would run upstairs shaking with fury. Ruefully I remembered the story of *The Good Woman of Setzuan*. Authoritarianism, I was painfully learning, was not so much ingrained as circumstantial.

I was distressed by my estrangement from Mary. Our friendship had been strained by the tensions in the house and the distance between us was growing ever harder to cross. Occasionally we could still talk as we had done about ideas and observations, but the ease of the exchange had gone. We no longer shared the same assumptions or wanted to live in the same way; our outlooks had split apart.

Brian, meanwhile, had dropped out of school and been stopped late one night carrying a minute piece of hash. Cursing his thoughtlessness, I had to go to court dressed up in my teacher-type clothes to defend his character. He was let off with a warning and I managed to look the part so convincingly that the policeman assumed I was the probation officer. There seemed to be some profoundly respectable welfare state ethos about my character. At the British Museum the security guards assumed I was a librarian, while taxi-drivers in east London took me for a nurse.

I continued to search for working-class University Extension students, busily pestering libraries from Durham to Exeter with queries. Cambridge University Press wrote saying they would like to look at the manuscript of my thesis. I explained it was in handwriting, but offered it just the same, whereupon a tactful note came back: 'Perhaps it would be best to wait until it is typed before submitting it here. I say this because the usual procedure is to ask one or two professional referees to advise the Syndics, and I will not be able to send it out until I have a typed version.'

My personal life might be messy and inconclusive, but a new decisiveness was discernible on the left that autumn. After that meandering summer in which so many currents had been swirling under the surface, a sudden change of purpose was evident along with a certain sense of being implicated in history with a capital 'H'. Just as 1967 had begun in 1966, 1968 was starting already. On 8 October the Bolivian military shot Che Guevara. I can remember the sobering shock of the photograph of his corpse along with Richard Gott's report on the front page of the *Guardian*. I started to keep a diary on 14 October after meeting Tariq Ali, who had recently returned from Bolivia, where he had been arrested with Robin Blackburn and Perry Anderson during the trial of the French writer on guerrilla warfare Régis Debray.

I was being pulled back into politics. On 22 October the Vietnam Solidarity Committee held another demonstration. It was the day after the Pentagon demonstration in the United States and was the first mass demonstration in solidarity with the Vietnamese National Liberation Front. Feeling groggy because hippie visitors had woken me up at four in the morning, I was nonetheless exhilarated by the size of the march, a great gathering of everyone I had ever known plus thousands more besides. I found an excited Bob in the crowd enthusing about the building workers' strike at the site of the new Barbican development in the City.

This Barbican strike signalled a new unruly militancy among young workers and the Labour government responded to them with a heavy hand. By November 2,000 police were down at the Barbican and mounted police broke through the picket line, confirming left-wing disenchantment with the Wilson government. The building workers' bitter anger merged with a widespread desperation among opponents of the Vietnam War, haunted by the photographic images of hunted Vietnamese being lined up, the Buddhist monks' self-immolation, the TV coverage of unrelenting US bombing raids. Yet Wilson, despite pressure from the Labour left, despite our demonstrations, remained resolutely in support of President Johnson.

Two disturbing letters arrived from Lawrence in California during

November. In the first he reported, 'The FBI doesn't know I'm in the country so there's no warrant out yet,' and described how one of his friends was 'in hospital trying to keep his leg on after stepping on a mine'. He was still asking for news of the surfboard – Lawrence retained a trusting faith in people. The next letter was on American National Red Cross notepaper. They'd picked him up in Hawaii, where the US Attorney had told him, 'Go to serve your nation or go to prison.' The lure of those big waves had been his undoing. When he refused to eat, they strait-jacketed him and kept him in jail under observation for a month, diagnosing him as 'a chronic schizophrenic manifested by severe hallucinations, loose associations and autistic behaviour'. In extremity, Lawrence's optimistic, nature-child personality was mutating. 'Went to a rally in Frisco against the war and for the Black Panthers last time I was *AWOL*. You'll be pleased to know a Marxist has captured control over the Peace and Freedom party.'

It was ironic that Lawrence, who just wanted big waves to ride and quiet ecstasy, was being strait-jacketed for refusing to kill people in a war he had simply turned his back on. He was in prison for not fighting Marxism, while I, the one who had lectured him remorselessly on Lenin, Trotsky and the Workers' Opposition, was simply scuffling about outside the American Embassy. I tried to imagine how I would face the military police, but my timorous imagination couldn't stretch that far. Lawrence's letter helped me to make a decision. The International Socialists were drifting out of the Labour Party and, along with the Young Liberals and the International Marxist group, were setting up a local branch of Vietnam Solidarity. I decided this was the place I would concentrate all my energy and left the Labour Party. I couldn't be part of an organization that supported Lyndon Johnson.

In Oxford that November I finally spoke at Raphael Samuel's meeting on working-class education, which turned into History Workshop 2. I was nervous and apprehensive facing the crowd of students in the hall at Ruskin College. I had given a talk on the Luddites at Hackney Young Socialists at which I'd been denounced by members of Militant, who had insisted the Luddites were being objectively reactionary because they should have realized that a modern proletariat had to be created by the factory system. I had told them I thought this was a daft way of thinking, but I had been on home ground. The Ruskin trade union men could have given me a hard time because I was describing a class experience which was not my own. Instead they came up to me and compared what I had said about the worker-students of the 1890s and 1900s with their own lives. It was reassuring that the personal details I had been unsure about regarding as 'history' were recognizable. Their generosity was to be a reminder, when the women's movement came along, that historical inquiry can travel over boundaries and does not have to be confined within specific identities.

In fact class in British society was changing noticeably by 1967. It wasn't, as Mary Quant and others have implied, that 'Swinging London' had become classless. But the relative prosperity of the previous decade, along with low unemployment, had resulted in a generation of young workers who were shedding deference. Young working-class women on the pill had acquired just a bit more space and confidence to break the rules. The Who hit in 1965 'Anyway, Anyhow, Anywhere' had heralded their arrival and by 1967 they were making their way in miniskirted droves through 'Swinging London'. I was impressed when two blonde sassy independent travellers visited our house. They had just gone round the world dancing in cages. I was sure I would never have had the bottle.

This was the year of two important sexual reforms: homosexuality between consenting adults and abortion were legalized. I can remember hearing the news of the latter and thinking, 'Thank goodness,' at the back of my head. But with little knowledge of the long campaigns behind the two reforms, I took them for granted, regarding the laws as simply keeping up with attitudes which I assumed were spreading inevitably through the land. In fact both these changes marked real shifts which were to alter assumptions.

Quite suddenly that December I started ruminating about being a woman in a spate of diary entries. Brooding on the masculine lens which filtered perceptions of femininity – 'State of being a woman seen through the eyes of men' – I was reinterpreting the women characters in books by male authors. For instance, I questioned the 'good girl', 'bad girl' dichotomy in John Braine's Room at the Top, a novel in which I had obediently loathed Susan and identified with Alice (especially after she was played by Simone Signoret in the film). I also began reconsidering Sartre's passive woman in the dressing-gown, a figure of dread for me because Bob had communicated her 'immanence' as a kind of female living death. Now I had stumbled into an insight about the obvious: those literary figures I had worried so much about resembling had simply been created out of men's hang-ups. It was all in their heads.

I tried to make sense of incidents I had observed with resentment, putting many uneasy feelings and responses together – a man at a party talking about a woman's buttocks as if she was meat, another calling girls 'bits'. Women, I noted, operated within the narrow spaces allotted to femininity, as assertive hip chicks, academic women, mother goddesses, geisha-type sex symbols, independent girly girls, being matter of fact or taking comfort in dismissing men. I thought we jumped in and out of these modes of being and that our discomfort about how to 'be' put us at a disadvantage in relation to men. There was an emphasis upon 'wholeness' in hippie thinking, and Mary had suggested to me that if these diverse forms of behaving and relating could only be combined it would make women much stronger and less dependent on men.

I puzzled over how this integration could happen. Even in resisting we seemed to 'map out certain areas of independence and compensate in others'. I was convinced the solution couldn't be found by simply working out an ideal of emancipation in your head, for the very ways women learned to be feminine came from a male culture: 'Women take on the attributes given them by men and parade them with pride. Very like the black/white thing.' Nor were we necessarily conscious of how we assimilated our femininity.

Before Lawrence had left, we had gone to see *Bonnie and Clyde*, the romantic film about two outlaws in thirties America, starring Faye Dunaway as Bonnie in a becoming black beret. When Bonnie adjusted her hair to please Clyde (Warren Beatty), I looked at her expression, taking her cue from a man's, and thought, 'I'd never be so submissive.' Lawrence turned to me in the cinema, saying innocently, 'She looks just like you often look.'

It was unbearable to think that there was nothing we could call our own. Women, I decided, *did* have a culture, though I observed that this took various forms depending on your class. I was aware that my education meant the way I saw myself and the world differed from many other women and that this self-consciousness isolated me. But I already knew that I was not entirely alone, catching a glimmer of a group, writing, 'Only our kind who operate in men's world can acquire a marginality which makes it possible to ascribe limits and areas to the assumptions somehow inherited. We become in fact half men.' (I'd been reading Genet.)

As I started to rethread and reinterpret previously disconnected memories, films and books about women came to assume a new significance. Peter Collinson's *Up the Junction*, based on articles by Nell Dunn, was kitchen-sink drama sentimentalized, but it was unusual in dealing with contemporary class dynamics from the vantage point of the woman. Despite its superficiality, I could empathize with the theme of the middle-class girl going to live in working-class Battersea. The very different *Persona*, Ingmar Bergman's tortured film about a woman who breaks down and starts to live the illusion she plays as an actress, left me with a profound anxiety which I could not articulate.

I returned to Simone de Beauvoir's writings, to find they had taken on a new relevance and clarity. From 1966 I had also been working my way through Doris Lessing's novels, discovering in *The Golden Notebook* a new sensibility which mixed the personal with left politics, a startling reflection of perceptions I had assumed to be purely individual. The essays of the left wing German psychoanalyst Karen Horney on 'feminine psychology' in 1967 made me realize that concepts of cultural hegemony, familiar from Marxism in relation to class, were being applied during the twenties to women.

Yet 'feminism' did not interest me. I knew it only as the suffrage movement of long ago or as a lobby of professional women for advancement at work. This narrow version of 'feminism' as the demand for external rights had no purchase on the personal relationships which preoccupied me. I associated even the broader term 'emancipation' with competing with men and regarded the claims of women in the public arena as 'men's attitudes' in reverse.

Adamant that I didn't want to be like a man, the evident contradictions in how to be a woman kept making me question my own emotions and relationships. I was aware of different kinds of desire, and wondered whether there was a connection between my sexual feelings and the cycle of my periods. I tried to chart moods and responses in a haphazard way in my diary, but the infinity of variables ultimately foxed me. I knew that I could simply want sex physically and not emotionally, but this was more or less impossible to assert publicly in 1967. Such an admission would be too likely to be met by derision from men and scorn from women.

I was also troubled because I knew that in some of my encounters with men sexually I could be as detached and controlled as they sometimes were with me. I was, I thought, 'using' them sexually for physical satisfaction. I interpreted this as an inversion of the traditional male approach to sex and thus a dead end which simply reproduced relations of estrangement.

I did not see men as a group as uniformly powerful or myself as a defenceless victim, for I had observed that men could be vulnerable and that they seemed to fear women. It was the contrariness within myself which concerned me. My desire to lose myself in passion locked with a ferocious resolve to hang on to myself. With some men I could contrive to be possessed physically but not emotionally. But I hankered after the total risk – to be annihilated and yet still there; to be taken over and remain intact. At the same time I was driven by a longing for a sexuality which was not about possession or being possessed, for forms of relating and loving I could hardly express or even imagine.

I was puzzling over the gap which divided these private musings about sexuality from 'politics' when the first hint of the existence of a Women's Liberation movement reached me. The news arrived unexpectedly and I nearly missed it.

I didn't want to go out on a cold December night to the first meeting of the East London Vietnam Solidarity Committee; I had to grit my teeth as I headed off down Mare Street to the Trades Council Hall. Sure enough it was all too familiar – another meeting dominated by unpractical but opinionated Trotskyist men. The new East London VSC group had no money. I brightly suggested a jumble sale; no one responded, so I piped up again. They kept cutting me out of the discussion as if I had never spoken. I was exasperated but it was a familiar pattern. The unconscious assumption was that because a jumble sale involved women – old women to boot – it was inherently 'reformist'. But they had no other suggestions for raising funds and I stuck to my guns. I knew how to organize a jumble sale. We had no money. My voice was beginning to rise. I was being overemphatic. Eventually the chairman begrudgingly agreed I could organize a jumble sale. The secretary equally begrudgingly consented to book a room.

The meeting moved on with relief to more serious matters, asking the comrade from the Stop It Committee to give his report. I waited for someone to come forward. Nothing happened. Then I heard something peculiar. From the back of the room came a male voice rejecting the offer to take the floor. This was an unprecedented event in my experience. Moreover, he was speaking in a modest mumble – I heard an American accent saying 'like' every third word. Like he could just talk like from the back like. Most peculiar! I turned round and saw a good-looking man in his late twenties or early thirties with longish dark hair, a white kaftan shirt and hippie beads. How on earth had he got to Hackney Trades Council and what was all this diffident stuff?

Henry Wortis, the comrade from Stop It, a group of Americans against the Vietnam War, did another surprising thing that night. According to the North American custom, he offered me a lift home after the meeting. In Hackney you walked or got the bus – there was still no feeling of any danger. But it was cold and a lift was welcome. I liked this American man with his quiet air of authority despite the libertarian front. He proceeded to tell me that they were shutting me up at the meeting. I grinned. People were always telling me I talked too much and men in left meetings often made me feel as if I was being unruly, which made me more defiantly unruly. But, Henry went on, it was because I was a woman. I couldn't believe my ears. This was an extraordinary thing for a left man to be saying. According to Henry, there was this thing called 'male chauvinism' and that's what had been going on in that VSC meeting.

I usually thought that I had a hard time because I wouldn't adopt the particular mannerisms acceptable for women in left groups, which involved holding your body stiff in an asexual neutrality and jabbing in the air to prove you were 'hard'. This I knew very well turned off every other woman in the room who was sitting there silent and alienated. I was determined not to be cut off from women by turning myself into a ridiculous martinet to impress men. I could acknowledge that the common deadpan response from men when I or another woman spoke *might* be because we had said something foolish. On the other hand, this was not how they behaved with men. If they disagreed with one another, they engaged and argued. Our remarks seemed, in contrast, to just fall into oblivion. It was as if you had never spoken. This made your voice falter or you would shout with the pitch just too high. I definitely didn't want them to be chivalrous, just for communication to be easier. Now Henry had produced a name for all these puzzling difficulties: male chauvinism. He explained that he knew this because his wife, Shelley, had been in a Women's Liberation group in Boston. Several groups in the United States had been started by women from the New Left.

I was to meet Henry and Shelley over the next two years as Women's Liberation groups began to form in Britain. But it was not until many years later that I learned about Henry's own political background. In the mid-fifties, during the McCarthy era, Henry Wortis had kept left debate going at his university – Madison, Wisconsin – through the secret Labor Youth League, acting as a bridge between the old left and the new. The historian Herbert Gutman described Henry and his fellow undergraduates in this difficult period as 'very funny, wonderful, free in their spirits, radical but a whole separate generation from the old left true believers'.

The dramatic events of 1968 were to relegate personal concerns to the back burner of consciousness. However, the new insight Henry had transmitted from the Boston Women's Liberation movement did not entirely go away and that 'male chauvinism' term was to churn around in the back of my head.

Right at the end of 1967, however, it felt like time to take a breath. John Hoyland wanted to know if I would like to parade around an architectural students' ball in a mask. A friend of his, a poet and puppeteer, was making elaborate papier-mâché masks. Though mine was an unartistic white paper bag with a red nose, we were a big hit on the tube, where we were treated as minor celebrities. We waltzed around the dance floor at the ball to oohs and aahs until it was time for the next act, when the architects quickly lost interest. A strip-tease had begun on stage. I looked at the stripper through the slits in my white paper bag with a queasy sensation. Yet another of those contradictions. How was I to regard her?

More masks, fairgrounds and people getting away and having fun appeared on television on 26 December in the Beatles' sly satire of 'straight' society, *The Magical Mystery Tour*. Again there was a strip-tease. As I watched the black and white television, I caught myself picking up their excitement. Suspended, I observed myself divided in two, seeing another woman's body through men's eyes. It was a moment of incongruity when the outer world and my own perceptions collided uncomfortably.

At the end of 1967 I was feeling profoundly disjointed and askew. I was not, of course, the only woman sensing that personal experience was shifting in the late sixties. It was as if some hidden plate deep under the surface of appearances had moved irrevocably, sending out tiny, barely perceptible seismic shocks which were shortly to contribute to an earthquake. After this politics was never to be quite the same.

CHAPTER 5

1968

Early in 1968 the Vietnamese National Liberation Front were advancing through the south. I heard about the Tet offensive in the dusty, dilapidated building in Tottenham Street where Adam Hart, the friend who had sent Lawrence to be my lodger, was living. We watched the flickering television with incredulity and then began cheering. The news was more extraordinary than the fusions and partings of the light shows Adam was doing. The commentator was showing how much territory the NLF had taken; the victims were turning into victors. A small group in Saigon had raised the red, blue and yellow flag of the NLF over the American Embassy. Though the embassy was later recaptured, nonetheless it was a decisive turning point and the first indication that we had entered an extraordinary year.

One of the fatal reflexes of left politics is surely the celebration of noble defeats, and since becoming a socialist I had conditioned myself to supporting lost causes. The NLF winning broke through this habitual pessimism. There is nothing as powerful as example and the Vietnamese resistance sent a sense of possibility flashing out over the airwaves all around the globe. If the Vietnamese could take on the mightiest power in the world, what about us?

My own Vietnam Solidarity efforts that January in Hackney were not exactly at the cutting edge, being rather the revolutionary equivalent of 'doing my bit'. The saga of the jumble sale for East London VSC was continuing. At the eleventh hour, with jumble bursting out of my bedroom, I discovered the Trotskyist secretary had considered himself too much the grand revolutionary to book a hall for the jumble sale. Suspecting sabotage and hardly able to move around in my room for boxes, I defiantly stuck up the notices in the newsagent's anyway:

'Victory to the Vietcong Jumble Sale, 12 Montague Road.' Sure enough, the tough gangs of elderly women who were regulars at all the local jumble sales were in the door, down the corridor past the 'Dialectics of Liberation' poster on the wall and bargaining fiercely. Then off they went, like the proverbial greased lightning, leaving sad little piles of debris in their wake.

The momentum of the jumble sale went with them. A few lost Hackney souls, bemused and aimless, were left ambling around my bedroom, evidently disorientated at finding themselves in a house. Indeed, one Caribbean man, who must have decided the solution to this oddness was that we were an extension of Mr Archie's business next door, propositioned Mary and me. I steered him past the 'Victory to the Vietcong' posters and out through the front door.

Over the course of 1968, many people, radicalized through CND in the early sixties and then disheartened by sectarian politics in the mid-sixties, were to become involved in the demonstrations around Vietnam. The police assault on the counter-culture was also to bring younger people into radical activity in defiance of 'the system' and 'the fuzz'. In the first few months, however, left politics continued to depend on tiny left groups who remained set in their inturned ways.

Early in 1968 personal worries rather than politics were preoccupying me. These were, as ever, a teenage Brian, with whom I could no longer communicate and who was soon to leave 12 Montague Road, and of course Steve, or rather the absence of Steve.

My whole relationship with Steve was about yearning really. I estimate it was around 70 per cent yearning and 30 per cent sex and relating. It consumed an extraordinary amount of emotional energy, though, regardless of the fact that actual contact was rare. Over these three years I would meet men, sex would come up, sometimes I did and sometimes I didn't. Some vanished, some were smitten and some I ran away from. Yet others became good friends. However, the obsessive returning to Steve went on – because the sex was always amazing and because he would intimate things I couldn't see myself but wanted to understand. Nothing was ever explicitly stated and I was never to unravel the power of the connection between us. I knew I was going round in circles, like a caged mouse on its wheel, but it took me a long time to get off. I carried on out of stubbornness, or perhaps because of wanting not to be afraid of knowing passion, of merging without being obliterated. When it ended, Steve wrote saying that I had always held him at a distance. Ostensibly, though, he had been the one who was always vanishing.

For several years after leaving Bob, despite my loneliness, I was terrified of becoming part of a couple again. The fishes growing on my skin made me shudder. A tragic love was in certain crucial ways safer than a reliable one. The times were as ambiguous as I was. By the late sixties sex was often not a big deal, though my generation of young women had been brought up to consider that it would be. This was just one of the splits we lived between. What happened and what we had been led to expect never seemed to be in sync. In 1968 practice had gone ahead of attitude and it was difficult to say, 'I just felt like it', 'I was curious', 'I thought I might as well', 'There was nowhere to sleep.' A grand romance balanced the other profligate and amicable sexual relationships which popped up in daily life. It was the 'real thing'.

I was nearly twenty-five, about to hit that old borderline which, only a few years earlier, had seemed to mean you were definitely grown up. But I wasn't feeling grown up at all. We had moved all the signposts anyway and nothing signified what it had done then. I had no clear idea how to live in the new space. Teaching seemed the only certainty which still made sense and I threw myself into work. I must have been looking conspicuously troubled, because Chris, the engineering student at Tower Hamlets, remarked with East End solicitude, 'You take things too hard, gel. You'll be a nervous wreck by the time you're thirty.'

Amidst the chaos of my house I had managed to acquire two responsible house members with whom I was friendly, a bass player called Stevie York and his partner, Helen, who made clothes for pop musicians, including Jimi Hendrix's drummer and the poet Pete Brown, who had been part of the jazz and poetry scene with Mike Horowitz in the mid-sixties. His song 'I Feel Free' had become a hit single for Cream in 1967. Pete had continued writing lyrics, though his real ambition was to be a singer in his own band.

I was teaching a new class of London Transport trainees, who all seemed to be budding poets, and to encourage them I persuaded Pete, whose grandparents had lived in east London, to come to the college in Jubilee Street. He started off in their class and went on right through the lunch hour. Some of the Port of London Authority messenger boys piled in, along with the group of engineering apprentices which included Chris and the hairdressing students. A great mélange of skinheads, greasers and long-haired Rolling Stones lookalikes sat listening intently to the tubby, hairy hippie. Pete was a great showman and extrovert, and the fact that he had written lyrics for Cream gave him God-like authority. It was all right to be weird: 'She was like a bearded rainbow.' It was all right to talk about your feelings: 'Sunshine of your love'. And you could be a sexual loser.

Pete left a wave of creative enthusiasm in his wake. In return my appreciative classes tried to teach me some useful things they knew about, like wig-making or how the London Underground signalling system worked. But the boys' main passion was for football and about this I hadn't a clue. Once in desperation, with ten minutes to fill, I said, 'Well, why don't you tell me about football?' 'Takes time,' replied a Port of London Authority boy on the back row, with just the slightest of hand gestures. His studied irony put my gaping ignorance firmly but tactfully in its place.

None of us noticed a bewhiskered bad fairy glowering at us in the wings. Rhodes Boyson was about to make an entrance, flapping his 'Black Paper' on education and fulminating against anarchy. Throughout the seventies, war would rage about education and about liberal studies in particular, until the Boyson brigade took power in the eighties. The right wing were to then caricature the teaching of the previous two decades and idealize the period before the introduction of comprehensive schooling.

Those day-release students I was teaching in the sixties had all gone to secondary modern schools and been branded as failures because they had not passed their eleven-plus. When they came to Tower Hamlets they found themselves for the first time in small classes and given individual attention. As a result the principal, Bill Fishman, kept finding students who decided they wanted to do O-levels. I was aware of the arguments against the selection of the supposedly 'academic' through the eleven-plus, but it was actually teaching young working-class people who had been excluded from grammar schools which made me discount the linear testing of 'intelligence' at a much deeper experiential level. Tower Hamlets showed me how the expectation of the teacher really does affect the pupil and convinced me of the importance of small classes. We had them in groups of twelve and this meant – as the public school system has always recognized – that everyone had some flash of interest which could be a starting point. Confidence and the encouragement of creativity and originality are the first steps in the desire to learn.

The right wing in education was to make standards their official ground. This was a red herring. You had only to look at the green-grocers' notices in the sixties to see that working-class pupils in the disciplinarian secondary moderns hadn't learned to spell. Covertly, their project was control and slotting people into predetermined destinies. In the late sixties an opening seemed to be appearing in the rigidity of the English class-bound education system. From the late seventies the right were to mobilize in earnest to extract revenge for that moment of freedom.

In between teaching and working in the British Museum, I had taken to hanging out in the Arts Lab, a conveniently neutral space where you could chat to friendly people, watch weird underground avant-garde films, look at exhibitions and eat a cheap meal. Around Covent Garden and Tottenham Court Road there were now a series of counter-culture centres: clubs like UFO, Middle Earth and the Marquee. I continued to dip in and out of the hippie world and my ex-boyfriend, the guard from Collet's bookshop who had taken me to the Hendrix concert, David Ramsey, came visiting that March, a skinny beanpole exuding cosmic despair about everything being 'plastic'. Since I had tripped around the Oxford cobblestones in high heels and my height-of-fashion black plastic mac, plastic had nosedived. First Claes Oldenburg's telephones had made it a bit of a joke. Now it had become the symbol of sterility and capitalist degeneration. Like modernity, disgraced by Wilson and his white heat of technology and complicity in the Vietnam War, plastic had fallen into ill repute by the late sixties. This distrust was henceforth to run counterpoint with anti-capitalism before eventually merging with Green politics. The differing elements of modernization were not distinguished or thought through, and layers of misunderstanding muddled into a flip response over the decades – a double bind that is still with us.

Edward Thompson wrote to me on 5 March, grizzling about the introspective druggy youth culture: 'I think it is neither better nor worse than other forms of psychic self-mutilation – but worse at the moment because it belongs to a culture so excessively self-absorbed, self-inflating and self-dramatizing. *Very* like Methodist revivalism, self-examining hence v. unhappy and not v. good at mutuality . . . the involuted culture you paddle in – that isn't "you" . . . do try to talk a bit about other worlds.'

Little did he know all was about to change – though not in the way he might have wanted. Early in March a mysterious call came from John Hoyland, after which normal life was not to return for several years. John wanted to know if I would be willing to do something slightly illegal which involved being collected early in the morning. He was friendly with a group of radical architects who had been cleverly changing the wording on posters in the tube. For instance, there was a George Peppard film, *New Face in Hell*, showing and they had overlaid President Johnson's face on the advertisements. I suspected it was something on these lines and, all for making subversion as funny as possible, I agreed.

Sure enough, the bell rang around 6 a.m. and a young man in a leather jacket stood on the front steps. As we drove off he explained the plan. The architects had produced stickers advertising the Vietnam demonstration which was to be held on 17 March. But these were stickers with a difference – they were designed to cover the faces of the new parking meters. Little teams like ours were out all over central London busily sticking away. We set to with zeal and had got through a few streets when a policeman appeared at our side. He told us to hand over our stickers and empty our pockets. To my horror, my kamikaze companion had pockets bulging with inflammatory stuff telling people to bring weapons on 17 March to defend themselves against police violence. My eyes were as wide as the saucer dog's. I thought we were done for. What kind of anarchist situationist nut had I been lumbered with? To my amazement, we were let off with a caution and told to go home. But as the morning wore on the police became less patient and other people sticking were arrested. Our cultural guerrilla action was not in itself such a big deal, but it felt like a marker.

In the Young Socialists there had been all those inherited rituals for doing things and it never occurred to anyone to deviate from them. Jokes were inconceivable; it was all deadly serious. Moreover, communication was a matter of words. You presented a reasoned case, then off it went to a printer and back it came in small black ink. In the late sixties the barriers between propaganda and everyday activities came down. For instance, one of the left-wing architects produced a vast number of paper shopping bags made from the NLF flag. I carried mine around Ridley Road market, hoping to sway shoppers to the cause as I stuffed it with oranges.

The night before the 17 March anti-Vietnam War demonstration, the Vietnam Solidarity Committee called a meeting to discuss tactics. Members of the anti-authoritarian German student movement had come over and were clustering at the back of the hall. Having been engaged in a series of confrontations with heavy German police, they were held in considerable esteem and we all spun round to watch them show how to make a human wedge to break through police lines. The other demonstration tactic introduced by the Germans that March was linking arms and chanting, 'Ho, Ho, Ho Chi Minh'.

On the day the demonstration had the buzz of a big march – around 25,000 people were there. It fizzled with defiance from the start, as we distributed leaflets with Gerald Scarfe's grotesque cartoon of the 'Special Relationship' – a lapdog Harold Wilson licking Lyndon Johnson's arse. Its ethos contrasted with CND's 'We the good people bearing witness' style. We were more angry than good and far less passive than was customary on British CND demonstrations, pushing against the police lines, arms linked at Grosvenor Square. I was briefly at the front and saw a few demonstrators get through the police lines and run towards the embassy. I pushed, but not too hard, because the police were really beating isolated demonstrators behind the lines with their truncheons. Then the horses started going right through the crowd, driving people back and sideways and trampling them in the crush. The police seemed to go mad. I suspect they were taken aback by behaviour they had not predicted.

It was still the case, though, that a demonstration in Britain was not synonymous in most people's minds with a violent clash with the police. Most people came dressed for a walk through London, not a battle. On 18 March the newspapers were plastered with a photograph of a young woman struggling as the police carried her off. Her skirt was pulled up to reveal stockings, suspenders and underpants. The hand of the policeman was raised. 'Spanked' was the salacious headline.

We didn't know, of course, that the My Lai massacre, where American soldiers killed women and children, had occurred on 16 March. Ignorant of the full extent of the American atrocities, we also tended to idealize the North Vietnamese as the embodiment of good. But we knew enough to be desperate to stop the relentless bombing, the napalm burning on flesh and the chemicals being sprayed on the land. Eddie Adams's picture of Nguyen Ngoc Loan executing a member of the Vietcong during the Tet offensive became the visible symbol of the brutality of the war.

The Vietnam Solidarity Committee's slogans against imperialism were only part of what it meant to oppose the American government's war in Vietnam. Beyond party and beyond sects, Vietnam came to symbolize a wider humanitarian struggle between the just and the unjust. Vietnam was to be my generation's Spain and the suffering of its people became imprinted on our psyches. I kept seeing the image of a strange white creature, lacerated by red wounds, the embodiment of pain.

The mood of desperate frustration was tempered by an awareness of the need to break through what seemed like a universally hostile media. The innovative Americans in the anti-war Stop It Committee came up with a plan to drop the slogan 'Oxbridge paddles while Vietnam burns' over a bridge during the Oxford and Cambridge boat race, thus catching the TV cameras and millions of viewers. We were all to arrive as individual spectators, each with a letter on a cloth banner concealed about our person. When we reached the river, however, it was evident that police were privy to the Stop It Committee's plans, for they had cut off access to the bridge. Conferring hastily, while trying to appear nonchalant, we settled for the riverbank. As the boats approached, we clutched the banners under our coats, then – whoosh! – out they came. We'd done it!

Jubilant and excited, we hurried back to Wisty Hoyland, who had been watching the boat race on TV. Wisty announced ruefully that, yes, our banners had shown up, but we had forgotten about the *direction* of the camera following the boats. As a result we had reached millions with the challenging anagram SNRUB MANTEIV ELIHW SELD-DAP EGDIRBXO. It was shades of Czechoslovakia backwards.

That April the assassination of Martin Luther King was followed by an attack on a leader of the German student movement, Rudi Dutschke, who was seriously wounded. Tariq rang round VSC supporters and a group of us left the rally in Martin Luther King's memory and headed off to protest against the Axel Springer press group, which had offices at the *Daily Mirror*. The right-wing Springer press had been pouring out the most vicious attacks on the student movement, contributing to the mood of hatred which had resulted in the shooting.

Our internationalism was implicit and simply taken for granted. It did not occur to us to justify or explain why we were connected to King or to Dutschke. These assumed attitudes of an era are often the most puzzling to people subsequently. One influence on us had been CND, which had always included peace protesters from other countries. There had also been the anti-colonial movements and the connection to southern Africa. Then came the war in Vietnam, along with opposition to the regime of the right-wing Greek Colonels. Indeed, Melina Mercouri was speaking in Trafalgar Square on 19 April and we were out demonstrating once more. This internationalism was much more than an abstract political idea, because the students who came from South Africa, Rhodesia, Latin America, the United States, Greece, Italy and Ireland brought information and radical ideas from their own milieux. Friendship and love affairs made the connections to other countries' predicaments all the closer. International relations were thus personal as well as political. Another letter from Lawrence arrived on Red Cross notepaper that April. He had been classed as schizophrenic and was in a mental hospital, but was suspected of being sane. 'Please don't say anything on the envelope against the war.'

Enoch Powell's notorious speech against black immigration, in which he referred to the River Tiber in ancient Rome 'foaming with much blood', brought the focus sharply back to the dangers of racism on our own doorstep. On 23 April I was going home to Hackney, sitting on the top of the bus, musing, when I caught sight of a clump of working-class men huddling defensively near the Houses of Parliament – East End dockers supporting Powell. I looked at them with a heavy heart. I would normally have seen a workers' demonstration and felt support. But this time we were on opposing sides and it hurt.

Their response to Powell's speech, which legitimated racism as a scapegoat for Britain's economic ills, made left political activity seem more urgent, more serious, regardless of any personal exasperation about sectarianism. It felt like a repeat of fascism in the thirties, a context in which individual concerns appeared less significant.

When I went in to teach the Port of London Authority messenger boys a few days later, they stood up as I entered, giving the fascist salute. We battled throughout the lesson, but there was no budging them. However, one boy – the ironic football enthusiast who usually seemed half asleep – was not having any of it. He had been arguing every day at work on the docks non-stop. His quiet courage was impressive. It was him and me against the rest. I used everything I could fling at them, from the music they liked to appeals to human decency and to ridicule at being taken for a ride by a man who was contemptuous of the working class.

We argued for several weeks. It was eventually to be the information on the flyer for a new, radical newspaper called *Black Dwarf* which Tariq Ali was editing that dented their support for Powell. Along with a big picture of Powell in Nazi uniform, it revealed that he supported 3 per cent unemployment as a solution to inflation. This information enraged the east London further education college students and Enoch Powell promptly ceased to be their hero. Ironically, by getting all steamed up about Powell's speech, they were later to become much more interested in political and social issues in general.

This volatility made me realize how important it is to keep arguing. Watching the apprentices change, and knowing them over several years, also made me aware how contempt for both women and blacks was so closely bound up with feelings of self-hatred. My battles in Tower Hamlets left me convinced that to counter racist views you had to dig around for what is behind them and start undermining at the source.

Of course this is not always physically possible, as I was to find on the 1 May worker-student anti-racist march to Transport House, when we carried the big flyers for *Black Dwarf*. A young woman from Hackney Young Socialists and myself tried to leaflet a group of dockers who were jeering from behind the police line. We weren't expecting a welcome, but we misjudged their mood. The knot of burly men surged towards us. I shall never forget the unrelenting hatred in their eyes – being women was not going to protect us. The police braced themselves and I had to eat my pride and feel grateful to the law for saving us. As we backed off hastily, one man spat accurately past a policeman's ear; venom hit my face. This was the fascist hard core and we had to concede defeat.

Throughout the march other dockers were wandering, defensive and troubled, arguing with all and sundry. I remember one mild, bewildered man in his fifties, wearing a cap, who kept repeating that he wasn't racialist and was in a tenants' association, but, 'You can only fill the cup so far.' An Indian demonstrator dressed in a smart striped lawyer's suit had adopted him and was instructing him on economic theory in a quiet and friendly manner. The docker was utterly disorientated by the encounter. He thought there was a fixed amount of wealth which was apportioned through the land. 'You can only fill the cup so far,' he responded, shaking his head. 'You are being misled,' his companion told him, benignly tapping the older man on the shoulder.

As I went down to get the tube I saw a man with grey hair dressed in a denim jacket and jeans. He carried a situationist banner from Notting Hill and was disgorging his scorn of the dockers in a posh voice. I stood there mutely, feeling wretched. I hated their racism, but I also felt that it was satisfying to a man like that to be able to despise workers. It fed into his feeling of being superior.

The New Left *May Day Manifesto*, which the Thompsons and Bob had been working on with a group of socialist intellectuals, was published by Penguin in a revised edition that May and launched at an evening meeting. Edward spoke supportively of the German students, but was critical of what he regarded as the provocative violence of some strands in the US left. In contrast, he praised the young people who had cut their hair and were campaigning for Eugene MacCarthy.

As I listened I felt torn between admiring their dedication and thinking how horrible it must be to go around with those American short back and sides haircuts.

The *Manifesto* in 1968 was edited by Raymond Williams and sought to ground a New Left politics in an understanding of what was happening in capitalism rather than the 'holy writ' of Communism or Trotskyism. It was ahead of its time in looking at Britain's position in relation to a global economy and pointed to several questions which were to become more relevant over the next decade, including the implications of communication, the nature of technology and the meaning of work. It criticized the implicit values of capitalism, while proposing realistic changes, challenging for instance the exalted faith in modernization which marked Wilson's Labour Party policies.

If we want to test the validity of modernization as an economic panacea, we have to see it in its real context: as not a programme but a stratagem; part of the language and tactics of a new capitalist consolidation . . .

It opens up a perspective of change, but at the same time it mystifies the process, and sets limits to it. Attitudes, habits, techniques, practices must change: the system of economic and social power, however, remains unchanged. Modernization fatally short-circuits the formation of social goals . . .

In more sober times the May Day Manifesto initiative might have been the basis for a regrouping of the left. But the meeting that night had a feeling of flatness and the Manifesto was to be side-lined. Its failure to strike a chord in 1968 among people my age was not to do with the prescience of its proposals but because of our political disposition. We were full of our revolutionary toughness even before the May events – a stance which infuriated our elders – and the Manifesto didn't have the frenzied intensity which was a feature of the resistance to the Vietnam War and now to anti-Powellism. It looked too respectable, too safe.

I was far more excited by Tariq's new paper, *Black Dwarf*. A group of writers and designers, which included David Mercer and Adrian Mitchell, aimed to start a non-sectarian radical newspaper in the spirit of Tom Wooler's early nineteenth-century *Black Dwarf*. The flyer announced, 'The New BLACK DWARF will not pick quarrels with other left-wingers – but with our principal enemy, Capitalism.'

Tariq was even more ebullient than usual at the May Day Manifesto meeting. He came sweeping down the aisle and took me off to meet Clive Goodwin, a left-wing literary agent who was the driving force behind *Black Dwarf*. Clive seemed very worldly and sophisticated to me. In his mid-thirties when I met him, he had been radicalized by Suez and involved in left theatre and TV. Banned from producing for TV after he said he smoked marijuana in an interview, he was an agent for, among others, Dennis Potter and the uncompromising Manchester writer Jim Allen. He was also closely connected to the talented group associated with first the Wednesday Plays on the BBC and then with the independent company Kestrel Films. I knew nothing about Clive's media world when I met him, but I was attracted to the concentrated energy. He was like a creative power pack – everything was purposeful, no waste, no scattering to the winds.

He was smooth and expensively dressed – unknown territory to me. But it was the contradictory bits that interested me; under Clive's eyes there were dark rings and the skin was crinkly and old-looking. I was to learn that his wife, the Pop artist Pauline Boty, whose interview I'd read in Nell Dunn's *Talking to Women*, had died the year before of cancer.

We went out for a meal and he offered me a lift home. Instead, I ended up staying the night at his flat in Cromwell Road, waking up in an alien world of expensive sixties modernity – no wooden CND bowls for Clive. Clive maintained a contrived distance, a detachment, which intrigued me and which I found sexy. He would retire like a brown tortoise into his shell and then suddenly an incredibly warm smile would flash out and the lines crease.

If the night-times were about pleasure, the days were all work and bustle. Clive directed a great team of helpers and was constantly on the telephone – a posh, modern, white telephone. This seemed an extraordinary way of organizing to me. In the Young Socialists few people had telephones: we communicated with Roneoed narrow strips of writing through the post. Clive, in contrast, moved fast. I suspect he saw me as a walking data base. In London I knew the activist left and had left-wing friends scattered all over the country. Just as Clive's left media world was unfamiliar to me, my academic and labour movement connections were *terra incognita* to him.

Within a few days of knowing Clive I was conscious of being handled. Despite his charm, he was far more overtly autocratic than was customary in the left I knew. Left-wing men could be exasperating about women, but they kept up the appearance of democracy. Democracy never entered Clive's head where women were concerned; he simply assumed it was the men's job to talk politics. Once he'd got the addresses from me, he sent me off up to the bedroom to stuff envelopes with the other women. I had acquired a respect for the mail-out, so I went meekly enough.

Thanks to Clive, I met someone up there who was to become one of my closest friends. Sitting on the floor, enviably slender in a close-fitting ribbed top, with ash-blonde streaks in her hair, was Sally Alexander. She waved her arms in extravagant dramatic gestures and was extremely funny, telling me how Clive had been sending her round to raise money from theatre people.

Sally, who had recently been divorced from the actor John Thaw, had a young daughter and was wondering what to do next. When I heard she was an Equity member, I told her there was this trade union college called Ruskin. 'You could go there, Sally.' And she did.

I was surprised by the interest she expressed in Trotskyist groups. My women friends rarely related to my love–hate preoccupation with understanding their fissiparous histories or the nuances of difference which divided them. Sally kept telling me to go on because the leader of the Socialist Labour League, Gerry Healy, was making a real bid to recruit left-wing media workers. I gave her as fair an account as I could, but I considered the Socialist Labour League and its bullying, authoritarian leader to be bad news. So I echoed the advice Brian Smith had given me when I joined Hackney Young Socialists: 'You want to stay away from them.'

Sally told me later that she'd repeated my warnings to Clive. 'How do you know all this, Sally?' he'd asked, perplexed. Clive himself resisted the SLL's blandishments doggedly. He was not susceptible to being guilt-tripped – one of the Trotskyist tricks of the trade. In the fifties he had put all his energy into leaving the Willesden working class, where his father had worked as a waiter. Poverty held no romance and he retained a horror of the smell of sweat. He'd worked his way up to Cromwell Road and was not apologizing. Clive was a socialist because he detested deference and saw that a large part of the upper-class establishment were pompous, incompetent confidence tricksters. He wanted to call their bluff. He once said to me, 'We've all been through the things people are made to believe are important and we've seen them for what they are. We've got to communicate that understanding.' Exposing the hold of the trappings of power and privilege and achievement really was the most subversive message of the late sixties, and Clive was utterly committed to this process of divesting authority of its cover.

When news came through in the first week of May of student demonstrations and barricades in Paris, Clive rushed over there and returned with an eyewitness account for *Black Dwarf*, written by the situationist Jean-Jacques Lebel, who had 'liberated' the stock exchange with a huge white banner decorated with a joint. In Hackney I silently prayed to the god of revolutions, 'Please don't let them be defeated.' I wouldn't let myself hope. My classes at Tower Hamlets pooh-poohed it all. 'Students,' they snorted disparagingly.

They hoisted me on my own petard, rising in revolt themselves and staging a mock trial. The manifesto of the 'Trial of Sheila' declared:

We accuse you of boring lessons about government. We are not interested in government. Government is something to do with upper-class people and students. We are working-class people and nothing to do with government. We're not interested in what students do. We want lessons about everyday things, e.g. sex.

We accuse you of brainwashing us. We accuse you of keeping us cooped up in classrooms and then wondering why we go mad the first time we're let out.

We say if we were let out more we would become used to it and not go mad.

Or throw things.

WE HAVE THEREFORE HAD A REVOLUTION.

As soon as the students went to the factories and young workers began to join the rebellion on the Left Bank, my Tower Hamlets classes changed their tune. 'Can you organize a march for apprentices?' they wanted to know. Demanding the impossible was one thing, but I wasn't able to conjure apprentices out of the air.

When the general strike of 12 May was followed by factory occupations it really did seem that all those industrial relations experts and sociologists who had said it could never happen were wrong. The French working class were cocking a snook at those who interpreted the world and all that seemed secure and settled was revealed as shaky and mutable. Along with many others, I'll never forget the extraordinary sight of power wobbling like a nervous jelly in those weeks. The actions of the French students and workers that May were to leave a lasting impression upon my politics.

De Gaulle called on the armed forces for support in June. The police stormed the occupied factories. It was over. It was true that they lacked any political alternative to de Gaulle and that the faith in spontaneous insurrection proved illusory. Yet the implications of May '68 continued to splutter long, long after. The anarchical young rebels had resuscitated questions about the purposes and meaning of work, the role of technology, the relationship between experience and knowledge, desire and reality, which were to resonate through the seventies. They demonstrated a presentiment of a new capitalism coming into being in which knowledge and communication would be of strategic significance. Yet they looked to this future, while re-enacting the past. Sadly their time-honoured barricades were not made of the stuff which could check the profit-led transformation which was to come. Work and the everyday *were* to be turned inside out by new technology, but not in the democratized, egalitarian or cooperative ways which we glimpsed in that extraordinary month.

Some friends went over to Paris but it always seemed to me that I should be in Britain, arguing through the political implications of what was taking place in France. This was certainly a less glamorous position to be in. History might have been happening across the Channel, but in east London the old routines continued to tick over. I was still doing open-air meetings, but this time for the East London Vietnam Solidarity Committee, one week in Walthamstow market, one week in Ridley Road. Local working-class shoppers were even less interested in Vietnam than they had been in joining the Labour Party. Regardless of their indifference, we all had to mount a little box and explain about the Vietcong. A photo appeared in the *Hackney Gazette* of me in my red 1900s tartan cap, but I had no talent as a street orator. My one moment of glory came when an old Ulsterman decided I was being unpatriotic and hit me with his umbrella. To my surprise, a bodyguard of enraged middle-aged women formed around me like an impenetrable blanket. 'Give the girl a chance to speak,' they bellowed.

There had to be some more effective ways of getting through to people than putting me on a box. I stumbled on a clue at a May Day meeting in Tower Hamlets attended by a curious assortment of libertarian dissidents from another era: Anarchists with long white hair from the Freedom Press, which had been operating since the 1890s from an alleyway near the Whitechapel Art Gallery, and free-spirited pensioners from the almost defunct Independent Labour Party. In the pub after the meeting, I told my woes about street-speaking to an elderly bespectacled man in one of those grey macs worn by the respectable demonstrators at Aldermaston. 'We used to do Living Newspapers, dramatizing the news,' he told me.

Excited by the idea of imaginative propaganda, I went into work at Tower Hamlets College and enthused to John Hoyland. A teacher who had done the projectionist course more thoroughly than I had observed, 'You could show films on a back projector from vans.' When I dropped into Tottenham Street, Adam Hart suggested adding light shows and the kinetic domes he was making.

I took myself off into the British Museum to find out about aesthetics and revolution. I rapidly became utterly confused; there were as many conflicts about art as between Trotskyist groups. I copied out the Bauhaus artist Josef Albers's declaration:

TO DESIGN IS
TO PLAN AND TO ORGANIZE
TO ORDER, TO RELATE AND TO CONTROL.

I liked the rhythm of the words. However, his vision of order, modernity and control sat uncomfortably with the delight in the irrational and the absurd which was erupting from the People's Workshop in the occupied Ecole des Beaux Arts in Paris. Their posters echoed the surrealists and Dadaists more than the Bauhaus group and neither resembled the documentary realism of 'Living Newspapers'. 'Living Newspapers', I later learned, had originated in Germany in the twenties when Ernst Toller had developed the use of montage, which later influenced Dos Passos in the United States. This technique was about to influence the visual arts, where instead of bringing new dimensions to 'the real', it transmuted into a strong impulse to destroy the significance of subject matter itself.

Amidst the conflicting views on art during the Russian Revolution, the name 'Agit Prop' caught my eye – the Agit-Prop train (much, much bigger than a van) travelling through that vast land. There must be a way to move from our closed citadels of revolutionary ideas into the everyday. When I turned up at *Black Dwarf* jabbering in excitement about Living Newspapers, domes, vans, Josef Albers and Agit Prop, Tariq listened. 'You should really go and see a guy called Roland Muldoon,' he said.

The cockney voice on the phone already had quite a history. Rebelling against the Communists who ran the Unity Theatre, Roland had formed the Cartoon Archetypal Slogan Theatre with Claire Muldoon in 1965. CAST was to be the first of the many alternative theatre groups to sprout in the late sixties and early seventies. Unlike the slightly older group of left theatre people whom Clive knew, CAST remained on the fringe rather than entering the mainstream. It used the shock tactics of the avant-garde while being defiantly not 'arty'.

Roland agreed to meet me at the Anti-University in Shoreditch. Modelled on the American Free School and echoing the 'Dialectics of Liberation' conference, the Anti-University had been set up by a curious alliance of anti-psychiatrists and members of the *New Left Review*. It aimed to 'destroy the bastardized meanings of "students", "teacher" and "course" and do away with artificial splits and divisions between disciplines and art forms and between theory and action'. Though these ideas, in a diluted form, were to percolate through the educational system over the next few years, in this radical enclave, in 1968, the dream was to be doomed. Life folded into learning too literally, turning the Anti-University into a dosshouse. The hope of a counter-institution was already sinking, like a pie lacking an eggcup, by the time I arrived to talk to Roland, and the atmosphere was bleak and besieged.

Roland looked like one of those travelling doctors in a Western.

His light-ginger hair stuck out uncontrollably and then continued downwards in his beard. He was all frizzy and fizzy and absolutely adamant that my idea of Agit Prop was old hat. It should be Agit Pop and attract young workers. We argued. Agit Pop was too flip – the revolutionary tradition (Rowbotham); young workers today wouldn't go for it (Muldoon). We had hit an impasse which we never resolved but, undeterred, within a few days we had rounded up a group of enthusiasts, including John Hoyland, to discuss forming a radical cultural group. Without any clear idea about what Agit Prop was, I would jump up at meetings and urge people to get involved. 'Agit Prop' was launched at Unity Theatre, which, almost despite itself, was serving as a centre for the cross-fertilization of ideas about left drama coming from groups which ranged from the Parisian Théâtre de l'Unité to the San Francisco Mime Troupe.

It was John Hoyland who was to be our Josef Albers and design, relate and control. He created the organizational structure for a network by methodically establishing a card index of artistic talent and would lovingly handle the cards in his boxes. We conceived Agit Prop as a kind of left-wing mix 'n' match between art and action. We hadn't taken into consideration one crucial factor: left campaigns didn't reckon that they *had* aesthetic needs. They *liked* their oblong black and white, wordy leaflets. Worse, 'aesthetic' was implicitly associated with effete.

For two months I had been almost constantly at meetings and 12 Montague Road had turned into a disaster area, with nobody except me paying their £1 a week into the house fund regularly. I resorted to leaving notes pinned by the telephone – we had a coinbox. Taps dripped but no one could wake up to let in the plumbers, even after they had called three times. Slogans in red paint appeared all over the walls of the house one night, denouncing me as a 'straight drag' for demanding the house fund money. I eventually cracked when a notice in red print, threatening legal proceedings about 'nuisances', arrived from the council. I might have been fighting the state in general, but I was terrified of the state in particular. I went to see Bill Fishman at Tower Hamlets College in tears towards the middle of May. I was going to sell the house; I couldn't bear the responsibility any longer. I put it on the market at the estate agent's at Lebons Corner.

Some of my anxieties scribbled earnestly in my diary that spring seem ludicrous now. For instance, I was concerned that my inability to believe in my own mortality would make the shock of death, when it came, worse. With hindsight this was rather premature. But the daily troubles look unbearable in retrospect and my delay in acting absurd. Desperation, however, finally made me ruthless. I swept everyone out of the house except Stevie and Helen on the grounds that it was going to be sold. Brian had left and Kathie and Mary were away. Peace fell. Life suddenly felt better again and I had second thoughts. The 'For Sale' notice was taken down.

Theresa Moriarty, a friend of Dorothy and Edward Thompson's son Ben, with dark-black hair and grey-blue eyes, moved in that summer. Theresa had grown up with Irish and labour politics in her family; she was interested in art and in history. At last there was someone to talk with about ideas.

On 1 June *Black Dwarf*'s first issue appeared. Big red writing all over its cover declared confidently: 'PARIS, LONDON, ROME, BERLIN. WE WILL FIGHT. WE SHALL WIN.' I agreed to go around the country to boost sales.

I recorded these *Black Dwarf* travels in a letter I never posted, reporting enthusiasm among the situationists of Newcastle, who were 'chuffed because of Lebel but they think *Black Dwarf* should be given away (I feel this is rather ultra left)'.

From Newcastle I went to Yorkshire, where I was on home ground, reporting, '163 *Dwarf*s sold so far ... *Dwarf*s have penetrated Leeds Gas Board, Burn Bridge bourgeoisie, tramps at St George's Crypt, Ripon Grammar School, a Welsh College, Tony Jackson and "Ultima Thule", Leeds CND, Tyne Tees television, the people in the Pack Horse in Leeds ... We have been rejected by Hebden Bridge library because we aren't local, by a Communist because we weren't the *Morning Star*, and by a man on the dole in Newcastle because there was nothing for him in the paper.'

People in the Northern left groups and in the labour movement were profoundly sceptical about a paper started by London trendies. This combined with the ingrained resistance among some socialists to anything new. I knew all this so well and knew that beneath it was also the loyalty. Once something was accepted, people would put themselves out, give their time, what money they had, and tolerate stuff they didn't particularly even want to read. I knew that to survive, we needed these readers who were already committed, even though we had the ambition of reaching far beyond the existing left. So I argued, persuaded, cajoled and hitched across country to York and then on to Hull with my bundle of *Black Dwarf*s.

The lorry driver who took me to Hull entertained me with incredible stories of women who hitched lifts without any knickers on, ready for instant sex, and of intricate and extensive wife-swapping arrangements on his Hull council estate. As we headed for the east coast, I ruminated on why all this sexual revolution had been missed by the sociologists writing on family and kinship. I told him *Black Dwarf* was the paper for him.

I reached Hull University around noon on a sunny, breezy Saturday, my black and grey jellaba, bought in Morocco with Lawrence the previous summer, over my mini-dress, clutching the 'WE WILL FIGHT. WE SHALL WIN' *Dwarf*s. The campus was bubbling with cheery rebellion. One of the third-year students had gone to Paris, joined the May rebels and returned inspired. He had walked into his finals exam, torn up his paper and acquired heroic status.

The students were sitting around in the sun, waiting for Senate to come back with a decision on their demands for representation. They were slightly bored and I did a great sale. The red 'LONDON, PARIS, ROME, BERLIN' covers were soon dotted all over the green of the grass. Pity we hadn't foreseen Hull, I thought, but there again it wouldn't have scanned. When Senate prevaricated about participation, the students voted to occupy the administration buildings and around 6.30 they swept me along with them.

I sat on the floor blissfully happy and kept on writing to *Black Dwarf*: 'Everyone is smiling at each other, food appears from nowhere. People give it to each other. The Commissions which have been created move into operation. [We used the French word, thinking the English "committee" was too rigid.] Blankets, food, toothbrushes are collected from the halls with incredible efficiency. There is total participation – no referring, deferring. Each student is himself [*sic*]. The organization. No them. Messages, donations, visits from staff and townspeople who support the sit-in. The sit-in becomes a celebration. Everyone is dancing, talking, grinning, giving their food away. Everyone IS. Next morning students with large brushes clean up. Books and papers are on sale. Prominently *Black Dwarf*. It is also up on the notice boards.'

Hull was one of a spate of occupations. Essex had been the first, triggered off by students' protest against a speaker from Porton Down, an experimental chemical defence establishment. Three students were suspended and eventually reinstated. As at Berkeley, military defence links and their financial connections to universities were issues which stimulated the demand for greater democratic control by students over the content and structure of education. Inequality was also raised. At Bristol students argued for young workers and students from less well-endowed institutions to have access to their facilities. Suddenly curricula and customs which had been meekly accepted by generations of students were being challenged all over the country. Even tradition-bound Oxford defied the unquestioned authority of the proctors, causing Adam Hart's liberal father, as professor of jurisprudence, to rush around trying to get a conciliatory compromise accepted by both sides.

As some of the student rebels were the most thoughtful social science undergraduates and graduates (a high proportion of whom were to turn into professors all over the globe), they were to write critiques of utilitarian and authoritarian forms of knowledge and theories of education which did have an impact upon higher education, though in such different circumstances that their social meanings were to be utterly changed. The late-sixties rebellions helped stimulate greater choice in the curriculum, continuous assessment and participant observer methodologies. This moment of revolt also generated numerous creative spin-offs – the growth of oral history, community arts and publishing, trade union resource centres, and a great number of other innovations which have long since ceased to seem revolutionary. It was to prove much harder to alter the whole structure of education than to add on new spare parts. The ideals of the late sixties survived most in women's studies, where, long after their broader origins had been buried, battles were to ensue about subjectivity, community, the role of the teacher, the relation between experience and theory.

It was from the occupied art colleges that some of the most exciting and utopian ideas were to appear in the summer of 1968. Hornsey was occupied on 28 May and I turned up, along with variegated socialists, tenants and trade unionists, to show solidarity. Charlie Posner, always to be found when exciting ideas about education were being discussed, recruited my doctor, Michael Leibson, to stave off an attempt to close the college on health grounds. Sceptical about socialism, Michael loved to take on authorities of all kinds and liked artists.

Revolt in the art colleges, which were run by local borough councils, was dealt with very differently from revolt in the universities. The councils were not tender about academic freedoms and were to take revenge with mass sackings and expulsions. The universities still retained their ethos of training an élite of professionals and rulers, and rebellious individuals (who were not women) were traditionally treated with kid gloves. In contrast, the art colleges combined craft skills with fine art and were more open to the bright working class.

Throughout the sixties they had been seedbeds for all kinds of unconventional speculation and behaviour. In 1969, inspired by the Ecole des Beaux Arts Workshop, they were challenging *both* the idea of the artist as a romantic individual *and* a functionalism which linked their work directly into industry. The surrealist André Breton's dream of taking art into everyday life was no longer confined to esoteric tiny groups.

Conflict at Hornsey had begun in opposition to incorporation into North London Polytechnic. In the furore of debate, students and staff went on to argue for a more flexible curriculum geared to students' changing needs, with greater choice between options. Ideas which had been circulating in the art schools took a political shape during the occupations. They included a fascination with flux and impermanence, along with a view of art as a shared creative process and a desire to break down the barriers between artist and spectator and between objects and art. From surrealism came a celebration of the contingent, the unexpected, the unplanned as a means of breaking up hierarchies in society as well as in aesthetics. These cultural perceptions were to affect community art and the libertarian strands in left politics during the seventies, afterwards reaching a respectable middle age in various branches of academic theory.

Even as form was metamorphosing into attitude in 1969, the art avant-garde was preparing to do a U-turn as conceptual artists began to document objects as concepts – famously turning attitudes into form. One preoccupation, however, persisted right through from the mid-sixties into the seventies. Hilary Gresty describes it as the desire 'to expose the relationship between perceptual and conceptual apprehension; to allow a little contemplation rather than to posit complete directive assertion'. This insight, in a period when new technology and the fast marketing of ideas were about to affect everyday life in all kinds of ways, was to have a profound influence on feminist, gay and black cultural politics. It also had obvious wider social and political implications.

Tom Nairn and Jim Singh-Sandhu, writing in *Student Power*, the collection edited by Robin Blackburn and Gareth Stedman Jones in 1969, noted that the art students' rebellion was not political in a narrow, schematic way. Indeed, their questioning of hierarchical forms of learning was to exert a pervasive influence on radical thinking. While the Hornsey students were less into '-isms' than the social scientists of the LSE, they were not completely without old-style socialist disputes.

Tom Nairn may have been thrown off the scent by the assiduous efforts of the president of the Student Union at Hornsey, an adroit politico and member of the Communist Party, Nick Wright, whom I met early that June. Nick, who was from a Luton Communist working-class family, was appalled by what he regarded as the rampant ultra-leftism of the *New Left Review* and the Trotskyist groups alike. Throughout the Hornsey occupation he was to conflict repeatedly over tactics, style and politics with a passionate Welsh firebrand, a member of the International Socialist group at the time, called Kim Howells (now a New Labour minister). Nick played a cheeky-chappie-style Mr Cool to Kim's 'ultra left'. In 1968 it was Kim not Nick who was in the majority.

By June the left grouping in the NUS, the Radical Students Alliance, was beginning to look too tame for many student activists. The Revolutionary Socialist Student Federation was to fill the gap for about eighteen months, before it auto-destructed in sectarian battles. In 1968 the *New Left Review* was propounding their theory of 'red bases'. The idea was that colleges were to become guerrilla bases, 'foci' for the development of revolutionary theories about politics and society – including education. The International Socialists, meanwhile, were telling students they should go out to the working class. Quite a lot of people like me were in between. I thought just getting redder and redder amongst yourselves made no sense and inclined to the International Socialists' position, with some uneasy twinges when it seemed to deny the relevance of the intellectual arguments within higher education.

I went to the founding meeting of the Revolutionary Socialist Students' Federation at the LSE on 14 June, straight from a discussion with my London Transport class about automation. Since their 'revolution' against me, they had acquired the habit of debating all manner of things. I decided to say to the RSSF students that the further education colleges received the least resources and that the young worker-students on day release spanned two worlds. It was important to open the RSSF to them.

I stood on the platform, feeling like a jelly before it sets. I had never spoken to so many people before. It was a warm, sunny day and I was wearing a black and gold summer miniskirt. To my horror, as I walked to the mike, I was greeted by a tumultuous barrage of wolf whistles and laughter. I remained frozen for what seemed an eternity. My eyes fixed on a face I recognized, an Italian postgraduate I'd met through Bob at Cambridge. His head was tilted back and his mouth was open. He was guffawing. I had ceased to be an individual and had become an object of derision. It was like a living nightmare. Stubbornness kept me in front of the microphone. I'd got up there and I was going to say what I'd meant to say. Somehow through the whistling and laughter I managed to speak about further education.

The tiny, anarchical dynamo Danny Cohn Bendit had come over for the RSSF meeting and Clive Goodwin threw an extraordinary party for him. This event, in the luxurious Cromwell Road flat, was more of a production than a party. Clive's speciality was bringing people together and this time he went over the top, assembling a gathering as motley as those space creatures who appear in the pub in *Star Wars*. The socialists collected together that night were of such different species, they could hardly recognize one another as belonging to the same universe. An International Socialist building worker from Glasgow was denouncing everyone for being middle class and enjoying the freely flowing alcohol, while a suave Ken Tynan sat languidly on a couch, laughing about how Princess Margaret expected you to call her 'ma'am' when she smoked dope. I felt gauche in an old, cheap, straight grey dress I'd turned up to keep it in style amidst such fashionably elegant people and was relieved when I came across Nick Wright from Hornsey College, who was feeling even more out of it than I was.

Clive's party even made the newspapers. A disgruntled Dennis Potter wrote an article headed 'Tea-bag Rebels' on 17 June in the *Sun*, comparing it to 'a benefit concert for clapped-out seaside donkeys' – he clearly hadn't enjoyed himself. Potter's 'Nigel Barton' TV plays in the mid-sixties about class and Labour politics had evoked the earlier Bevanite left; his response to 1968 was one of abhorrence. I didn't register the article at the time. Nor did I consider how Clive's commitment to *Black Dwarf* and the May 'Events' affected his relationships with people from his own circle. His friends came from other worlds to me. Suddenly there were all these slightly older writers and directors around who, despite being far more sophisticated than I was, were so evidently clueless about the organized left and the history of the socialist movement. Just as I had bumped into bits of the New Left and then spent years working out all the nuanced differences between them, Clive's group introduced me to another set of cultural and political puzzles.

I was drawn to Clive's communicative skills, so acutely attuned to immediacy. Clive the entrepreneur and gambler could deal with the mutability of the era. He enjoyed his deals and making money. 'I've just made £1,000,' he once boasted, showing me the cheque. Being the daughter of a salesman, I respected commissions on sales, even though my capitalist propensities had been overlaid by Methodism, the beats, Oxford and socialism. Having landed in circles where money-making was not the thing, Clive's touching delight in the material seemed to be left over from the fifties and slightly quaint. On the other hand, I admired his capacity to sell visions. With hindsight, Clive was ahead of his time; it was as if he could sense a brutal new capitalism was in the offing and was saying desperately, 'We've got to get there first with *our* version of flexibility.'

Part of his risk-taking was his mixing of people and his generation-jumping. He was a kind of cultural explorer, through friendship and through sex. I found all these qualities enticing. Yet I was never completely at ease with Clive and I do not think this was simply a personal response. There were tensions between his generation of left-wingers, politicized during Suez and the Cold War, and people like me who were in their twenties during the sixties. Trevor Griffiths, a friend of Clive's, was to dramatize these conflicts in his play *The Party* in 1973, where a TV producer (modelled on Tony Garnett) calls together a drunken playwright (based on David Mercer), a man from Agit Prop theatre, a young Trotskyist woman and a male socialist lecturer.

You tend to define your sense of a rebellious identity against the people who are just ahead of you. Then, as time moves on, the distinctions blur. I was to be left with a vague perception of differing assumptions and a shyness because so much was never to be stated as my sexual relationship with Clive petered out into a political friendship that summer.

With the poet Christopher Logue, whom I met through Clive, dissimilarity did lead to conflict – which was ironic, for he had been another of my schoolgirl idols. His rasping voice, the spoken equivalent to Bob Dylan's penetrative singing, was already familiar because I had played his 'Red Bird' record of poetry to jazz over and over again in my Leeds bedroom. One beautiful warm spring evening in the middle of May, Clive, Christopher, Bob, a young woman from Hackney Young Socialists and I met in the Cromwell Road flat to go out for a meal. It started badly when Christopher ordered me to fetch his drink. Leeds gruffness came to the fore. 'Get it yourself,' I snapped. Whereupon the young woman from the YS, who was only seventeen, dutifully went and handed it to him. 'That,' declared Christopher in his scratchy voice, 'is real emancipation.' In the posh restaurant Clive and Christopher enthused about how under socialism the working class would all eat like this. At the time this sounded an incredibly complacent acceptance of privilege. 'What are you doing to yourselves?' I screamed, and ran into the ladies. When I eventually emerged, Christopher said to me that he had never been so bullied by a woman since his mother. I sat sullenly wondering to myself what she had been like.

Cornered, without any way of expressing how I felt, I had become irrational and impossible. This self-ostracism was partly an intuitive reflex, a sense of being annihilated by the way men behaved – my 'bullying' was about more than a posh meal. But Christopher had accurately spotted the rectitude. The extraordinary sequence of events during 1968 led my generation to believe we were moving in the same direction as history. We considered that, unlike our elders, we had no apologies to make; we hadn't justified labour camps, we hadn't compromised. In contrast to the fifties, when both Stalinism and the Labour Party had loomed large, we were convinced that we could make everything anew. Unlike the fifties New Left, we did not see any need for a politics with space carefully hewn out for doubt. This sixties certainty was simply brash at first, but it was to harden as hope of fundamental change evaporated over the next decade. The righteousness, which passed into the libertarian left social movements, festered as an internal problem, eventually providing the triumphant right with the stick of 'political correctness'.

There are no easy answers to the question of how you live in a world you want to change radically. Edward Thompson once said to me that in the lean, ascetic faces of old Communist workers who had renounced everything for their beliefs there was also a terrible bitterness. We were less abstemious in the late sixties. I loved shopping for clothes or books or records, though I did not equate spending money with having a good time. Our conviction that revolution was approaching inclined us to the view that to travel fast, you should travel light, reducing needs rather than making them become more elaborate.

The sense of urgency resulted in various political short cuts. My honeymoon with *Black Dwarf* ended abruptly on 5 July, when the second issue appeared with the headline 'Students the New Revolutionary Vanguard'. I sat on a pile of papers in the *Dwarf* office and wept. I couldn't abide vanguards. Tariq maintained that the designer had forgotten to put in a question mark. But I suspected the ideological influence of the *New Left Review*, whose office was upstairs. At least in the Bolshevik party the 'vanguard' had been tried by experience; I thought the *New Left Review* simply assumed it could be self-appointed – and, being in their own image, would necessarily be young men like themselves. Intellectuals in my opinion might be ahead on some things, but they remained way behind other people on others.

I went home and pounded out my dislike of vanguards into an article called 'The Little Vanguard's Tail', which later appeared in the underground paper *Oz*. The little vanguard was only very small but it was very hard and its job was to 'inject . . . the unorganized lumps and clusters' with 'correct ideas'. One day the trusty lumps had rebelled and shouted a warning to the clusters: 'Keep an eye on your vanguard. Vanguards get out of hand.' Whereupon a commune of clusters proposed an alliance with the lumps, generously suggesting that the lower-level cadres might like to join in and get 'a bit squelchy and squashy sometimes. More human altogether.'

I stepped back a little from *Black Dwarf* that summer and Agit Prop came to take up most of my time. It had mushroomed into a network of about 100 people, who ranged from members of antiquated socialist tendencies which pre-dated Leninism to alternative types from the underground. The latter were making Roland Muldoon from the CAST group restive; he was noisily claiming that the hippies were taking over. Roland was always leery about his proletarian 'cred', even though his shaggy locks would have made him indistinguishable from the hippies to the uninformed eye. A further reason for his ill-humour was the beginnings of another theatre group, the Agit Prop Players (later to become Red Ladder), whose approach to drama he considered to be fundamentally flawed. Long after the theatre groups themselves had vanished, he continued to battle it out with former members of Red Ladder – like old rivals still jousting after the tournament had come to an end.

Special Branch, meanwhile, appeared to have decided that Agit Prop was some command centre for Rent-a-Mob, calling on John and Wisty Hoyland with questions about the 'organization'. Like the Trots and the *New Left Review*, the police were attuned to vanguards. If they had but known it, our position was closer to piggy in the middle, caught between warring left factions.

Agit Prop that July was busy organizing a 'Revolutionary Festival' which we hoped would generate support for the Vietnamese struggle for national liberation in a less aggressive way than the militant demonstrations. This alone was enough to make us suspect of reformism by the Trotskyists, especially as one component of the festival was to be the arrival of members of the Young Communist League riding white bicycles which they'd been collecting for the Vietnamese. The British Communist Party by 1968 was trying desperately hard to be modern, but it creaked along so ponderously that it was always a few years behind. White bicycles, for instance, had been pioneered by a group of Amsterdam Anarchists, called the Provos, as a cooperative solution to traffic jams – a utopian move thwarted when the communal bicycles had been stolen and resprayed. Now the YCL had revamped the idea and were sending them off to a Communist Youth festival for the war effort. The ingenious Vietnamese would divide the wheels in two and attach goods to them.

Organizing the festival meant that I spent a lot of time in an outhouse off Upper Street, Islington, belonging to one of John Hoyland's radical architect friends, with a gang of Young Liberals from Hackney, anarchists, various apprentices and Theresa Moriarty. Like the art nouveau architect Charles Ashbee at Chipping Campden, we were strong on ideas but weak on implementation. Apart from Theresa, who was going to study art at the John Cass Institute, we possessed few artistic skills. We laboured away regardless, producing Coca-Cola bottles with French riot police helmets you could knock off with tennis balls and a big picture of Karl Marx with a baby on his knee. We cut holes in the board so you could stick your heads through either Marx or the baby's face. This innovation in left propaganda was inspired by a photo of me aged four in Whitby, my head through a picture of a girl in a grass skirt with a bunch of bananas, with 'Bongo, bongo, bongo, I don't want to leave the Congo' written in a bubble by my right ear.

I did make a brief official appearance as the representative of Agit Prop at a meeting with the police about the festival. Also there was the current leader of the Young Communist League, a young worker with film-star good looks, and Jack Straw, from the National Union of Students, who had ended up having to hang out with the Communists when everyone else turned into 'revolutionaries'. They spent ages discussing routes. With no grasp of geography, I kept quiet, sure that the Agit Prop/Revolutionary Festival types would ignore any arrangements anyway.

We were misunderstood all round. If the Trotskyists regarded us as 'soft', we were distinctly dodgy to the Communist Party. The *Morning Star* choked over 'revolutionary', altering our advert to 'Festival of the

Left'. The North Vietnamese, for their part, were utterly perplexed by 'Agit Prop' and Fei Ling Blackburn acted as our anxious ambassadress. The hippie underground also divided. Among those in opposition was John Peel, who gave us backhanded publicity by announcing on his radio programme that he definitely wouldn't be going.

I had been overdoing it. Just before the festival, a mysterious insect had bitten me in the Islington workshop. The bite had become infected and an enormous carbuncle appeared at the bottom of my left leg. When I finally limped off to a doctor I was so dazed by exhaustion and pain, I misunderstood the dosage instructions, taking the painkillers as if they were the antibiotics and vice versa. By the morning of the festival on 20 June I was out of it.

In Trafalgar Square I was compèring speakers from various left groups and campaigns, who instead of the customary box were speaking from an imitation TV box made by an art student at Chelsea College. I became embroiled in a furious argument with an extreme and obdurate revolutionary with long black greasy hair from the LSE who refused to speak from the box. I stomped off defeated in a temper, my leg cushioned by painkillers. Through a haze I could perceive that otherwise everything was going according to plan. The white bicycles and the YCLers duly arrived. John Hoyland acted as master of ceremonies, a role for which he has a natural talent, introducing Mick Farren and the Deviants in tight black-leather trousers, which made ascending on to the plinth problematic. They proceeded to play amidst purple smoke, followed by Pete Brown, who had managed to put a band together. Agit Prop Theatre Group made a début appearance. Adam Hart came along with a friend of his, a kinetic artist called Phil Vaughan, and blew golden plastic bubbles, much liked by children. Graham Stephens brought his pioneering inflatable – a first at a left demonstration.

Our efforts to communicate appeared to be working. People began to gather, intrigued by the bubbles and bands. An advertising friend of Roland Muldoon's had designed us leaflets which were intended to show the horror of the war. In an effort to describe the effect of napalm, he had written in large letters, 'Pour a gallon of petrol over your baby. Let it burn.' One woman screamed as I gave it to her. He was to go on to have a successful career in advertising, but our over-effective leaflet became a malevolent legend – the left advocated burning babies.

As the afternoon wore on we marched round and round Trafalgar Square, chanting, 'Ho, Ho, Ho Chi Minh' and bearing aloft a big hamburger made out of papier-mâché. A human body was squashed inside, the blood oozing out like tomato sauce. The irate police slashed at Graham's squashy plastic inflatable with knives and impounded the hamburger, which they seemed to regard as the equivalent to our standard. The hamburger artist declared stoically that he could always make another one. But I was upset to lose it, being too Yorkshire and waste-not-want-not for the spirit of auto-destructive art.

After the festival, with my carbuncle slowly healing, I found time to take stock for the first time since March. It seemed as if I had lived through several years during the last few months. I had learned to think for myself about politics and I felt responsible in a way I could not have imagined before. Moreover, I had glimpsed that rulers can totter. Once you've seen this happen, you don't forget – even if the world does appear to go on much the same. But it was hard to think clearly; we were being pounded by circumstances. In so far as I could grasp anything amidst the dizzy momentum of events, it was not to let ourselves get isolated, to keep on going outwards beyond the 'revolutionary' student milieu.

Many people I liked and respected in 1968 were in the International Socialist group, which had assimilated William Morris and left Independent Labour Party strands of libertarian socialism into its Trotskyism and was beginning to attract dissident and thoughtful trade unionists. Bob, who started to have a relationship with Theresa that summer, was around again at Montague Road and we talked about joining. I tried to banish my unease, then went away for a few days and thought better of it. In the meantime, he had become a member. As I dithered, he said, 'You can't do this to me,' and I signed up. Now, instead of recruiting for the Labour Party, off I went with Bob to sell *Socialist Worker* at a clothing factory in Shacklewell Lane. I didn't know then, as I shivered in the early-morning chill, that we were part of a long tradition of agitators. Mary Wollstonecraft used to walk down that lane from Newington Green to discuss the French Revolution with a radical clergyman who lived there. Our only regular customer was a tall, beaming young African who told us he was a prince learning the clothing business. Bob thrived on the early mornings of course, but I would be wrecked, returning home to find the sensible Theresa just getting up for breakfast. 'Workers have to get up at this time every morning,' I told myself, finding solace in penance.

Throughout that hectic spring and summer, personal feelings removed themselves from the foreground. My sexual encounters were all snatched in between meetings and somehow the customary emotions didn't settle upon them. It was as if intimacy had acquired an almost random quality. The energy of the external collectivity became so intense, it seemed the boundaries of closeness, of ecstatic inwardness, had spilled over on to the streets. While creativity bounced through the world at large, the libido defied borders and appeared in some peculiar way to have been shaken out into the everyday. I thus caught a glimpse of the peculiar annihilation of the personal in the midst of dramatic events like revolution – just a glimpse, of course, for the spring and summer of 1968 were not actually revolutionary times. In retrospect, revolutions seem puritanical, although that is not how they are experienced at the time. It is true that this readiness to put self aside subsequently increased the danger of merging individuality into the collectivity, though in times of ferment and upheaval this is never apparent. In such periods the distinction between inner and outer shifts and the significance of sexual encounters fall into a new relief. Caught in that maelstrom of international rebellion, it felt as if we were being carried to the edge of the known world. Then that July we were left marooned in a lull – the summer lull.

Sure enough Steve reappeared that July, and sure enough passion erupted again. What was I doing for the holidays? He would meet me in Paris on a motorbike. But I was getting wise. 'If no Steve by 1 August I must go somewhere,' I wrote in my diary. On 28 July I announced, 'No Steve shown up.' Dorothy Thompson came to the rescue and took me off on a plane to Paris to join her younger son, Mark, in a flat owned by some French historians. It was a beautiful little place, stuffed with books on Marx and history, which I read happily. When Dorothy left I was put in charge of Mark, then sixteen, and a group of his schoolfriends. There was no sign of Steve.

Mark and I decided to hitch down to Torremolinos to visit Roberta, who was in a flat owned by her father. On the journey my main concern was to keep going in the right direction and I routinely fended off lorry drivers, now considering myself an adept hitchhiker. Years later Mark told me he had gone through agonies of anxiety, feeling unable to defend me and convinced that I was about to be raped. Safely ensconced in one of the new Torremolinos holiday blocks, where ants were the only danger, Roberta and I persisted in turning up our noses inconsistently at the other holidaymakers, whom we termed the 'tourists', on the crowded beach. We spent happy evenings dancing in a club which let us in for nothing in the hope that we would bring in male customers. The news that the Beatles' shop, Apple, was giving clothes away reached us, but we remained unaware of the Chicago demonstration in the United States, and of the tanks going into Czechoslovakia.

I was determined to show Roberta Formentera and, when Mark set off for Morocco, we began hitching. 'We can sleep on the beaches,' I said chirpily. I had not allowed for us both being women. Hitchhiking across Spain with a woman, I was to learn, was really not the same as with a man. This ill-considered odyssey was, however, to attach me more deeply to Roberta.

Formentera was no longer the cooperative paradise of the previous year. A certain stratification was apparent between the long-terms, bronzed and cool, dressed in the delicate faded mauves, blues and fawns which tie-dye had made fashionable, and the indigent others, whom we joined, sleeping in bags in the woods because it was now unsafe on the beaches.

Back in London I arrived in the *Black Dwarf* office wearing a man's old-fashioned shirt with a round collar which I had dyed lilac. I was showing off my suntanned legs, but there was an intensely serious mood and no one was interested in frivolous things like a Formentera suntan. The *Dwarf* had been raided while I was away, with the ironic result that we had sold out. Some 15,000 copies were gone, thanks to Scotland Yard.

In September I noted in my diary that I was conscious of a tension 'between desire to cut all my hair off, wear no make-up, look out and be', and an equally strong urge to 'cover up'. Irresolute, I went out and bought new clothes. I decided I was looking much older and felt relieved.

I was equally ambiguous about the underground's celebration of the irrational, remaining torn between belief and scepticism. Early that October Graham was taking a new inflatable to Hampstead Heath, where David Medalla and his artistic commune, The Exploding Galaxy, who lived near me at 99 Balls Pond Road, planned to do their *Buddha Ballet* – a kind of prototype of performance art. As we danced on the grass, I did feel an extraordinary sense of open delight being generated within the little group, which appeared to spread outwards to embrace passers-by. I did, however, retain sufficient scepticism to suspect that part of our popularity came from the startling beauty of Graham's partner, Myrdel. One aspect of the hippie underground was the loving playfulness which it is easy to be cynical about. Looking back, I think they had an insight which I would value more now than I did then. Everyday relating was to be assailed by a much harsher set of attitudes at work, in the streets, in public services, in the media. Competition, fear, distrust and self-assertion won out and we socialists had no means of naming the shift in individual behaviour.

Something else was there in play power too. In 1968 I hardly noticed the more worldly aspects of the underground, which were to tune into the changes in capitalism. When a young student who used to ring me up for his newsletter to get Agit Prop information launched a magazine called *Time Out* that autumn, I didn't regard it as a particularly significant event. Papers were starting all the time. The difference was that Tony Elliott's was to last. Hippie culture, like the Victorians, had its self-made men and these ingenious entrepreneurs discovered that you could market ways of living.

An upper-class bohemia had also grafted itself on to the underground by 1968. Class snobbery merged with the élitism of cool which was one element in the underground. The 'do your own thing' sense of individual liberation was turned into a justification of living completely for yourself. Elements of this self-absorption were also to persist, transmuting into the ruthless selfishness which would come into ascendancy in the late eighties.

During that autumn of 1968 the connection between the inner and outer forms of consciousness which had seemed possible a few months before was wearing thin. The over-simplified polarization which resulted tended to be presented as changing society or changing yourself. First Roland Muldoon and then John Hoyland were to contrast the Beatles and then quietism with the Rolling Stones in *Black Dwarf*. John Lennon was eventually stung to reply, 'I'll tell you something – I've been up against the same people all my life. I *know* they still hate me. There's no difference now – just the size of the game has changed. Then it was schoolmaster, relatives, etc. – now I'm arrested or ticked off by fascists or brothers in endless fucking prose.' In response to John Hoyland's admonition about the need to 'smash' capitalism, he added a PS: 'You smash it and I'll build around it.'

In theory I wanted the 'revolution' to combine the Johns and be about changing the outer world and building a new one within. In practice I had no idea how you could live this total revolution personally, trying in vain for balance in my own life and steering between the extremes of inward preoccupation *and* the denial which featured in the sectarian left.

When Sally Alexander took me along to hear Gerry Healy speak to a group of her media friends at Tony Garnett's flat, neither she nor I was thinking about my being a member of International Socialism. We had reckoned without that old bruiser Gerry Healy. In the discussion I remarked that the boys I was teaching would begin to change their political attitudes in general if one prejudice towards women or black people could be shifted. Gerry Healy responded with a ferocious aggression which reminded me of arguments with my father; it was as if he was beating me down with words. Well practised, I answered back, which incensed him so much he looked as if he was about to have a heart attack. 'If you were a Marxist,' Healy bellowed. The playwright David Mercer decided he wasn't being fair. 'How do you know this girl isn't a Marxist?' he demanded. 'Have you spoken to her before?' Gerry Healy's mouth opened like a goldfish. Conversing with someone to ascertain what they thought was not his style. He knew everything already without ever listening. I couldn't understand why all these gifted people Sally and Clive knew bothered with his bombast.

*

Clive asked me to photocopy excerpts from the original *Black Dwarf* that September, assuring me he would pay the bill. I went through every issue in the British Museum and found it fascinating – so fascinating that the final photocopying bill came to a monstrous £25. Clive was scathing; not because of the money, but because I'd wasted time producing piles of material for no practical end. 'We can't use this,' he said contemptuously, and the gulf between the media and the historian's craft opened at my feet.

Inadvertently, by sending me back into the British Museum, Clive had reawakened my love of history. He was always particularly tough on me in relation to political ideas or writing, while being endowed with an uncanny ability to draw creativity from people without looking as if he had ever been trying. Towards the end of that September I knew I wanted to write; what, I was not sure.

I had abandoned my thesis completely that summer as politically irrelevant. That autumn a meeting with a tutor in the Workers' Educational Association, Jim Fryth, provided a bridge back to historical work. Jim, an open-minded Communist Party member since the thirties, combined labour history with an interest in contemporary trade unionism. This combination of past and present, along with his whimsical humour, made him seem much younger than his years. He was to show me, by example, how to teach adults, in the process becoming a close friend. Meanwhile, my first WEA class of Guildford housewives was to give me insights into the lives of intelligent suburban housewives a little older than myself whose discontents could not be encapsulated in terms of either class conflict or student revolution.

Edward and Dorothy Thompson also rounded me up that October to talk to their classes at Warwick and Birmingham universities about University Extension. Many of Edward's Warwick students were left wing and the surroundings were informal. At Birmingham it was more stiff and proper. After Richard Johnson introduced me, I was beset by a powerful urge to slide under the table and make my escape through everyone's feet. I couldn't let Dotty down, though, so I kept my nose above the table and delivered.

The atmosphere at their home in Leamington Spa was strained. Dorothy and Edward disliked *Black Dwarf* and were horrified by events in the United States, where the violent Chicago demonstration had been followed by the arrest and shooting of Huey Newton. They were similarly alarmed by the escalating invocation of violence accompanying the build-up for the anti-Vietnam War demonstration planned in Britain for 27 October. 'There is nobody for you to trust and so you have to respect those who don't deserve respect,' Edward exploded as one of the students at Warwick argued with him. I wanted desperately for him to be with us. But the divide was there and wishing didn't make it narrow. I remembered that conversation with Lawrence Daly – the New Left that might have been.

Towards the end of September I had a nightmare of a sea monster, its head back and its mouth open in a scream although no sound came out. I felt pity towards its agony and then saw it carried a baby. A wave of love and protection consumed me for the baby, when two rocks moved in and crushed it. I associated the monster with my obsessive preoccupation with Steve. I was weary of subterranean emotions which went nowhere.

Nick Wright popped up again at a dance at the Royal College for the sacked art school teachers and attached himself to me. 'I like him but that's it,' announced my diary on 5 October. Nick wasn't going to be shaken off. He invited me out. I was amused by such formality and had a good time. He made me laugh and I could sense he was a bit shy, which made me want to tease him. When we woke up the sun was shining on us through my bedroom window and Nick wasn't shy any more. I was still brown and felt light-hearted and cheerful. This time I really had managed to meet someone I liked. No more blinding passion, I said to myself. Here was a warm, jokey human being I could be with and talk to.

I could hardly get a word in edgeways. Nick, who seemed to think he had landed in a hornet's nest of Trotskyists, argued all the time. The only thing that caused the ceaseless assault to falter was sex. Then off he would go again. He took on the whole household. Bob was often around visiting Theresa; Nick liked him but argued just the same.

I was constantly being put on the defensive, retaining plenty of doubts of my own about Trotskyism and being always more at ease with Agit Prop. Just before the Vietnam demonstration, I was downstairs in my tiny basement kitchen with a woman from the Poster Workshop, thinking up slogans for posters: 'Remember Whose Violence We Are

Marching Against', 'We Are All Foreign Scum', throwing in 'Workers' Control' for good measure.

By that autumn the student left had become a news story. We could see ourselves reflected back in the media. We had initially imagined that if we could put our case, reach enough people, they would be convinced. It was of course much more complicated. A lot of the coverage was overtly hostile; to the xenophobic gutter press we were indeed 'foreign scum'. The liberal media's representation was more perplexing. After being temporarily winded by the 'Events' of May in Paris, they were beginning to employ derision. On 24 October I watched a television programme of Nick during the Hornsey sit-in and the Agit Prop street theatre performing in Petticoat Lane. Along with Tariq and the International Socialist student activist David Widgery, they came over as reasonable enough, but by over-emphasizing the role of tiny Maoist sects the programme was skewed to make the student movement cranky. I was not conscious then that it is how a programme is framed which creates the impact on the viewer, but I knew something was wrong.

As media hysteria about the march mounted and the argument about whether to go to Grosvenor Square continued to rage in the Vietnam Solidarity Committee, Tariq was under tremendous pressure. He had become exceedingly exposed as an individual figure in the media, branded as Mr Student Revolutionary, even though he was not connected to any group of students. I suspected that it was this isolation which caused him to join the International Marxist Group.

Just before the October demonstration, Tariq asked me to write a short article about the history of direct action in British radicalism for *Black Dwarf*. Though I had been selling the paper since May out of personal commitment, it had never occurred to me to actually write in it. The unstated assumption was that political writing was something men did.

I had continued to jot down comments about women in my diary, but the experience of being a woman remained personal, even though several public events had affected me. I had been annoyed when the Ford sewing machinists' dispute over grading during the summer was headlined as 'Petticoat Pickets' and when Rose Boland, their spokeswoman, said, 'It isn't about pay, it's about *recognition*.' 'Recognition' rang a bell. I could see how *women* workers were put down as women, remembering the hostile response to the Hull fish-house worker, Lil Bilocca, who had campaigned the previous February against unsafe trawlers after a disaster in which forty fishermen died. A Women's Rights group had been formed in support of the campaign in Hull and a new national organization called the National Joint Action Committee for Women's Equal Rights (NJACWER) had come into existence after the Ford strike. These initiatives from working-class women preceded the emergence of Women's Liberation as a movement; indeed, they influenced us, serving along with the Vietnamese guerrilla fighters as what are now called our 'role models'.

Anger was to galvanize me. That summer I'd heard that Clive had held a meeting with David Widgery and his friend, who was also in IS, Nigel Fountain, and they had jokingly suggested putting pin-ups into the paper to raise sales. I had stormed into the office, pinning a furious poem about Rosa Luxemburg and wanking into revolution on to the wall. At an IS students' meeting early that autumn, David Widgery joked about how the founder, Tony Cliff, should follow the example of another Trotskyist leader and find a young wife. Everyone laughed and I was outraged. I went up to David after the meeting and asked if he'd heard about Valerie Solanas and the Society for Cutting Up Men. He didn't look at all worried. After he left, I glanced at the three other women in the group, afraid they would sneer at me. Instead we went to the ladies' and began talking. This was really my first-ever women's meeting – a crucial glimpse of how connection to other women makes it much easier to express disgruntlement.

By 25 October the LSE was occupied again and people were pouring in with sleeping bags. An Agit Prop Poster Workshop had been set up in the building. Defying the sombre 'struggle gear', increasingly worn on the left, which marked you off as a breed of professional revolutionary, but mindful of the miniskirt fiasco at the Revolutionary Socialist Students' Federation meeting, I headed off there in an olive-green bell-bottomed satin trouser suit, bought in my September spending spree. The trouser suit shocked some friends of Kim Howells from Hornsey College who had joined the Socialist Labour League. 'Don't you find that your clothes put off the working class?' 'No,' I replied point-blank. But I felt sad. A few months ago they had been warm, idealistic human beings; now they had been turned into zombies by the SLL.

In the bowels of the LSE the posters were coming off the silk screens at a great rate, hanging in serried rows from the ceiling like incendiary pillowcases. In their midst was Bert Scrivener, the tenants' activist from the Agit Prop Poster Workshop, who had turned himself into a one-man pensioners' wing of the RSSF, adding his own slogan for the march, 'Freeze Rents Not Wages'. Bert was enjoying the anarchy, for he loved movements and taught me the term 'ground-floor politics', which he considered to be more appropriate for an urban setting than 'grass roots'. When the press besieged the Poster Workshop in Camden, looking for wild, hairy, revolutionary youth, they would be met by the canny Bert, who parried their questions with, 'This is nothing to do with politics, it's the rent campaign.'

A massive 100,000 people demonstrated against the war on 27 October. I watched the south London section coming across Waterloo Bridge, the Vietnamese and red flags flickering in the wind, and felt a lump coming into my throat. All those years of campaigning and now so many people. The majority avoided confrontation by going to Hyde Park. At the point where the routes diverged, no one was directing people. It was impressive to see people thinking and deciding what they were going to do themselves.

I was to learn from a CID man who came round after I reported a robbery that November that the feeling among the rank and file of the police was that the demonstrators who went to Grosvenor Square should have been 'mopped up'. This personal hostility among the police had been contained by orders for restraint from 'on top'. This antagonism, as in the United States and France, was class-based: we were spoilt rich kids to many police officers. I think the police also feared the spontaneity of the 1968 left, which horrified them by its disorder. Like the Communist Party, the hierarchical police mind was distressed by the unpredictable behaviour of youthful rebellion.

Demonstrations are partly an expression of collectivity and partly a political drama acted out on the streets. Their theatrical and symbolic significance is extremely important, for they literally demonstrate opinion. The fact that they are exceptional events also means they have obvious limits. Mick Jagger wrote 'Street Fighting Man' and sent it to *Black Dwarf* after the demonstration. This street-fighting-man image had no sooner crystallized than it was being challenged from all sides from within the anti-Vietnam War movement. This big demonstration was in fact to be a watershed. Not only had the whole event been the subject of fierce arguments; it was becoming increasingly evident to many of us that simply escalating the violence and getting into fights with the police detracted from the main issue of the Vietnamese resistance to the United States. 'Remember Whose Violence We Are Marching Against.' The impasse was to lead many people into local community politics.

When I next arrived in the classroom at Tower Hamlets College after 27 October, I received a surprise. 'Where were you?' berated scornful youthful voices. Several apprentices had, unbeknown to me, decided to demonstrate. And being young East End toughies, they had gone off to Grosvenor Square., The May 'Events' had started them thinking, but it was the tenants' campaign over the summer and autumn which had made them take the big step of demonstrating with the reviled 'students'. Their mothers had been coming back from tenants' marches angry about police violence against working-class people. They had gone to Grosvenor Square to avenge their mums.

The combined upheavals of 1968 led many of the boys I was teaching to become interested in the history of revolutions. They wanted to know how they had occurred, what had happened and why. I started by telling them about the English Revolution of the seventeenth century, in the London they knew: the apprentices petitioning the Commons and the Puritans drilling near Liverpool Street on Artillery Row. Modern sociological terms such as 'social inequality' made them go glazed until translated into direct expressions: 'The rich are getting richer and the poor are getting poorer.' So I tried an older metaphorical language which bridged direct experience and abstraction, a connection missed in contemporary left politics. I read them bits of Gerard Winstanley about the 'inner and outer bondages' and explained how Milton had come to write in the *Areopagitica*, 'To be still searching what we know not by what we know, still closing up truth to truth as we find it . . . even to the reforming of reformation itself.'

Some theoretical concepts made immediate sense to them because of their work and familiarity with trade unions. In one lesson that November I described what Marx had said about alienation and asked them to write an essay about a society in which work was no longer alienated. One engineering apprentice handed in an account of a place where no one ever went into work regularly. Instead they wandered about enjoying themselves, wearing labels describing their various skills. So when the pipes leaked you would just take to the streets and hail some plumber who was mooching around, who would come and fix the pipes. I was unsure whether there would be much demand for historians.

A group of engineering apprentices decided they wanted to form their own RSSF at Tower Hamlets. This was a very big deal. Not only was the name Revolutionary Socialist Students' Federation a mouthful, it required a leap into a series of alien identities – declaring themselves 'students' as well as 'revolutionary' and 'socialists'. It also meant meeting with a long-haired hairdressing student who always looked sleepy because he took mandies (Mandrax). For skinhead engineering apprentices to go the pub with a hairdresser was a mini-revolution in itself!

The driving force behind this remarkable diplomatic initiative was a boy who had been radicalized by a Maoist shop steward who used to sell him an unreadable paper in tiny print called the *Worker*. A more personal experience had affected him very deeply. A child was being beaten at home in his street and he had tried to get adults to report the violence. The woman who had called the NSPCC was someone who was despised by everyone because she was a prostitute. This had made him question not simply politics but sexual attitudes and personal values.

The boundaries of assumption about where politics began and ended seemed to have been infinitely extended by the extraordinary happenings of 1968. Actions and organizational structures which would have appeared remarkable a year before had now become quite ordinary. The international student rebellions had extended to young workers and the mobilization of schoolchildren. Colleges and factories had been occupied. The Civil Rights movement had begun in Ireland. So much had been condensed into a few months, it was difficult to reflect upon the implications. It is not surprising that we believed ourselves to be creating a completely new kind of politics.

The tempo of transformation slowed down towards the end of the year, creating a space in which I realized that by being so preoccupied with the optimistic hopes of change I had evaded dwelling on anything shadowed by doubt or pessimism. Immersion in the external events of the previous year had led me simply to stack the painful, buried feelings about my parents, especially my father, on one side, as if they were lumber to be deposited from a fast-moving train. I was to learn that you cannot detach yourself so easily from your inheritance – personal and political.

It seemed evident to me that I had pushed my passivity about dealing with the outside world on to Bob. My struggle to leave him had been about my own terror of dependence and both the dependence and my terror of it went back to my childhood relationship with my father. I was exasperated with myself for jumping from one dependency to another. I continued to carry internally many of the early-sixties existential concerns about detachment. Refusing to make any allowance for my own emotions, I had assumed a very austere attitude to sexual relationships and was liable to be surprised when they affected me in ways that I could not reason away. I was constantly taking elaborate precautions not to be 'dependent', only to be hit unawares.

Nick, who I had lined up to be my normal and reasonable love affair, had mysteriously gone missing. Early in December Steve suddenly wrote from a 'Station Biologique' in France, where he was watching dolphins and birds from some tree, asking if he could come and stay because he had an interview for a job in the Virgin Islands. I wrote and said I didn't want him to reappear. I wasn't going to sit miserably mooning about two unrequited loves.

Black Dwarf that autumn had been shedding editorial members because of conflict about the Socialist Labour League. Bob was invited to join and he suggested that they should ask me. I was unsure whether I was up to being on the editorial board. Even though I resisted the assumption that men did the left politics, it was incredibly hard to have confidence as a woman. You were on your own. In fact I was to find an ally, the *Black Dwarf* secretary, Ann Scott, then aged seventeen. On 5 December Tariq, Clive, Fred Halliday and Bob decided, according to the minutes, to 'meet regularly at 11 a.m. on Fridays at Dwarf offices. Only to be altered under emergency conditions.' They also agreed to 'get Sheila to be in charge of women coverage of *Dwarf*. Ask her to be on the board.'

Two immediate factors were behind this decision. First, Bob had been in an argument with the *New Left Review* men about the Soho strip clubs, which were multiplying in the sleazy side of Swinging London. He maintained that any principled socialist man should be prepared to strip in protest outside the clubs against the insulting treatment of women. The *New Left Review* men had told him he was being puritanical and old-fashioned in his attitude to socialism. I had nothing personal against the occasional strip club – the one nearest to the office was perfectly friendly and gave us their tea-bags when we ran out – but they were multiplying in Soho and I sided with Bob, giggling secretly at the thought of the *New Left Review* men doing a strip-tease. The second factor was less utopian. The International Marxist Group, to which Tariq now belonged, supported the National Joint Action Campaign for Women's Equal Rights, which had been lobbying Parliament that October.

On 13 December I went to my first meeting of the editorial board, although I had already started to commission articles. It was decided that I would help Fred Halliday, who was regarded as something of an expert on sex and the family (and thus on women) because he had read Reich and knew about psychoanalysis, to do a special women's issue. Fred wrote a long article on the 'family' and I zealously busied myself collecting other articles. Through Dorothy Thompson, I contacted Audrey Wise, then an official in the Union of Shop, Distributive and Allied Workers; I asked the single mother with the Valerie Solanas targets on her lavatory wall to write about having a baby; and Ann, whose mother worked for Family Planning, did an article on contraception.

I then sat on my stool in the basement by the gas fire and began writing furiously myself. Out came all the concentrated thoughts and impressions which had been unconsciously accumulating. It was the kind of article I would later recognize as one that boils up inside. In the spirit of '68, I knew I must write not from received authorities on 'women' but from my own observations and feelings. In retrospect, this resolve related to a wider cultural shift towards subjectivity. I had been hearing it in the music ever since the Beatles sang 'Help' at the end of 1965. It joined to the outer world in the politics of Black Power. I had read other combinations of the personal and the political in Simone de Beauvoir's writing and in Doris Lessing's novels. Karen Horney's ideas about masculine hegemony had also been playing around at the back of my mind over the last year. I had *become* a woman and I should begin with my own perceptions of what this meant. I made a list: 'Me; Hairdressing girl; Brentford nylons; Birth control; Unmarried mothers; TUC USDAW; Ford's women: strip-tease girl . . .' Now suddenly all those scattered experiences could take a new shape. As the words splattered out on to the pages, it felt as if I had reached a clearing.

CHAPTER 6

1969

When Tariq showed me the layout for the '1969 Year of the Militant Woman?' issue of *Black Dwarf*, my heart sank. The designer, who usually worked for *Oz*, had heard 'women' and thought 'ridicule'. On the pink cover a cartoon dolly bird looked out from a 'V' sign, holding a hammer and sickle. Below this image he had drawn a woman in a boiler suit in comic-book style, her pocket buttons substituting for protruding nipples. The articles I had collected were overlaid with images. It had been so hard to get those words out into the light of day, now you could barely read them. 'Women's liberation' in the designer's mind seemed to evoke everyone taking their clothes off, so he had scattered photographs of Marilyn Monroe, Yoko Ono and John Lennon with nothing on over the pages. Tariq, to his credit, took them out, costing the paper £70 – a vast sum in 1969. But I missed a nasty little personal ad the designer had inserted: 'DWARF DESIGNER SEEKS GIRL: Head girl type to make tea, organize paper, me. Free food, smoke, space. Suit American negress.' This was the seedy side of the underground: arrogant, ignorant and prejudiced. It explains the anger which was shortly to cohere among many women who worked on the underground papers.

Nonetheless, regardless of sabotage, there it was, the *Black Dwarf* women's issue, with Audrey Wise on why more than equal pay was needed at work, information on Lil Bilocca's campaign for safety on the trawlers in Hull, Ann Scott on birth control, ideas about community involvement in child care, and Fred Halliday on 'Women, Sex and the Abolition of the Family'. Across the centre spread were the words I had written in my Hackney basement. Thoughts I had mentioned only to friends, scribbled in my diary or sent in a letter had now gone off into the world. Anxiously I read what I had written about inequality at work, the struggle to combine jobs with child care, the lingering taboos on women's sexuality, and asked,

So what are we complaining about? All this and something else besides – a much less tangible something – a smouldering, bewildered consciousness with no shape – a muttered dissatisfaction – which suddenly shoots to the surface and EXPLODES . . .

We want to drive buses, play football, use beer mugs not glasses. We want men to take the pill. We do not want to be brought with bottles or invited as wives. We do not want to be wrapped up in cellophane or sent off to make the tea or shuffled in to the social committee. But these are only little things. Revolutions are about little things. Little things which happen to you all the time, every day, wherever you go, all your life.

Everyday details such as these were not part of the language of politics in 1969.

I was still raw from exposure when a trade unionist from Hull whom I knew slightly stopped me at a meeting at the LSE and remarked scathingly that it must have felt good to let out all my 'personal hang-ups'. I could feel humiliating tears starting in my eyes when Ann Scott lashed into him with icy fury: 'It's not just Sheila who thinks this.' My assailant backed off in amazement. I had been rescued by another woman and one some years my junior. I snuffled my gratitude to Ann from the depths of my heart and learned in that moment how important it is not to be an individual alone. We needed one another!

Not all men were hostile by any means. Henry Wortis told me he liked the article; Edward Thompson wrote from Warwick University that January, 'I liked your piece in BD very much: a lot in the space, a new style, not patronizing, not NLRish, sometimes poetic.' The most remarkable tribute came from the Boston Women's Liberation movement; the May 1969 women's issue of the radical newspaper *Old Mole* reproduced my article with powerful and moving pictures. When Danny Schecter, then a radical student but later to become a well-known journalist in the United States, handed me a copy at a meeting at the LSE, I was overwhelmed that words I had written from my own experience could be relevant to women in another country. In the early years of Women's Liberation these international practical exchanges were to be vitally important; they confirmed a feminist consciousness which often felt fragile.

Ann Scott's passionate defence signalled a much closer connection among young radical women. I had always had strong individual friendships with women since being at school, but my intellectual and political friendships tended to be more generally with men. While these were to continue, after *Black Dwarf* came out that January I found myself just talking and talking with women friends with a new-found excitement. We all seemed to be going in a similar direction. Things suddenly began to connect, to make sense. It was as if we were discovering a new way of seeing which at the same time had always been somehow part of our awareness. Nor was it only women I had known for a long time who seemed to understand this mutuality of recognition. Whereas before new women might be potential sexual competition, now a glance or a smile communicated reassurance.

The small clusters of middle-class women talking to one another coincided with a new spirit among working-class women. The demand for equal pay, raised in the Ford's dispute about grading rights, was being taken up in workplaces around the country; bus conductresses were also insisting that there should be women drivers. That January, while the Transport Workers' Union Central London Bus Conference discussed how to deal with proposals for 'one-man buses', the women occupied the building during the lunch break.

My life had turned into meetings during 1968 and the momentum of what was to be known as the 'extra-parliamentary' left was not abating. On 24 January the Central Hall Westminster was packed for the debate 'Reform v. Revolution'. Michael Foot and Eric Heffer put the case for 'reform', Tariq and Bob argued for 'revolution', while I ran up and down the aisles with bundles of *Black Dwarf*s – this was a great selling opportunity.

By 1969, however, the millenarian hopes of 1968 had given way to a recognition that total transformation of the globe was going to take a little longer than we had figured. Yet 'Revolution' continued to be invoked with little definition of how and what this would entail, because it seemed self-evident to us that the Labour Party's proposition of reforming in bits did not challenge the existing structures of class and power. We had lived through the disappointment with Labour in relation to the unions and foreign policy, and we tended to take the reforms of the 1945 government for granted. It seemed to follow that only a fundamental transformation could alter social inequality. We never imagined that this was going to come from the right and actually make Britain *more* unequal. It was to be Margaret Thatcher on the extreme right who would suss out how to make a leap into the unknown appear to be common sense.

The dramatic moment of the *Dwarf–Tribune* debate came when an impassioned Robin Blackburn (in a green army-surplus greatcoat) rushed up to the mike and announced amidst cheers that 'the comrades' had taken down the gates. These were of course the infamous security gates erected by the LSE authorities. They symbolized to the student movement what Barbara Castle's attempts to curb strikes with compulsory ballots, cooling-off periods and fines represented to the unions – authoritarian control.

Indeed Edward Short, the Labour Secretary of State for Education, was profoundly hostile to the students, saying it was time that 'one or two of these thugs are thrown out on their necks'. Robin was eventually to be sacked, not for taking the gates down – he had been in a seminar at the time – but for expressing sympathy with the students' action. Remembering the habitual drunken violence of upper-class young men at Christ Church in Oxford, for which they would be reprimanded and fined, the LSE hysteria about the attack on the gates seemed to me out of all proportion. They had become a metaphor of power.

That January I set off to various universities, taking copies of *Black Dwarf*. At Essex I found the students planning a Revolutionary Festival for 10–12 February and they decided, partly because of our women's issue, to include a session on 'women'. I got a lift down with Jean McCrindle and Sally Alexander to what was to be our first public meeting. Although unsure what to expect, we were charged with a powerful sense of anticipation. I remember the intensity of our talking and the feeling of shared discovery. Ideas, in these early days of Women's Liberation, seemed to just spring out of a process of recognition. This connection of experience was all the more remarkable because it was an exchange of perceptions which had been so private.

All those reactions, those vagrant thoughts which you had kept to yourself, suddenly came to acquire a new social meaning.

With the new-found affinities came a corresponding realization of distances. I sat in the back seat of the car thinking how Sally and Jean had a bond which I could not share, for they both were the mothers of young daughters. Despite our common perceptions, I was conscious of being just slightly apart. I was a detached, atomistic one, not a mother. There were things I did not know. Contrary to the stereotypes, the early women's movement was respectful towards the women with children – they were our equivalent to the Marxist proletariat. But this remained abstract. Motherhood persisted as the uncrossed barrier and was inwardly mysterious to me. There were whole realms of my friends' lives which I could not comprehend. This early intimation of closeness and separation was to be replicated over the years in the women's movement in various contexts. I think this was because the utopian longing in our politics for union, 'sisterhood', carried with it the opposite awareness of being necessarily, as individuals, apart. The two polarities were difficult to negotiate.

It was a freezing winter's day and the isolated campus of Essex University had the air of a besieged space station in some bizarre science fiction other-world. I trailed around with Roberta, lifting the long dresses which we now wore, to prevent them from becoming sodden in the much-tramped snow. Also sludging along with us was the film-maker Jean-Luc Godard, who was looking for revolutionary students to include in his film *British Sounds*. Radicalized by the May 'Events' the previous year, Godard was defying the film as art object and making throwaway works which could help finance the left. Unluckily for him, the Essex students, who were heavily influenced by the situationists' critique of the 'spectacle', were suspicious of all film-makers and dramatists, regardless of politics. The tenacious Godard did manage several interviews, though, despite this suspicion of the 'bourgeois' media.

The iconoclastic anarcho-situationist politics combined with the bleak and remote setting of the campus to make the Revolutionary Festival a chaotic and fraught event. The women's meeting, held in a large lecture hall, was electric with tension as Branka Magas from the *New Left Review* began to read a theoretical paper. She held her head down, speaking in a low voice with a Yugoslavian accent. Now this was a cat-on-a-hot-tin-roof kind of meeting, not an academic seminar. You could feel the currents of emotion charging around the hall. Reason and analysis did not cut much ice that day. Yet the fight for her space to speak undisturbed felt like a life and death struggle. Again we were being treated with ridicule. One of the students came in laughing with a woman on his back. Someone threw toilet paper from a balcony and it cascaded down in long white tendrils. The lights were turned on and off.

In the discussion a sedate member of the Communist Party (which was regarded as the equivalent to the right wing) tried to take another tack. When a woman complained about having to type the leaflets, he stood up to explain that there had to be some division of labour, as not everyone understood what should be put in the leaflets. By this time the women in the audience were in an angry mood and we hissed and booed.

One man, at least, was appalled by the men's response. A visiting German student stood up in the left corner of the room and spoke with a calm authority. He warned the men that they would be making a big mistake if they failed to listen and acknowledge what the women were saying. In Germany already the men's derisive reaction had created a very bitter rift. Despite the hysteria-edged political ethos at Essex, his words carried conviction. There was a pause; people were reflecting.

We weren't about to let it go at that and announced a follow-up meeting. Two men came along to this smaller meeting. One was a bearded Sikh Maoist from Hemel Hempstead, who told us we should read Mao, Lenin and Stalin. Things went from bad to worse when the other man there declared that we sounded like a women's tea party (shades of Potter's tea-bag rebels) because we kept giggling in high-pitched voices. Militancy was being thrust upon us.

When those of us from London exchanged addresses we discovered a group formed by North Americans was already meeting in Tufnell Park. We fixed a time to make contact again, knowing something momentous was happening but with no idea just what it was. This realization was offset by the intensity surrounding us; we had grown accustomed to taking the unusual for granted. Claims for 'liberation' were sprouting everywhere.

*

On 14 February, in the midst of rebellion at the LSE, *Black Dwarf* came out with the headline 'Create 2, 3, many LSEs'. The *New Left Review* had developed the idea of red bases from Régis Debray's ideas about guerrilla strategy. The 'vanguard' view of the students had merged now into this peculiar conviction that universities and colleges were to become liberated territory, bases for intellectual guerrillas combating ideology. My friends in the International Socialist group had their own version of that *Dwarf* headline: 'Create 2, 3, many balls up'. At the *Black Dwarf* editorial, while Fred Halliday defended red bases, I argued against them, along with Bob and Kim Howells, who was aware of the demoralization at Hornsey College after the occupation.

I stayed in IS for eighteen months, because they provided an alternative to the dead end of simply escalating student militancy within institutions. Another reason was more personal: I was friendly with and respected the commitment of many IS members. I was not to prove a very successful recruit, though initially things went well enough. I had been allocated to 'youth work' by the Hackney International Socialists – nearly twenty-six and feeling pretty elderly, I concluded they must regard me as young at heart. But I was not complaining, because 'youth work' provided a means of wiggling out of those early mornings on Shacklewell Lane with the African prince. Instead I organized meetings on sex and psychology, or why terrorism was only the correct tactic if you happened to be in the Russian Revolution – all more interesting than bothering about points of order in the Young Socialists. David Widgery came along to the Britannia pub (now Samuel Pepys) in Mare Street from his flat above an electrical shop in Islington's Chapel Market to speak to my youth group on rock music. Going back on the 38 bus, I decided to relent about the Solanas feminist terrorist hit list. After all, we weren't in the Russian Revolution, and he was only twenty-two and wearing a particularly beautiful, antiquated brown-leather jacket.

Other aspects of my youth work involved organizing the leafleting of schools. The ulterior motive was to recruit proletarian Hackney youth, who would then be able to raise class issues about education in the Schools Action Union. In fact, I really liked the young organizers of the Schools Action Union, which included some lively sixth-formers from Camden School for Girls who were in contact with the French lycée rebels of 1968.

The International Socialist idea of a worker–student alliance was not a chimera in 1969. Left trade unionists felt betrayed by Labour and a new confidence had developed among workers. They were resolved not only to resist the attempt to get more work out of them but to demand a greater share of profits. The result was to be a unique period in industrial relations in which workers took the offensive. Though 1969 has been eclipsed by the attention which has focused on 1968, it was to be a year in which the basis for the working-class militancy of the early seventies was being laid. There was a sixties generation in industry, as well as in student politics and radical popular culture, and they were to be hammered the heaviest in the long run.

On 24 February Ford workers came out on strike against management's attempts to curb resistance in the plants and the Ford stewards invited the students to join their demonstration. Resistance had been building up since the publication of Barbara Castle's White Paper 'In Place of Strife' in January, proposing a month's cooling-off period and the threat of prosecution through the new Industrial Relations Court. Ironically, industrial action was being politicized by Labour's emphasis upon state intervention in disputes. In retaliation, the shop stewards and militants on the shopfloor were adopting arguments for democracy and control within the workplace. One Ford worker I met on the march, inspired by the TV drama about an occupation of the docks, *The Big Flame*, written by Jim Allen, declared, 'We want to see the big flame all over.'

At an Agit Prop meeting during February, Hubert and Dorothea, two German left-wing students who were friends of the injured Rudi Dutschke, now staying in London with a member of International Socialist active at Ford, suggested that we should go out to Dagenham with a street theatre play. A group of us went off, very shyly, and performed *Stuff Your Penal Up Your Bonus*. It was not great drama but the Ford workers welcomed support and laughed anyway, urging us to come back.

We were at Ford when a massive 4,000-strong meeting voted to stay out. Not only did I witness for the first time the incredible power of workers in a large plant, but the stewards amazed me by doing the most complex mental arithmetic for the darts score in the pub after-wards while drinking pint after pint. Yet they were inordinately grateful when I typed and corrected the spelling in one of their leaflets. They were cynical about the multitude of sects who came leafleting. 'Like the Salvation Army,' one man remarked wearily. They also viewed the smoother left intellectuals askance, comparing them to the type of younger personnel officer who arrived at Ford with a liberal approach and commenting grimly, 'They turn out the worst.' I became friendly with some of the stewards who would gang up with my next-door neighbour from Jamaica, Barbara Marsh, to tease me for being middle class and knowing only bookish things. But amidst the banter they were as romantic about 'students' as we were about workers. After the strike they decided they wanted to go to a Revolutionary Socialist Students' Federation meeting in Manchester to 'thank the students'. I rang up Claire Brayshaw, the tiny, round ex-Communist who had befriended me when I was at university. She did not bat an eyelid at being asked to put up seven Dagenham shop stewards. They came back delighted by Claire and still drunk on the talk, incredulous that students would talk about politics non-stop for three days.

The Agit Prop expedition to Ford made me think more specifically about the process of communicating across class boundaries. 'Com-munications' had been the theme of a May Day Manifesto meeting that January which had included Raymond Williams on the structure of the media industry. Perry Anderson had talked about something I didn't understand, but was to hear much more about in the future, called 'semiotics'. But it was the more immediate problems that confronted us on *Black Dwarf* which really engaged me. During 1968 we had been carried along by a tide of militancy when the accelerating impetus of the student movement and the anti-Vietnam War demonstrations provided us with a constituency. By 1969 we could no longer ride along on that wave of conviction. Radical activity was not abating, but it was diversifying, appearing in the workplace, in schools, among squatters, tenants, women, the black community and within radical culture. This fragmented radical movement did not have any automatic affinities. I wanted *Black Dwarf* to reach outwards, not only to students but to workers, and be a means through which these differing kinds of radical movements might communicate with one another. However, there were problems of both style and content. We were never to find how to communicate with the differing potential readerships – the 'left' in the broad rather than the narrow sense of the word.

My apprentices at Tower Hamlets College had made me aware how words could have several simultaneous interpretations. Quite everyday political language changed its meanings in their heads. 'Capitalism' they interpreted as 'freedom', 'fascism' meant 'against the government', while 'democracy' was translated as 'government'. A metaphorical form of writing which created pictures and told parables, before arriving at an abstraction, could act as a bridge between direct experience and abstract thought, but this was absent from the sociologically influenced 'left theory' of the period. Consequently a lot of our writing just went over most people's heads.

At the end of February Tariq went home to Pakistan, where a student revolt had acted as a catalyst for a broader rebellion. While he was away, Douglas Gill, whom Bob and I had brought on to the board, edited the paper. Douglas decided that *Black Dwarf* should become a left-wing version of the *Daily Mirror* in order to gain popular appeal. There were two snags about his approach. First, the *Mirror* was aiming at a set of reforms grafted on to the existing society, a bigger piece of the pie. We were meant to be baking something else entirely. Yet we had no idea how to connect this abstract 'revolution' with the everyday. *Black Dwarf* began to sound as if it had a permanent frog in its throat. The second difficulty was that *Mirror* journalism was a special craft skill which none of us possessed.

I knew something was wrong, and was puzzling away about it, when, shortly after Tariq had left for Pakistan, Gus Macdonald, who was then working on the TV current affairs programme *World in Action*, happened to wander into the *Black Dwarf* office. The small Anarcho-syndicalist group Solidarity were stapling together the Rone-oed pages of their magazine on Tariq and Ann's big working table. Gus picked up an issue and pointed to the dialogue quoted in an account of a strike. Solidarity's politics emphasized the consciousness which came from the rank and file. They were completely opposed to the vanguardism of the Trotskyist groups. It was the voice from below which mattered to them, not the direction by generals from on top.

Gus said to me he could never understand why the left didn't realize that they had a tremendous asset in access to people's voices. 'Of course!' I thought to myself, and after that quoted copiously.

I landed bang in the middle of a communications problem of my own when Jean-Luc Godard offered to include Agit Prop in *British Sounds*, which he was making with Kestrel Films for London Weekend Television. Aiming to catch specific instances of left organizing and consciousness, Godard had decided he wanted to use my *Black Dwarf* article on women. He aimed to do an *Oz* in reverse. His idea was to film me with nothing on reciting words of emancipation as I walked up and down a flight of stairs – the supposition being that eventually the voice would override the images of the body. This proposal made me uneasy, for two quite different reasons. I was a 36C and considered my breasts to be too floppy for the sixties fashion. Being photographed lying down with nothing on was fine, but walking down stairs could be embarrassing. Moreover, while I didn't think nudity was a problem in itself, the early women's groups were against what we called 'objectification'. New and powerful images were being projected all around us in the media. Contesting how we were being regarded and represented had been one the sources of our rebellion. Where did you draw the line over images? Why on earth did the pesky male mind jump so quickly from talk of liberation to nudity, I wondered? On the other hand, Agit Prop needed to move out of John and Wisty Hoyland's house, because they had a new baby. We were trying to raise money for an office.

Godard came out to Hackney to convince me. He sat on the sanded floor of my bedroom, a slight dark man, his body coiled in persuasive knots. Neither Godard the man nor Godard the mythical creator of *A Bout de Souffle*, which I'd gone to see with Bar in Paris, were easy to contend with. I perched in discomfort on the edge of my bed and announced, 'I think if there's a woman with nothing on appearing on the screen no one's going to listen to any words,' suggesting perhaps he could film our 'This Exploits Women' stickers on the tube. Godard gave me a baleful look, his lip curled. 'Don't you think I am able to make a cunt boring?' he exclaimed. We were locked in conflict over a fleeting ethnographic moment.

In the end a compromise was settled. The Electric Cinema had recently opened in Notting Hill and needed money. A young woman (with small breasts) from there agreed to walk up and down the stairs and I did the voice-over. When *British Sounds* was shown in France, Charlie Posner told me the audience cheered as I declared, 'They tell us what we are . . . One is simply not conscious of "men" writers, of "men" film-makers. They are just "writers", just "film-makers". The reflected image for women they create will be taken straight by women themselves. These characters "arc" women.' As for Godard's intention for making a cunt boring, I cannot say, except that a friend in International Socialism told me that his first thought had been 'crumpet' – until the shot went on and on and on, and he started to listen.

British Sounds was to have an unexpected series of repercussions which I did not grasp at the time. Humphrey Burton, then head of arts at London Weekend Television, refused to show it. The ensuing row fused with the sacking of Michael Peacock from the board of LWT in September 1969. Whereupon Tony Garnett and Kenith Trodd from Kestrel, along with other programme-makers, resigned in protest. LWT decided to go for higher ratings and brought in an Australian newspaper owner called Rupert Murdoch. The last thing *he* wanted to do was to make a cunt boring.

News of the Essex women's meeting had spread by the time a small group of us gathered again in London on 3 March. Jane Arden, the author of an avant-garde feminist play, *Vagina Rex*, made a dramatic entrance in a big, broad-brimmed hat, fashionable on the King's Road. 'Stupid hat,' I thought to myself cattily. She addressed us with majesty, telling us we had to head a movement. Hackles went up all over the room; we were intensely suspicious of leadership and, as fugitives from being bossed by the men, did not take kindly to it from women. We were determined to create a democratic collectivity which gave all women the space to develop – an unforeseen outcome was that we implicitly tried to subdue extreme figures. The early Women's Liberation groups were to establish a consensus of tentativeness as an alternative to strident militancy.

In the free-for-all combat of the student movement, men who could assert charisma or just sometimes aggression would tend to hold the floor. While the Revolutionary Socialist Students' Federation had a rhetoric of participation, its anarchic style of meetings effectively excluded most women. Whereas women might have had a secondary role in the more hierarchical Young Socialists, at least there we had been allowed a nominal position.

Now we were desperate for autonomy. One man came to the meeting and refused to leave unless we gave him a 'political' reason for his exclusion. 'We need to be able to talk to one another before we can work out any political reasons,' I replied. I did not equate this all-women discussion with a total separation from left politics. Autonomy meant space, not a severing from the left. Implicitly we saw this as indicating another approach to politics in general. The thoughtful Dorothea observed how the women's revolt in the German student movement had also spoken for the 'little men' who were similarly crushed by the 'theorists'.

Roberta was there, frowning in concentration as the two North American women from the Tufnell Park group, Sue Cowley (later O'Sullivan), blonde and petite with her pixie face, and Shelley Wortis, a serenely imposing figure with jet-black hair, spoke about child care. Unlike the approach usually taken on the left then, in which new relations in the family were to follow a 'revolution', they were intent on making changes in the here and now. Along with their anti-authoritarianism and belief in participatory democracy, the North American women brought into the British Women's Liberation movement a belief in prefiguring a desired future in the way you organized. They also possessed an openness to new realities and perceptions and a respect for knowledge rooted in experience. The influential New Left thinker C. Wright Mills had argued the need to translate personal problems into social issues and this concept was to have a particular relevance to women.

The combination of radical influences at that first meeting made it one of the most exciting events I have ever experienced; we stayed on for hours, discussing and discovering, and when I came away I was still thinking about it. In the left sects, all necessary 'correct' knowledge was already parcelled up; after this women's meeting, it seemed that *nothing* was already known. I began to recast my memories, wondering how I had been affected intellectually by studying at an all-girls' school and deciding that I deferred to men intellectually.

The fierce mood of democracy in the early days of Women's Liberation was to be empowering. Just as the avant-garde in art was to reject
any hierarchy of subject matter, we were blotting out all distinctions
between differing kinds of knowing. On reflection, I believe a more
equal balance between theorizing and tacit understanding is preferable.
Like many anti-authoritarian movements, we were to discover that an
extreme rejection of hierarchy could result in a denial that anyone *did*
have differing degrees of understanding and thus something to pass
on.

The conviction that 'liberation' meant changing the world and yourselves was prevalent in the student left. But what about the impact of
self-expression on others? The LSE had erupted again after summonses
were issued against some students and lecturers, and I spent the evening
of 10 March with Vinay and the International Socialist students, wiping
the slogans off the wall. 'It's not fair on the cleaners,' we told the
'libertarians' who accused us of acting as 'guards'. Introducing subjectivity into politics had its downside.

On the back of an International Socialist leaflet 'Support LSE',
which must have been produced around this time as it was protesting
against Walter Adams's lock-out of the students, I scribbled ideas
about women's position in red ink. Women, I noted, defined men only
in oblique ways, through irony, through intonation. The 'differences'
between women were frequently more 'apparent than the universalizing
features'. I considered there to be different levels of consciousness and
'very limited traditions of struggle' (I was to learn how mistaken this
latter view was through studying women's history!). Having read my
Mao and Trotsky, I considered that the resolution of the 'theoretical
contradictions' in women's position would be through practice: 'a real
task of life' rather than exclusively a process of intellectual understanding. Eric Hobsbawm's *Primitive Rebels* had suggested to me that
this new consciousness might not develop through formal political
structures. Christopher Hill's essay on *Clarissa* indicated that a moral
protest against women's predicament had appeared in the novel long
before it attained any political expression.

I wondered how the 'confusion' and 'conflict' affecting women like
me had arisen. A key factor seemed to be the split in how we were
regarded sexually and in the 'persona' (Bergman had given me a new

word) permitted in the public spheres of politics, intellectual culture and academic life. While women were accepted in an abstract way in an intellectual or academic milieu, men appeared to find it 'difficult' – I wrote 'impossible' at first, but crossed this out as too pessimistic – to permit women also to be sexual. You were expected to be one thing or the other: 'Bed/intell' I called this split in my own shorthand. The notes ended grumpily with an obvious borrowing from Black Power: 'Men's job not to tell us what we're like, which they do all the time. Start to explore what they are like in relation to us.'

By March 1969 the euphoria of May '68 had metamorphosed into the 'past'. On 3 March I wondered in my diary about 'this strange optimism that flashes through the world, that last year was smattering, shimmering . . . Where does it come from?' During the late sixties so many ideas flew around, springing from differing sources at the same time and going through several permutations, that we could not track their course or their implications. For instance, occupying spaces was a preoccupation of the situationists, but it was also what the US Civil Rights movement had done when they sat-in on buses or at restaurants. It was of symbolic significance again in the North of Ireland marches through 'Protestant' territory and reappeared as metaphorical space in the idea of 'prefigurative' alternatives in both the US New Left and the German SDS.

Because so many new radical streams continued to emerge, it still seemed possible to graft the transformatory consciousness of 1968 on to everyday resistance. A former student from Tower Hamlets College turned up and took me off to interview a young working-class couple squatting in north-east London. The squatters had been inspired by one of their relatives, a defiant man in his fifties who could remember the spontaneous squatting after the war. 'Squatting,' he told me, was 'like unions, people sticking together' – a local memory of direct action and collectivity had persisted. The squatters were to be brutally evicted by builders, even though the young woman was pregnant.

Housing was a material need which also raised wider questions about how to live and how space was owned and controlled. Before Christmas Agit Prop had considered occupying Centrepoint, the giant skyscraper near Tottenham Court Road tube, kept empty so the rents would increase. But the plan had leaked and the housing activist Ron Bailey had urged us not to do it. He feared violence and the accompanying bad publicity would rebound on his homeless families. Our modified scheme that March was to stage a demonstration.

Eight of us duly turned up outside the tall building at the crossroads of Tottenham Court Road and Oxford Street. The police, who must have thought Agit Prop was some kind of nerve centre of revolution, had blocked all the traffic off around Centrepoint. We had decided to try and look respectable and so I wore my short red Chelsea Girl military-style coat, a slightly out-of-date evocation of the *Sergeant Pepper* cover, which was my idea of 'respectable'. Ken Loach's film *Cathy Come Home* had become a symbol of the plight of the homeless and we had a long banner, 'Cathy Come to Centrepoint'. It was sunny but very windy that day and we had not remembered that the tall Centrepoint building acted as a wind trap. We could hardly hold the banner straight. However, our leaflets, with the picture of 'Cathy' with her baby and the heading 'Cathy Come to Centrepoint: It's Empty', vindicated the attempt to communicate more graphically. Cabbies put their hands through the windows to take them; even the police read them sympathetically.

Our action at Centrepoint proved you could get the optimum cover-age from a minimal deployment of demonstrators! Not only were the TV cameras whirring but the *Guardian* solemnly reported:

A rather disorganized march was led by Mr John Hoyland, an artist [I think they got the wrong John Hoyland], who wore a giant black and red mask and carried a placard bearing a slogan in the shape of a speaker's bubble in a cartoon . . .

Mr Bob Rowthorne [*sic*], a lecturer in economics at Cambridge, said the group did not want to see homeless people accommodated in Centrepoint but wanted to protest against the money wasted on the skyscraper.

I was wilting under the ceaseless round of activity and complaining hopelessly in my diary about my inability to get any work done: 'Every time I get a few days something new happens.' Though my thesis was slipping into the void of abandoned PhDs, I retained an interest in the long conflict over knowledge which has been part of the history of working-class education in Britain, writing about this in the 14 March issue of *Black Dwarf*: 'To know that we want something is not in itself sufficient. We must know what we want and, what is more important still, how we are to get it, in other words we must first understand before we can transform.'

Agit Prop had become involved in planning meetings to hold a unifying conference of the left, an initiative backed by Raymond Williams from the May Day Manifesto group, the Communist Party and the Young Liberals. The idea was to develop alternative socialist policies and to set up local left forums. I added the Left Convention to my weekly round of meetings and joined the group on education. Bob was coordinating the economics 'commission' with help from a young Cambridge graduate, Hugo Radice.

Our attempt to forestall the sectarianism of the left groups was to prove futile. The International Socialists denounced the Left Convention and as a result Bob was to leave IS and join the Communist Party. The economics commission, however, did survive, turning into the Conference of Socialist Economists and eventually producing the journal *Capital and Class*. Every ten years or so there seems to be a similar venture to the Left Convention. This was to be my first time around.

A peculiar thing about left politics is that you set out to do one thing – in this case, to create a structure for left debate and unified campaigns – and instead quite different consequences ensue. The positive outcome of the planning meetings was that I made several new friends. Among them was Ben Birnbaum, a trade unionist from the east London clothing industry. Ben was full of perceptive observations about politics, based on his experience of activism in the unions, the Communist Party and the East End community, explaining, for example, how a sense of Jewish identity against fascism had stimulated commitment to trade unionism. He pointed out that important interactions between culture and the workplace were missed by the syndicalist-influenced left. He also approached leadership very differently from the anti-authoritarian student left. 'A cadre,' Ben insisted, was someone who you could 'always rely upon to organize in a shop when the need arose'. Related to his view of responsibility was his respect for craft skill, which went against the distrust of the skilled worker on the libertarian left. Ben's observation of the clothing trade had convinced him that to possess a skill developed a strategic frame of mind which could be the basis for a consciousness of the need to organize. I was learning again how words could assume differing meanings and Ben made me qualify my absolute certainties about how to organize.

The Left Convention had revealed the political differences I had buried when I joined the International Socialist group. Members of IS considered that my involvement with the planning meetings was due to Nick's influence. It was assumed that women were semi-permeable membranes who absorbed men's ideas through the semen. 'You've been fucking with a Stalinist,' hissed a man in Hornsey International Socialists, pinning me against the wall at a party. This attitude was a mix of male sexual control and a religious feeling that the group should be your whole life, with sex only permissible within the boundaries. It was, of course, anathema to me. No one was going to tell me what I should or should not do.

The reality was that Nick, the organization man, took a cynical view of the Left Convention himself. Moreover, we had not seen much of each other during those months. My emotional energy continued to be largely consumed by the endless round of political meetings and demonstrations. Nick said to me in March that he found me 'unreal', I think because I was ceasing to exist as a private person.

One profound misunderstanding between us was that I retained my existential refusal to make demands. Nick expected demands, saying if I nagged him he'd be around more. I couldn't imagine anything more demeaning. Though Nick and Steve were completely dissimilar, I had managed to reproduce similar patterns in the two relationships. On one occasion Steve had grumbled about me getting off with other men and this had made me angry enough to respond with the observation that if the spaces between his visits were smaller perhaps I wouldn't. I was surprised when he said sorry. I was so bothered about dependence and independence, the most obvious complaints stuck in my throat. This convoluted pride might have been ostensibly self-defeating, but it was part of how my sense of myself as an autonomous person had developed. It was to be modified over the years, by having a child and by growing older, but it has never completely gone. I can recognize the same responses among several friends – not only in Britain. Some future psychoanalyst might identify the Greco–Piaf syndrome in women of a certain age.

On 21 March I received an ominous phone call from the *Daily Mail*, which was waging a campaign against leftists in higher education. They wanted to know what I taught in liberal studies. Around this time Tower Hamlets College told me they did not have any part-time hours for me next term. It felt like a kick in the stomach. I had been there longer than many full-time staff. But Bill Fishman had gone to Balliol and the union wasn't interested in part-timers. It was Ben Birnbaum and another older Communist trade unionist I had met in the Left Convention meetings who really understood the hurt of losing a job, and they made attempts to get me work. I was eventually to find some teaching in a boys' school in Shepherd's Bush called Christopher Wren.

Several people from the planning meetings, including Ben, were going to the Institute of Workers' Control conference at the end of March, which that year was up in Sheffield, where Jean McCrindle was now living. The IWC conference had grown to 1,000 people and assumed a greater significance through the participation of trade union leaders such as Lawrence Daly from the miners and Huw Scanlon from the engineers. By 1969, the IWC not only had an influence on the left trade union leadership but, less visibly, was creating a space for the early networks of shop stewards to develop – these were to become extremely important in the seventies labour movement. It was effective because it was independent of parties and groups. Amidst the working-class men there was a knot of middle-class socialists, among them Bob, Gus Macdonald from the film-workers' union, who spoke at the plenary, and Clive Goodwin, with the tall blonde woman who worked as his assistant, elegant and efficient as ever, but balking slightly at the overwhelming proletarian masculinity of the gathering.

Audrey Wise spoke on 'Women and Workers' Control' and, on the suggestion of one of the organizers of the IWC conference, Tony Topham, we held a women's meeting there. Along with Jean McCrindle, I contested the view taken by some Trotskyist women there that you had to concentrate on getting rid of capitalism first and *then* women would be all right. By this reasoning Women's Liberation as an autonomous movement was 'diversionary'. The argument was to recur many times in the early days of Women's Liberation.

In one of the breaks, Ben Birnbaum introduced me to a small bird-like woman in her fifties called Gertie Roche, a left-wing trade unionist in the Leeds clothing industry, who had left the Yorkshire Communist Party along with the Thompsons in the exodus of 1956. Gertie was to be swept into the leadership of the 1970 clothing strike. In a sudden rebellion, the workforce, who were predominantly women, surged through the streets of Leeds, from factory to factory, pioneering the mass picket before Arthur Scargill and Saltley Gates. Gertie, who was also to help the new Women's Liberation group in Leeds when it began to meet, asked me shrewdly when I visited her, 'And you, are you emancipated in your own life?' It was reassuring to hear the flat Leeds tones, so familiar from my childhood, expressing radical opinions.

Gertie, like Audrey Wise, acted as a link between Women's Liberation groups and an older working-class left influenced by a non-Stalinist Marxism, and both of them enabled me personally to understand more about the relationship of working-class women to trade unions. My neighbour Barbara Marsh was to act as another 'bridge person' for me. Her accounts of the everyday prejudice she encountered in terms of race, class and gender helped me see how these were intertwined and led me to admire how Barbara never let herself be consumed by bitterness. While sympathetic to some of my 'Women's Liberation' propaganda, Barbara took other bits with a pinch of salt. A staunch Catholic, she was opposed to abortion. But we became and stayed friends despite our differences.

My first contact with an actual Women's Liberation consciousness-raising group was to be a visit to the Tufnell Park group early that April. Shelley Wortis invited me to talk about women in the French Commune and I gave them an excited summary of Edith Thomas's *The Women Incendiaries*. Thomas's account of women's action in the streets complemented the 'history from below' I had learned from Richard Cobb. The contemporary inspiration of the women active in Palestine and Vietnam encouraged an interest in the history of women's role in revolutionary movements in the early days of Women's Liberation not only in Britain but also in the United States.

The Tufnell Park group was not at all like my experience of meetings in the Labour Party rooms on Graham Road or the pub room in the Britannia. There the chairs had been in rows. In the house on Dartmouth Park Hill everyone sat around on chairs or on the floor. Shelley acted as a linchpin for the group, but the atmosphere was quietly cooperative. You could hear yourself think and half-formed ideas could be developed collectively. The consciousness-raising approach of the early Women's Liberation groups could go badly wrong, when a consensus coalesced into a perspective which could be hard to contest. But when the anti-authoritarian insistence on everyone participating worked, it could be magic.

Early that April I read Juliet Mitchell's essay 'Women: The Longest Revolution' once again. But my own interests were in the processes of consciousness rather than in the structures of subordination. I wanted to understand how new perceptions of oneself appeared both through public action, such as strikes, and through personal sexual experiences.

Pondering on my own desire to be overwhelmed sexually, which I thought conflicted with my equally strong wish to be independent, I ruminated in my diary during April that men and women carried both potentials: to overwhelm and be overwhelmed. I concluded that the differences in how these were generally expressed arose because we had been 'socialized into the "male" and "female" roles'. By the time you slept with your first man, I decided, you had already been educated into a submission so pervasive that 'even the non-submissive girl . . . will doubt herself'.

From my own observation of the two areas of the public sphere familiar to me, politics and academia, I had deduced that women related differently to politics and to ideas. I believed we took intellectual criticism more personally, were less inclined to lose ourselves in abstractions and less likely to become sectarian. Unable to conceive at this point that women might become sectarian in *different* ways, I optimistically imagined that women would play an important 'de-alienating role' in radical politics. I was convinced that women could make a unique contribution to radical thinking about behaviour, responses, everyday existence and consciousness.

I had stumbled into a dilemma which did not go away. The stress of an oppression which spanned the public and private spheres could reduce women to being simply victims. The idea of women as carrying an utopian alternative was attractive because it presented a way of escaping from a politics of victimhood. More generally, it was part of the search for the means of moving from life as it was lived to life as it might be, which was so important in the radicalism of the late sixties.

Our utopianism, however, raised some complicated issues. As a *potential*, the recognition of opposing values presents a way of imagining an alternative way of being. The problem comes when these congeal into a fixed ideal of 'women' as all good and 'men' as all bad. In the light of what has happened since, I would be more wary about women necessarily behaving differently from men in politics. More generally, while the utopian impulse is a vital part of any movement for change from below, it requires a fluidity between reality and desire to be maintained. And this is of course easier said than done.

In April 1969 I reflected in my diary that a distinguishing feature of the revolutionary left was that unlike academia, where women could put the personal aside, you had to live out a split between public and personal. You were expected to act in a removed manner as a thinker one moment and as a sexual woman the next. And when it came to sex, you would be 'treated persistently as an object'. I thought that having to live this split explained our 'terror at assuming a total responsibility' and our tendency to 'look for a man to hide behind' when it was necessary 'to confront people'.

Looking back, I don't think it was the case that all my sexual experiences could be summed up as 'objectified'. The early-sixties belief that action was morally justified by a subjective 'authenticity' assumed a new permutation in the early Women's Liberation discussions of 'OK' sex as opposed to 'objectified' sex. What started in the late sixties as an impulse to consciously democratize sexual relations ended by imposing prescriptive restriction in the early-eighties feminist movement. Sex in theory was to move away from sex in practice.

In the late sixties my actual sexual feelings and behaviour were infinitely varied. I was as capable of wanting momentary sensual pleasure as a man, but this was a barely permissible female thought then and so when it was 'lust' it still just 'happened', while 'love' continued to justify everything. Most sexual encounters fitted neither of these extreme polarities. I would 'fancy' men, for instance, a lighter feeling than either love or lust. Or I would just be curious about a man I hardly knew: 'I wonder what he'd be like?' Sometimes sex would come up as an expression of closeness with political friends whom I was fond of but did not particularly desire. In other cases, it remained muted, below the surface of friendship.

I was puzzled. Even the friendliest of men seemed to find talking about sex difficult. Things that were perfectly obvious to women appeared to be alarming to them. 'They are afraid,' I noted in my diary on 13 April. 'They wince.' I was puzzling over the contrary expressions of sexual desire and consciousness: 'The man who makes strong statements about male dominance can desire himself to be dominated in bed.' The assumption that everything might not be as it seemed was something I took for granted, but many intellectual Marxist men appeared to find this very peculiar.

Though exasperated frequently by men's behaviour and attitudes, I certainly did not see them as universally predatory, which is the retrospective caricature of the sixties. I was hurt by some men, but I know I hurt people too. I was, moreover, aware that there were pressures on men to compete and succeed which I was glad as a woman to escape. It seemed evident to me that these expectations of masculinity affected how men behaved. Instead of simply blaming individuals, which I regarded as a dead end in the same way as what I called 'the achievement principle' of women getting into top jobs, I wanted to make differing kinds of relationships and ways of being women and men possible.

I was already troubled by two questions which were to cause many an anxious debate in the seventies, asking my diary, first, whether the prevailing culture of masculinity was *only* a consequence of capitalism or was there some underlying structure which we were to call 'patriarchy'? Second, I wanted to know whether we should concentrate on changing the attitudes and behaviour of the revolutionary left or try 'to reach women in general'.

My involvement in the Left Convention education commission and my persistent chat about Women's Liberation led George Gross, the Hegelian Scotsman who was editing a series of May Day Manifesto pamphlets, to suggest I should write one on women, enabling me to

develop the original *Black Dwarf* article. I originally wanted to call
this pamphlet 'Women's Liberation and the Whole People Question'.
I thought 'wholeness', a theme in the late-sixties counter-culture, could
overcome the personal sense of division. It also intimated that the
specific experiences and interests of women were of general relevance
and could contribute to a search for a different kind of socialism from
the Trotskyism of the sects. But George Gross argued it would be
better to use the term 'new politics', which he said was being used in
the US New Left. 'Women's Liberation and the New Politics' was to
be the result.

While I was writing away, the International Socialist group was
turning more 'Leninist', which meant in practice that the centre could
strengthen its control over the new membership. By April discussion
papers were sprouting all over the place and I produced my own, the
'Magic Marxist faction' – part spoof, part plea for a left politics which
could appeal through the imagination. I knew I was powerless and
thus resorted to fantasy. But the joke contained a kernel of serious
conviction. The document was about a magician who was otherwise
known as Comrade 'Y'. His magical endeavours were of an alchemical
sort, for he lived in a baked bean tin which he was trying to turn into
magic Marxism. As all the other discussion documents were prefaced
by quotes, so was mine: ' "Socialism is an integral vision of life; it has
a philosophy, a mysticism, a morality", Gramsci. "Magic has the
power to experience and fathom things which are inaccessible to human
reason", Paracelsus. "All theory must be able to enter its own belly
button and be born again", Comrade "Y".'

Early that May I was trying to think about the symbols of power
embedded in the culture of daily life. Re-reading Alexis de Tocqueville's
writings on the French Revolution of 1848, I was struck by his story
of a fireman who participated in the workers' assault on the National
Assembly. The man mounted the rostrum and then stood there utterly
unable to speak. Silenced by the trappings of customary power, he
was humiliated and paralysed. As I read de Tocqueville's sardonic
account, it was as if I could feel the words choking deep down in the
nameless fireman's throat.

I had taken out my childhood glove puppets that April and, inspired by the friend of John Hoyland's who had moved from masks to making puppets, began painting their faces and making them some new clothes. One was Barbara Castle in a fur hat and boa and one was a cheeky-looking red-haired youth made for me as a child by two 1956 Hungarian exiles – they had gone on to create the TV marionettes Pinky and Perky. In my version of *Punch and Judy*, he put Barbara Castle's White Paper into a sausage machine in defiance, not only of her but of the policeman and a skeleton ghost of capitalism. My puppet box was the adapted TV from the 1968 Agit Prop Revolutionary Festival.

The May Day demonstration against the White Paper that year was a massive 200,000 strong. I did the puppet show in Victoria Park on a sunny spring day, still wearing my bright-red military coat. In a break between performances one of the dockers who had supported Powell in 1968 came up to me with a baffled expression: 'You lot were on the other side to us last year.' It was indicative of the swirling momentum of those two years. We were all turning somersaults in great waves which kept on pounding against every customary assumption of politics.

I lost my beloved Paris nosebag that day. Its strap had broken many times and I had repeatedly sewn it together. I always carried it with me, despite the inelegant, bunched-up stitching. It was stolen out of the puppet box, leaving me without any money. I was stranded in Victoria Park and began seriously thinking I would have to sleep the night in the box – I never considered just leaving the thing and walking home. Finally, about 8 p.m. someone managed to get a message to a friend in the Young Liberals who arrived and rescued me in a car with a roof rack.

Amidst the mass movement of predominantly male trade unionists, a smaller mobilization among trade union women was occurring with the aim of extending Barbara Castle's commitment to equal pay to a wider definition of equal rights. When the National Joint Action Committee on Women's Equal Rights held a demonstration that May, even though it rained about 1,000 trade union women, their perms carefully covered by umbrellas, tripped smartly dressed to Trafalgar Square in high heels.

I ambled happily around, snatching interviews as the rain dripped from the rims of their umbrellas, jotting down their improvised banners. 'Barbara gets hers so why not us?' I knew that this demonstration

expressed the pent-up frustration of women who had been campaigning, in some cases since the forties. Only many years later was I
to learn that a similar agitation for 'rights' among trade union women
also ran parallel with the emergence of Women's Liberation in the
United States. In both cases the mobilization of working-class women
has been neglected in the histories of the sixties and of the women's
movement.

'Something is stirring,' I wrote in *Black Dwarf*, 'something which
has been silent for a long time.'

Not only the International Socialists but also the International Marxist
Group were closing up in this period. When Tariq returned from
Pakistan towards the end of March, I commented in my diary, 'Behaving
strangely. IMG have cavils and mysterious power scenes about him.'
One result of the editorial board's complaints about the long Trotskyist
treatises which now kept appearing in the paper was that John Hoyland
and I were to do a 'youth' issue. This comprised such honorary youth
as David Widgery, who had been developing his own kind of political
writing in *Oz*; his 'Cabbage Water Cock Up' sputtered in staccato
style over the page. We also included part of a speech by a German
SDS member, Helke Sander, asking the student men at a conference
in 1968 why they talked only 'at home about the difficulties of orgasm'.
In Germany as well, women were contesting the scope of politics and
the boundary between public and private experience.

The most remarkable piece was part of a manuscript Charlie Posner
had given me, compiled by a radical Italian priest from the words of
his peasant pupils. It described, in language of great clarity and beauty,
the cultural silencing which was preoccupying my thoughts, demonstrating how political ideas can be expressed from personal experience.
It was later to be published by Penguin as *Letter to a Teacher*.

Towards the middle of May, Fei Ling Blackburn and I went to a
Revolutionary Socialist Students' Federation meeting, which I hated,
writing to Roberta, in another letter I never posted, 'They move and
talk like men.' Those of us who saw ourselves as 'Women's Liberation'
regarded women in left groups as interlopers. We suspected them of
seeking to impose alien male Leninist concepts; a veritable fifth column.
I could conveniently forget that I was in a left group because the

International Socialist group was so completely dismissive of Women's Liberation that it did not have a 'line' on us. Paradoxically, while the leadership simply felt we should not exist, individual women IS members or the girlfriends and wives of IS members were the ones who actually played a key role in starting the early Women's Liberation groups in many cities.

Another political paradox was that while assuming our little groups were discussing entirely new questions about women's position and being fiercely resistant to the imposition of an already established line, the feeling persisted that 'answers' were hidden in some body of thought. I urged Roberta, who was having a difficult time studying anthropology with Evans Pritchard in Oxford, to make contact with Fei Ling. 'She knows about French stuff, theory things,' I declared. Again it was Paris, the mecca, which must have the answer to all theoretical quests. The emphasis on direct experience and collective democratic learning, associated with the North American idea of consciousness-raising, was distrustful of received theories and focused on immediacy. On the other hand, the rush of ideas and upsurge in awareness encouraged us to read and stimulated intellectual inquiry in all directions.

In my case, wondering what had happened before to women led me to rethink the history I had learned. An important early influence was to be a Swiss student at Ruskin College called Arielle Aberson, who was writing a thesis on the consciousness of the French student movement of the 1860s which preceded the Commune. She and I met through Roberta for the first time towards the middle of May and excitedly discussed Edith Thomas's writing and the work of the French historical sociologist Evelyne Sullerot, who wrote *Histoire et Sociologie du Travail Féminin*. Arielle encouraged me to write first the pamphlet 'Women's Liberation and the New Politics' and then the books which grew out of it, *Women, Resistance and Revolution* and *Woman's Consciousness, Man's World*. Tragically Arielle was to be killed in a car crash in the early seventies; I dedicated *Women, Resistance and Revolution* to her memory.

By the time I wrote to Roberta, around 18 May, that swell of external political activity in which I had been immersed since the spring of

1968 was finally beginning to slacken. At last I had time to catch breath and begin to consider my personal predicament. My friendship with Bob was still very important, but the old tensions between us were niggling away more overtly now. We were, I think, finally separating, long after we no longer had a physical relationship. Bob was deeply committed to his relationship with Theresa, who was soon to move away to live with him in Cambridge. And I was feeling isolated. 'I suddenly had a wave of great loneliness – coming as these things always do with me after a time when I've felt integral and free-wheeling,' I told Roberta, adding, 'Oh dear, I don't want a husband, what is wrong with me, but often I am lonely.'

By May I knew my relationship with Nick had become stuck. I couldn't talk to him about my personal feelings and the connection between us had begun to drift. In retrospect I think that part of our initial attraction had been based on political disagreement. We had come up with a late-sixties left version of being attracted to what was forbidden. However, by May I could hardly be bothered to argue in defence of IS because increasingly I was coming to identify with Women's Liberation. Nick didn't go away entirely but continued to wander in and out of my life throughout the rest of that year.

Material reality was finally getting through to me. My part-time teaching money from Christopher Wren school was late in arriving and I was utterly broke by the middle of May, surviving only on a £5 loan from Clive Goodwin – £5 was still a considerable sum. I once took a man who claimed to be a US draft dodger all the way from Hackney to Cromwell Road to get £5 from Clive for him to 'escape' to Holland (he was back within a few days and we eventually realized he was an agent). However, £5, even in 1969, would not last long.

Christopher Wren school, on a Shepherd's Bush housing estate, was a shock after Tower Hamlets College and my Workers' Educational Association classes. At Christopher Wren the head and his deputy seemed to see the boys only when they were sent up to be beaten. I was appalled by the arbitrary violence of the older teachers, who hit the boys for no clear reason. The boys responded with a defiant anarchy which was then held down by harsher and harsher reprisals. When some of the fifth form broke out in the lunch hour and stole cars, the head's reaction was not to deal with what was going wrong, but to issue orders that all of us would be locked in. Towards exam time he altered the timetable without any consultation, so we all found ourselves teaching classes with whom we had not built any relationship. Keeping order was thus far more difficult.

The small boys in this alienated environment took their revenge on female teachers by grabbing their bums in the corridors. These crimes would be much tut-tutted about, along the lines of the original sin of boys, by the middle-aged male teachers in their blazers. There seemed no higher authority to which you could appeal, so I decided direct action was the only feasible defence. A group of tough four-year boys became my bodyguards, marching protectively behind the two miniskirted dresses I wore through that summer, one white with red spots and one a pale blue shirtwaister. When they were in lessons I adopted an ingenious sideways walk, with my bum sidling along the walls.

Teaching was hard work in this milieu. Again I found myself arguing about Powell's ideas. The area was more solidly white working class than east London and did not have a comparable political history. The revolts of 1968 had made no visible impact here at all. Reading William Golding's *Lord of the Flies* one day with a class, I asked them if they knew of any example of people living in cooperative ways. They looked at me blankly, then a voice from this bleak council estate mused reflectively, 'The hippies.' Play power rather than street-fighting man had penetrated the concrete.

At the end of that June I struggled with my conscience. Methodist duty said I ought to stay on, to leave would be running away. But I couldn't bear it and quit. When I subsequently went to teach at Starcross (formerly Risinghill) in Islington in 1971, I realized that schools didn't have to be like Christopher Wren. Everyone smiled at you in the corridors at Starcross, and the liberal head had an open door for pupils and parents alike.

A mix of my experience at Christopher Wren and the *Black Dwarf* on 'Youth' gave me the idea of a liberated alternative 'Living School'. The name came from the Living Theatre, but in fact 'living' was a word which kept surfacing through the sixties in the visual arts as well as in drama. There were 'living sculptures' and 'living cities', for example. I collected a planning group together consisting of members of the Schools Action Union, Vinay Chand and a Young Communist League clothing worker who was a protégé of Ben Birnbaum. The aim was to bring the Schools Action Union in contact with the apprentices who had been radicalized through 1968 and 1969. On 14 June *Black Dwarf* announced an 'anti-authoritarian project' to be held at the LSE at the end of July, adding, 'The school will be organized to allow a maximum amount of choice of activities.' Along with discussions on education and the 'industrial situation', there were to be music, films, acting, poetry, songs, inflatables, 'art and fun'. We decided there would be no oppressive timetable, just an infinity of creativity in lots of little rooms.

A right-wing Conservative woman in the House of Lords made a fuss, asking why the LSE was to be used to propagate 'subversion'. We were banned by Walter Adams and Living School had to be rapidly rescheduled in that old home of free thought, Conway Hall, in Holborn. The 'anti-authoritarian' school started amidst conflict. A big, bearded film-maker from Germany called Gustav Schlacke, showing films made by his new group, Cinema Action, was to take up most of the morning insisting that we should all storm the LSE. Fiercely protective of the Schools Action Union, who were already having a hard time at their schools, and of the radical teachers who had come to talk about education, not go into combat, I argued that this was irresponsible. Eventually a disgruntled Schlacke led a small, militant raiding party off to the LSE in Houghton Street and Michael Duane, the white-haired libertarian former headmaster of Risinghill, was at last able to speak.

Conway Hall had fewer rooms than the LSE, but we utilized every inch. John Berger showed the Schools Action Union and Ann Scott how to make silk screen posters in the basement, Stephen Sedley (now a judge) talked on law, a left trade unionist discussed the White Paper with apprentices behind the stage. A Communist Party official tramped upstairs into the Conway Hall's turret to lecture on Marxism. The Schools Action Union members were either anarchical or incipient Maoists, or a bit of both, and argued with him heatedly. They were stuck in that turret for several hours, blocking up a room.

The idea of Living School was that the sessions should continue as the spirit moved them. As we had no timetable, we had no time limit and consequently it was not easy to find which space was free. This most 'anti-authoritarian' of projects ended up highly centralized and, because I was the only brain keeping track of who was where, the centre became me. It was like being the face on the computer in the TV sci-fi spoof *Red Dwarf*. This living timetable was far more exhausting than teaching in a normal school. But at the end of the day everyone (except Schlacke, I guess) was happy.

Vinay took a collection for Asian strikers at a factory called Punfield and Barstows, and they sent support for our challenge to an 'unquestioning acceptance of the decisions our "betters" have decided to channel us towards'. Living School also showed a short film made by the Tufnell Park women's group, which ended with a tribute to trade union women like Rose Boland from Ford.

While organizing Living School, I was also writing the pamphlet for the May Day Manifesto group. There are some things you write because of an external reason, but others are obsessive, they witter inside you. These are the undeniable ones, the kind that come from within. While I was driven to write, it happened that Bob and Theresa, along with Adam Hart, his brother Charlie – a musician in Pete Brown's band – and Phil Vaughan, a kinetic artist, who were all now living at 12 Montague Road, began a major reconstruction job in our bathroom and toilet because the floor was rotten. They applied an original combination of Phil and Theresa's art school training and Bob's useful O-level in carpentry and his advanced mathematical skills to replace it. Experimentation took time and for several weeks we went to the lavatory by balancing on the supporting lathes. The end result was to be a merging of the bathroom and lavatory and eventually a two-door bathroom.

My ears were filled with the noise of honest manual labour banging away on the bathroom floor upstairs as I wrote and rewrote my pamphlet. But writing, like lust, banishes ethics and duty. So I sat on my stool (unergonomically, in retrospect, though such a concept never entered my head at the time) for three weeks, with all the ideas and reading of the previous few months welling up inside me and tumbling out on to the pages. I wrote about how women were contained in a series of acceptable ways of behaving, of the minutiae of subordination, of the difficulty subordinated groups had in finding a theoretical language to contest the power of prevailing assumptions. I considered how women accommodated, how we beat a retreat.

I drew on my personal observation, as I had done in the *Black Dwarf* article, quoting Barbara Marsh saying, 'We women are just shells for the men', and one of the Guildford middle-class housewives in my Workers' Educational Association class, who told me that she could be herself only in the bath. The hairdressers' version of social stratification gleaned from one of my further education classes also found its way into 'Women's Liberation and the New Politics'.

> The Queen
> pop singers (various grades)
> employers
> principal of college
> vice-principal of college
> teachers
> hairdressing students
> black people
> mothers.

I included a practical and somewhat dutiful section on equal pay and training, but the innovative aspect was my attempt to trace how silence is broken by a new consciousness and how women's grievances had historically taken differing forms. I had no idea, of course, that I was to pursue these two for the rest of my life!

From my reading of Gramsci came the word 'hegemony', which I adapted into 'male hegemony', finding parallels with the writing of Frantz Fanon, Eldridge Cleaver and Stokely Carmichael. Black Power provided a crucial language of cultural domination, because it gave voice to a subjectivity obliterated in Marxist versions of socialism and thus suggested a connection between individual experience and political resistance. It was very difficult at this point to validate personal experience which did not fit the existing theoretical canon, but the movements of the late sixties gave me the confidence to insist on the need to connect. I was able to pick up on a few scattered pieces of contemporary testimony from women. For instance, Ronald Fraser had edited a series of oral interviews in the *New Left Review* on work. These were published by Penguin in two collections and in one of these Suzanne

Gail's essay on housework appeared. The recognition that housework was both a material activity and one with effects on consciousness was of course to become an understanding of the women's movement in the seventies. However, in 1969 it still seemed revelatory.

I was also realizing that there had been a past. In the British Museum, I had found Wilhelm Reich's *The Sexual Revolution* and from his references I discovered some of the books of Alexandra Kollontai which were translated into English. Kollontai gave me a completely new insight on the Russian Revolution. It began to seem as if there had been a conspiracy to conceal daily life and women in the histories I had known before. I combed through books now, looking for references to women; Fei Ling had recommended some on China, while Christopher Hill's work brought insights about the seventeenth and eighteenth centuries. I began, moreover, to transpose other experiences and see new connections. For instance, de Tocqueville's fireman, dumb on the tribune of popular power, made an appearance as the symbol of cultural silencing. I was fascinated by a printed extramural lecture called 'Education and Experience' which Edward Thompson sent me on the tension in English culture between class and theoretical knowledge, from the Romantics through to D. H. Lawrence. 'Education and Experience' was to be something which I read and re-read at many different times in my life – it is now fortunately available in the collection of Edward's essays edited by Dorothy Thompson, *The Romantics*.

The content of what I was saying really demanded a new way of writing about politics, because through a mix of subjectivity, history and theory I was trying to probe beyond what was taken for granted. Again it was the extraordinary upheavals of the late sixties which made me brave enough to risk a new form of communicating – and one vital inspiration was the manuscript of *Letter to a Teacher*.

I was able to seize the chink of space which opened that June as the frenzied momentum of the last year and a half began to slow down a little. But it still felt like sending out messages into the unknown. Despite my loneliness in the writing, 'Women's Liberation and the New Politics' was to sell very well and was republished as a Spokesman pamphlet, where it had a few more years' life.

*

After Living School, Juliet Mitchell, who was involved in a group in south London based on a mothers' and toddlers' 'One o'clock Club', told me about a Women's Liberation Workshop meeting and I went along. The London groups were growing and a newsletter, which was initially called *Bird*, then *Harpies Bizarre*, had been started. This soon became *Shrew* and the name stuck.

The Tufnell Park group, influenced by Dorothea, had decided to follow the example of the German student movement and set up an anti-authoritarian crèche. The Germans used to squat empty shops, creating their alternative child care in those 'Kindershops'. The idea was that the children played freely while the adults discussed Marxist theory. Sue Cowley reported in *Shrew* that summer that it hadn't worked. 'The kids were happy,' but the adults in Tufnell Park had sat around without much to say to one another.

This was to be one source, however, for the idea that men should participate in child care. Shelley Wortis, who was a child psychologist, began to do research about 'father deprivation' to counter the literature about the crucial nature of the mother–child bond. In contrast to the traditional nursery campaigns, which had not challenged the sexual division of labour, the Women's Liberation approach was for adults of both sexes to participate. Like the Germans, we believed in anti-authoritarian play. 'Kindershops' were examples of the 'prefigurative alternatives' which were being taken up by radical movements in many countries. In Paris they called their alternative childcare '*crèches sauvages*'.

I began going to the meetings of the nearest local Women's Liberation group, in Islington, that summer and we spent several weeks talking about our personal experiences in childhood and adolescence. But after my Young Socialist/International Socialist initiation into left politics, I felt uneasy about meeting just to *talk*. I formed an alliance with a woman in the Communist Party and a practically minded single mother from the recently formed pressure group Gingerbread, who also wanted to 'do' something. We started a nursery campaign – all three of us – and I was back knocking on doors, in Islington not Hackney this time. We knocked and knocked, but our public meeting for more nurseries attracted only one or two bemused local women and an articulate middle-class man who was a member of the Play

School Association, an organization which helped to give mothers a few hours' break.

It took several years before the Women's Liberation Workshop actually developed a nursery campaign and many disputes about whether you should set them up yourselves or lobby local authorities. After the May 'Events' the idea gained credence that making demands on the state would cost radical movements their autonomy; they would be assimilated and controlled through an all-pervasive 'permissive tolerance'. I did not accept this view entirely, but like many others I was affected by the fear of 'cooption'. It was assumed that while reforms might be granted, you would lose the power to exercise direct democratic control over daily life and thus the meaning and purpose of the gains would be lost. This argument was to meander round and round in the Women's Liberation movement until eventually the desperate need for child care began to produce interesting hybrid forms which combined community control and state funding.

The late-sixties emphasis on creating alternatives stimulated the formation of radical cultural groups in film, theatre, publishing and journalism which overtook the attempt through Agit Prop to provide a single umbrella; Agit Prop was to evolve into a political information service. I remained, through personal interest, politics and friendship, closely involved with this creative aspect of left politics, which was to become an important part of the non-aligned socialism of the seventies.

Towards the end of July, Roberta brought Marc Karlin, a member of the newly formed left film group Cinema Action, to 12 Montague Road. When she went back to Oxford, Marc was to stay in the house and become one of my closest friends. He had been in Paris during May '68, where he had been influenced by the radical film-maker Chris Marker's interest in the work of the avant-garde in the Russian Revolution. Modelling themselves on the Russians who travelled to film the workers, Cinema Action had been filming a strike near Liverpool just before Marc arrived in my house. His first encounter with Northern working-class women in the tenants' movement on Merseyside had made a deep impression upon him. My first memory of Marc was that Roberta and I argued with him in the kitchen when he said *working*-class women were oppressed, but not middle-class women. His first memory of me was somewhat different. When Roberta opened the front door I was sitting on the lavatory, from which, to his horror, I proceeded to greet him. I think this must have been because, in the wake of all the bathroom building activity, the doors didn't get put back on for a while.

My PhD thesis on University Extension was now looking like a gigantic white elephant. Eric Hobsbawm, my supervisor, proposed cuts and also the inclusion of women students who were pupil-teachers, who were often from working-class backgrounds, but by this time I could not bear to return to the sources and unstitch it. As Eric's clear and rational voice sentenced to extermination my lovingly discovered worker-students from Hebden Bridge and Woolwich, a despairing tear started to trickle down my face which I concealed by turning my head away to the window. As we sat there in his office at Birkbeck College, a student demonstration passed noisily by outside. My thesis, I decided, was just not politically relevant.

Writing 'Women's Liberation and the New Politics' had made me interested in elaborating my ideas historically. Roberta met Robert Hutchison, then working for Penguin, at a conference on anti-imperialism that summer and he said, 'Tell her to write a synopsis and send it to me.' I had no idea how to do this, so I sent him a list of chapter headings. These were to form the basis of what became *Women, Resistance and Revolution* and *Woman's Consciousness, Man's World*, except that my initial plan was even broader in scope. Because we had so little to go on, I thought I had to encompass the history of the world all in one book. There was an intimation that I might have bitten off more than I could chew. 'I'm very interested in what I'm doing. But I'm terrified it gets to be too big a job,' I told my diary ungrammatically. I had no way of knowing that I was sketching out in red ink a lifetime's work. Yet I must have regarded the notes as a kind of record, for the scribbled pieces of paper were, in the strange random way of scraps of past thoughts, to survive and surprise me decades later.

When I went to see Robert Hutchison in Penguin's friendly, slightly scruffy offices in John Street, Islington, he looked at my list and suggested that I go away and write a sample chapter, pointing at random to the heading 'Russia and China' and saying, 'What about this one?' So I took out Reich's *The Sexual Revolution* again in the

British Museum Reading Room and scoured the big blue catalogues
for every name mentioned in the book. Then I checked through all the
headings on 'women' which a librarian showed me in a little back
room. A bibliography by Lucinda Cisler from the United States helped
me track down a few more references. I drew some blanks. 'I want to
find out about women and revolutionary movements,' I told a bemused
Fawcett Society on the telephone. The library of the Anglo-Chinese
Friendship Society proved more fruitful.

By the time my sample chapter was ready that autumn, Robert had
left Penguin and Neil Middleton was doing his job. When I arrived in
trepidation to see my new editor, Neil was puzzling over whether he
should publish the I Ching. 'Why not ask the I Ching?' I piped up, the
hippie taking over. Neil looked surprised but did just that and the I
Ching, of course, recommended its own publication.

When Neil sent me the contract for my first book, I could hardly
believe that someone would pay me to do what I was always doing
anyway. Neil told me later he had never encountered anyone able to
write who was so unconfident; he was an indefatigably encouraging
editor and convinced me to have the courage of my own convictions.
Very few women wrote about left politics and ideas in the late sixties.
Many of my women friends were educated and thoughtful but terrified
of the definitive externality of print. I was just the same, but I think I
had been lucky in the people – men as well as women – who showed
faith in me. I had also gained just that bit of extra confidence because
of Tariq's gamble in letting me write for *Black Dwarf* the previous
year.

The response to the *Black Dwarf* article and then the May Day
Manifesto pamphlet helped me to believe that I had something to say.
I began to express thoughts which arose through collective activity,
not just out of my own head. I wrote down what I perceived, a
crystallization of what I saw and heard around me. I was helped greatly
by the radical assumption that an individual contributed something
which would be taken and reshaped by others, rather than some
timeless statement of intimidating genius. Bob remarked to me
around this time that my political significance was as an example.
People could look at me and feel convinced: 'If she can do it so can I.'
I laughed but I think there was truth in what he said. I seemed often

to bumble almost unconsciously into doing a lot of things in my life which have then connected me to some broader radical mood in the culture.

The Penguin contract was to solve my failure to earn money. Early in September, still suntanned after another visit to Formentera with Roberta, I was striding through Ridley Road market in an old, short denim skirt, carrying my brightly coloured paper 'flag bag', when a stall-holder hailed me with an offer of work. I hesitated. A fat old baker from Kossoff's had already proposed a job stripping for the bakers who worked through the night. But this was above board – £6 for Friday and Saturday on the biscuit stall. This was a lifesaver, £6 being just about a week's survival. So it was the British Museum Monday, Tuesday, Wednesday, Thursday, and the biscuit stall Fridays and Saturdays. My new employers taught me to chant, 'Buy your biscuits – lovely broken biscuits,' to attract the pensioners, the indigent and the thrifty. The two quick-witted stall-holders had to do my calculations as well as theirs because I remained unable to add up. They put up with this and with my peculiar politics for longer than might have been expected because the owner of the stall had his eye on me. He would take me off to the Norfolk Arms on Sandringham Road and buy me rum and Cokes.

If I don't fancy someone to start with, drink has never inclined me to them. I was too polite to tell him this as I thought it might hurt his feelings, so instead I explained I had this book to write on women and revolution which meant I had to be in the British Museum Reading Room. It took him a while to believe me, but eventually he did and I got the sack.

The biscuit stall had tided me over until my Workers' Educational Association classes began again that October. My Harrow class were studying Russian Revolutionary thinkers and as ever I was learning from my students. One old man, who could remember the impact of the Russian Revolution upon the east London working-class Jewish community, informed us, 'People said that a new saviour had arisen in Russia. He was called Lenintrotsky and was taking from the rich to give to the poor.'

*

Working at the biscuit stall, however, had prevented me from going to the editorial meetings at *Black Dwarf*, where John Hoyland, Adrian Mitchell and Vinay Chand were becoming more and more on edge because of Tariq's tendency to slip in International Marxist Group propaganda. The paper was beginning to turn into an organ of the Trotskyist Fourth International; only Tariq's irrepressible delight in mischief and flair as a communicator made it readable. I knew trouble was imminent.

You could hardly move for acrimony that autumn. *Black Dwarf* criticized the leading figure in the International Socialist group, Chris Harman, for attacking Ho Chi Minh at the memorial meeting marking the death of the Vietnamese leader. It was true that some Trotskyists had been killed in the forties in Vietnam, though the International Socialists had not stressed the point while increasing their numbers through the Vietnam Solidarity Campaign. A memorial meeting for the dead Ho Chi Minh seemed to me a divisive time to raise the issue. Whereupon Hornsey IS moved that I should be expelled. Expulsion was an extreme measure in 1969; only one other person had actually been expelled then, a Labour MP accused of racism. I knew I was being punished not only for disagreeing with Chris's action but for my refusal to be controlled by the ethos of the group. Hornsey IS had a particular rivalry with Nick Wright and indeed one of the prime movers was the same man who had accused me of 'fucking with a Stalinist'. The conflict was ironic, because Nick and I were drifting apart and my general perspective on domestic politics, such as the emphasis on working-class resistance, was completely in accord with IS at the time.

On 19 October shop stewards from Ford, Chrysler, Vauxhall and British Leyland held a historic conference in Coventry. They met to compare wage rates, because they had resolved to demand 'parity'. The meeting was closed to the press, but because of my status as scribe and typist Ann Scott and I were allowed in by the Dagenham convenor, Sid Harraway, to report on the conference for *Black Dwarf*. There was only a tiny group of women workers present; otherwise Ann and I were surrounded by a tidal wave of trade union masculinity.

Sid Harraway, a Communist, had been active at Ford since the forties. He was generally of a rather stolid demeanour, but he had a look in his eyes as if something miraculous had happened. Despite my ignorance of the car industry, I could sense the tremendous significance of two telegrams he held out to show me. They were from workers at Alfa Romeo in Italy and Ford in Belgium. What I was seeing in Sid's hand that day was a new kind of working-class internationalism which was to grow up alongside the official international trade union structures and was, in some instances, to challenge the bureaucratic remoteness of the unions. We were living, in fact, through the first signs of changes in the global organization of production, though we were only dimly aware of what was afoot.

After the Coventry meeting, I sat down at my kitchen table with one of the stewards who worked in the Ford paint shop at Dagenham and interviewed him about the new challenges the stewards were facing. The most politically astute stewards recognized the need for new forms of organizing. 'Improved communications means important inter-union contact from the bottom as well as the top. The realization is growing that these links must become international. Assembly operations could be and have been transferred to Ford workers in other countries,' I wrote, unaware how pertinent all this was to be in the future.

Tariq still groans about 'Cars and Consequences', which he insists was handwritten. In fact, it was typed, but on my mother's 'Made in India' twenties typewriter and on especially thin paper because I took a carbon copy, giving it an archaic appearance. Sadly, by the time it appeared war had broken out at *Black Dwarf*.

The clash came over an article Tariq put in without the rest of us on the editorial board seeing it. Headed 'Southern Africa Betrayed', it accused the African National Congress of corruption and deliberately sending rebellious members to their deaths. Vinay discovered similar material was being circulated by the South African police to discredit the ANC. It was bad enough that we were publishing an unbalanced sectarian piece of hatred without any reference to the ANC's viewpoint. Even worse, it seemed we were also unwittingly helping the South African apartheid regime.

That weekend, the consequences of our sectarian divisions in London struck home with a devastating personal force as, troubled and miserable, I began to envisage what people imprisoned by the apartheid regime might feel on hearing that a socialist newspaper far away was attacking them. It was this that made me take an unprecedented and, for me, frightening initiative. I called an editorial meeting and tried to get the centre spread removed. We lost and a compromise was to be a critical letter signed by John Hoyland, Adrian Mitchell, Vinay Chand and myself in the Christmas issue.

This conflict was personally very painful. Tariq was an old friend and I have never had much stamina for political conflicts with people I liked. The editorial board meetings where we had laughed and joked were now grim and gloomy and I dreaded them. I was also downcast because the non-sectarian left paper I had loved had become fraught with bitterness. Left papers are real heartbreakers and money-burners and ever afterwards I would hold something back. Once bitten, twice shy, as they say. One of the snags of having a love affair with a left-wing publication is the grief it brings. Just as we had been carried along by the optimism of 1968, now we were being sucked under by currents of profound distrust.

While the left was splintering in rancour, Women's Liberation was growing. The Islington group had moved its meetings to my house that autumn. This Dalston group expanded each week. Unlike most movements and organizations, which are generally pleased about recruitment, we were thrown by our rapidly increasing numbers. We had learned from the North American model that consciousness-raising rap-style groups should be small in order to enable everyone to participate and also to connect personal experience with a broader social picture. Instead of little groups of around ten women, we would attract transitory and heaving crowds of up to fifty, all packed into my bedroom.

We were from differing backgrounds and our political views, interests and concerns varied greatly. I remember a white working-class Enoch Powell supporter and a black woman cleaner whose husband started to lock her in when he discovered where she was going. A grey-haired woman in her fifties turned up with her daughter one night: Lucy Waugh was from a Walthamstow working-class family, her mother had been active in the local Women's Co-operative Guild, and as a young girl Lucy had done typing for Sylvia Pankhurst. Lucy, along with her daughter Liz, were both to become involved in the early-seventies campaign to organize night cleaners, in which Sally Alexander also took part. For two years Liz and I would tramp around the deserted City at night stopping women with plastic bags. 'Excuse me, are you a night cleaner? Would you like to join the union?' and Marc Karlin was to document the Women's Liberation campaign in his film *Night Cleaners*. Among the women who came to the Dalston Women's Liberation group was my friend from St Hilda's, now back from South Africa, Hermione Harris, and when we divided into three smaller groups early in 1970, I joined Arsenal Women's Liberation Workshop, which met at Hermione's house, near the football ground.

The rapid sprouting of groups in different parts of London was making the original general meeting unwieldy. We agreed we would send representatives and that each group would produce *Shrew* in turn so that no centralized single perspective would dominate. These approaches to organizing were in marked contrast to both the Labour Party and the Leninist groups. At the time, it seemed to me that the North American women just created this differing vision of how to organize which somehow made complete sense. Only when I read more about the history of Civil Rights, the New Left and the US student movement was I to realize that our Women's Liberation approach to politics was rooted in the ideas and assumptions of these movements. Over time people forgot their origins and they were called in a political shorthand simply the 'feminist' way of organizing.

In November 1969 women's history appeared for the first time at the Ruskin History Workshop when one of the trade union women students gave a paper on factory women's work in the morning session. A male trade unionist stood up in the discussion and said that a man should earn enough to enable women to stay at home and care for the children. I challenged him, stressing the importance for women of the collective experience of workplace organizing.

That lunchtime Roberta, Sally and Arielle, along with Anna Davin and myself, started talking about the need for more discussion about women. At the next plenary I announced there was to be a meeting for people interested in talking about women. I had missed the obvious *double entendre* and the announcement was greeted with guffaws, which made us extremely cross. A group crammed into a tiny student bedroom at Ruskin that teatime, talking excitedly. I proposed a History Workshop on women but a North American, Barbara Winslow, who was more aware of developments in the United States, pointed out that we had not had any general conference on women. And so, out of Ruskin History Workshop, was to come the first Women's Liberation conference, held at Ruskin the following February.

For once the prognostication of a left paper had been vindicated by history; 1969 really had been the 'Year of the Militant Woman'. While staying in Oxford, I was finishing an article for *Black Dwarf* summing up the year. In 'Cinderella Organizes Buttons', I noted the militancy of nurses, lavatory attendants, factory workers and teachers, mentioning the National Joint Action Committee for Women's Equal Rights, the Revolutionary Socialist Students' Federation meeting, the appearance of the magazines *Socialist Woman* and *Shrew*. I added that discontent was coming from many sources, criticizing the tendency to try and 'zone off' the economic from other aspects of women's subordination. I believed that differing aspects of experience overlapped, the stories and myths of childhood being part of our consciousness as well as the sociology of work and daily life. I ended the article with a tribute to Lil Bilocca, from the Hull trawler campaign; Rose Boland, from Ford; the bus worker Kath Fincham; the post office worker Daisy Nolan; and 'all the women you never hear about' – a preoccupation with silence and invisibility I was to take into my interest in the women 'hidden from history'.

Though in retrospect the emergence of a movement appears as inevitable, at the time our organizing felt fragile. We had no idea what response we would get to the conference we had begun to plan (500 people were to come). We were thinking on our feet, developing ideas from, as it seemed, scratch, and were surprised when an older generation made contact. One former suffragette who came to our planning meeting in London that December told me, 'Of course you're very lucky to be allowed to use halls. They banned us.' This generation were like political grandmothers to us, closer to our wavelength than the political mothers – the left women in the generation which preceded ours. Formed by the thirties and forties, they would often remonstrate with us for identifying as 'women'. They had had their own struggle to be independent, political activists and saw the 'women' tag as restrictive; to us it was liberatory.

Women's politics seemed full of hope and possibility, in contrast to the left, which was increasingly depressing. At *Black Dwarf* the conflict over the ANC article continued to be bitter and the question of my expulsion from IS rumbled on. Ann Scott had gone to Cambridge that October, so I was unable to discuss what I wrote with another woman of similar views on the editorial board. When John Hoyland was critical of my article summing up the year I felt stranded. I was beset on all sides by divisions and conflicts among people with whom I had previously been close.

The problems in participatory collectives become all too clear when these groups are riven by disagreements. Belatedly we started talking about the need for a constitution. Now it was the turn of *Black Dwarf* to produce discussion papers. These were written in deadly earnest, even though neither side was really listening to the other.

In opposition to the International Marxist Group, who wanted a Leninist 'vanguard' paper telling everyone what they should think, I produced a long eight-page statement which took its title from William Blake: 'One Law for the Lion and Ox is Oppression'. I argued for diversity and debate: 'We can't appoint ourselves as an all-knowing élite ready to issue orders to the masses.' We could learn not simply from the Bolsheviks but from a variety of radical traditions – Utopian Socialists, Anarchists, Anarcho-syndicalists, Guild Socialists and Third World revolutionary movements. I said that the circumstances we were facing required new approaches to organizing. We needed to consider not only external structures but the micro ones – the relations and responses among individuals. This idea had come from a spectacular confrontation early in November between Ronnie Laing and Gerry Healy from the Socialist Labour League. Laing posed the question why individual German soldiers in the First World War accepted the order to fight for their country, suggesting that the psychological approaches to child-rearing, in particular the restraints on masturbation, current in the early twentieth century encouraged absolute obedience. This psychological perspective was of course anathema to Gerry Healy, who erupted in fury. I was amused to see Laing handle his opponent with the accomplished ease of a therapist and the egocentric conviction of a charismatic leader.

Writing my 'Lion and Ox' discussion document was personally a monumental undertaking. I was bringing together a whole range of insights gleaned from the tumult of the last few years. Politically, however, it was a dead duck. Fred Halliday walked out as I finished the eighth page, saying, 'I disagree with you 100 per cent.' Fred liked vanguards at the time.

I had begun to develop stomachaches when I thought of editorial meetings. When 'Cinderella Organizes Buttons' was to be discussed, just before Christmas, I mounted the stairs to the office in dread and retired to think in the lavatory. What should I say? As I sat brooding and staring at the door, suddenly the subversive thought occurred to me that I could escape. I didn't have to go through this ordeal, I could run away. I scuttled back down the stairs and rejoined Roberta in the pub nearby. Anthony Barnett, terrier-like, tracked me down. I retreated into the pub lavatory. Anthony stood outside, demanding that I come out and discuss my article rationally and politically. I refused to budge. Roberta stood guard for half an hour until Anthony finally gave up and she hissed through the door, 'It's all clear now.'

A week or so later, on the way back from the dentist's, I sat in a café and wrote two letters. In one I resigned from IS before they got round to expelling me. In the other I announced I was leaving *Black Dwarf*, suggesting that they sit round imagining they had cunts for two minutes in silence so they could understand why it was hard for me to discuss what I had written on women.

John felt particularly betrayed by my resignation. However, three decades later he was able to laugh about the embarrassed hush which fell as Tariq read out my letter. It was Anthony who, after about forty-five seconds, became the first to gulp in protest, 'This is outrageous.' Everyone agreed that indeed it was so.

But I was in a mood to burn my boats, throwing myself into the Women's Liberation movement more or less exclusively for the next decade, until the election of Margaret Thatcher in 1979 made me feel the need to connect back to a wider movement of resistance against the harsh policies of neo-liberalism.

As we prepared for the first Women's Liberation conference, the movement I envisaged was to be an entirely new kind of politics – no leaders, no ego trips, no more sectarian disputes. It would assert the claims of working-class women, not only those of the more privileged, and it was going to be about bread *and* about roses. In the words of a woman trade unionist I discovered in the report of the 1968 Women's TUC Conference, we wanted 'more than the promise of a dream'. What actually happened was to be in some ways much more than we initially imagined and in some ways very much less – a paradox which holds true for many political and social grass-roots movements.

Notes

Acknowledgements

p. ix **'Labyrinth' where all kinds**: Mike Savage, 'Walter Benjamin's Urban Thought: A Critical Analysis', *Environment and Planning: Society and Space*, vol. 13, 1995, p. 206.

Introduction

p. xv **He who seeks to approach**: Walter Benjamin, quoted in Mike Savage, 'Walter Benjamin's Urban Thought: A Critical Analysis', *Environment and Planning: Society and Space*, vol. 13, 1995, p. 208.

p. xvii **To provoke ... the 'source of all philosophy'**: J. P. Sartre, 'The Theater', interview in *L'Express*, translated in *Evergreen Review*, vol. 4, no. 11, January–February 1960, p. 150.

CHAPTER 1
1960–61

p. 8 **The word** *dépayser*: Judith Okely, *Simone de Beauvoir*, Virago, London, 1986, p. 45.

p. 11 **How do you feel, girls**: quoted in Alison Leonard, *Telling Our Stories: Wrestling with a Fresh Language for the Spiritual Journey*, Darton, Longman and Todd, London, 1995, p. 93.

p. 14 **Will be a revenge upon**: Simone de Beauvoir, *The Second Sex*, Penguin, Harmondsworth, 1972, p. 364, quoted in Okely, *Simone de Beauvoir*, p. 110.

p. 29 **Art back into society**: Fine Artz Associates' Manifesto, quoted in Robert Hewison, *Too Much: Art and Society in the Sixties, 1960–1975*, Methuen, London, 1986, p. 51.

p. 40 **The familiar**: J. P. Sartre, 'The Theater', *Evergreen Review*, vol. 4, no. 11, January–February 1960, p. 150.

CHAPTER 2
1961–4

p. 61 **In 1916 Emma Goldman:** Margaret Anderson, quoted in Richard Drinnon, *Rebel in Paradise: A Biography of Emma Goldman*, University of Chicago Press, Chicago, 1961, p. 143.

CHAPTER 3
1964–6

p. 121 **In the formation of any socialist programme:** Charles Feinstein et al., (eds.), 'Beyond the Freeze: A Socialist Policy for Economic Growth', London, September 1966, p. 24.

p. 125 **There was definitely a group identity:** Duggie Fields, quoted in Julian Palacios, *Lost in the Woods: Syd Barrett and the Pink Floyd*, Boxtree, London, 1998, p. 63.

p. 125 **The first mission of the American radical is to escape:** Frank Bardacke, quoted in Abe Peck, *Uncovering the Sixties: The Life and Times of the Underground Press*, Pantheon Books, New York, 1985, p. 28.

CHAPTER 4
1967

p. 134 **In folk tradition:** Ian Macdonald, *Revolution in the Head: The Beatles' Records and the Sixties*, Pimlico, London, 1995, p. 116.

p. 162 **Very funny, wonderful, free in their spirits:** Herbert Gutman, quoted in Paul Buhle (ed.), *History and the New Left: Madison, Wisconsin 1950–1970*, Temple University Press, Philadelphia, 1990, p. 49.

CHAPTER 5
1968

p. 175 **If we want to test the validity of modernization:** Raymond Williams (ed.), *May Day Manifesto 1968*, Penguin, Harmondsworth, 1968, p. 45.

p. 176 **The New BLACK DWARF will not pick quarrels with other left-wingers:** *Black Dwarf*, pre-issue publicity flyer, London, May Day 1968.

p. 187 **To expose the relationship between perceptual and conceptual apprehension:** Hilary Gresty (ed.), *1965 to 1972: When Attitudes Became Form*, Kettle's Yard, Cambridge, 1984, p. 5.

p. 189 **A benefit concert for clapped-out seaside donkeys:** Dennis Potter, 'Tea-bag Rebels: Dennis Potter's Verdict After a Night with Red Danny', *Sun*,

17 June 1968, quoted in W. Stephen Gilbert, *Fight and Kick and Bite: The Life and Work of Dennis Potter*, Hodder and Stoughton, London, 1995, p. 204.

p. 192 **inject . . . the unorganized lumps and clusters**: in Sheila Rowbotham, 'The Little Vanguard's Tail', *Dreams and Dilemmas: Collected Writings*, Virago, London, 1983, pp. 50–53.

p. 199 **I'll tell you something**: John Lennon, 'A Very Open Letter to John Hoyland', *Black Dwarf*, vol. 13, no. 9, 10 January 1969.

p. 203 **It isn't about pay, it's about recognition**: Rose Boland, quoted in Sabina Roberts, 'Equal Pay: The First Step', *Socialist Woman*, March–April 1969.

p. 205 **To be still searching**: John Milton, *Areopagitica*, Douglas Bush (ed.), *The Portable Milton*, The Viking Press, New York, 1949, pp. 191–3.

CHAPTER 6
1969

p. 211 **So what are we complaining about?**: Sheila Rowbotham, 'Women and the Struggle for Freedom', *Black Dwarf*, vol. 13, no. 9, 10 January 1969.

p. 213 **One or two of these thugs**: Edward Short, quoted in David Caute, *Sixty-Eight: The Year of the Barricades*, Hamish Hamilton, London, 1988, p. 325.

p. 221 **They tell us what we are**: Sheila Rowbotham: 'Women and the Struggle for Freedom', *Black Dwarf*, vol. 13, no. 9, 10 January 1969.

p. 225 **A rather disorganized march**: *Guardian*, quoted in David Widgery, *The Left in Britain*, Penguin, Harmondsworth, 1975, pp. 374–5.

p. 235 **At home about the difficulties of orgasm**: Helke Sander, quoted in *Black Dwarf*, vol. 14, no. 17, 16 May 1969.

p. 240 **Unquestioning acceptance of the decisions**: message to the Living School: 'Why We Are on Strike at Punfield [and] Barstows', quoted in Widgery, *The Left in Britain*, p. 396.

p. 241 **We women are just shells for the men**: quoted in Sheila Rowbotham, 'Women's Liberation and the New Politics', May Day Manifesto Pamphlet, 1969, reprinted in Sheila Rowbotham, *Dreams and Dilemmas: Collected Writings*, Virago, London, 1983, p. 29.

p. 241 **The Queen**: ibid., p. 21.

p. 252 **All the women you never hear about**: Sheila Rowbotham, 'Cinderella Organizes Buttons', *Black Dwarf*, vol. 15, no. 27, 10 January 1969, reprinted in Widgery, *The Left in Britain*, p. 420.

p. 255 **More than the promise of a dream**: Miss J. O'Connell, Draughtsmen and Allied Technicians Association, TUC Report, London, 1968, p. 455.

Further Reading

In the course of remembering the sixties I checked facts in a range of political, social and cultural histories. What follows is a selection for people who want to read on.

Ali, Tariq, *Street Fighting Years*, Collins, London, 1987.

Ali, Tariq, and Watkins, Susan, *Marching in the Streets*, Bloomsbury, London, 1998.

Araeen, Rasheed, *The Other Story: Afro-Asian Artists in Post-war Britain*, Hayward Gallery, South Bank Centre, London, 1989.

Brett, Guy, *Exploding Galaxies: The Art of David Medalla*, Kala Press, London, 1995.

Buhle, Paul, ed., *History and the New Left: Madison, Wisconsin 1950–1970*, Temple University Press, Philadelphia, 1990.

Cant, Bob, and Hemmings, Susan, *Radical Records: Thirty Years of Lesbian and Gay History, 1957–1987*, Routledge, London, 1988.

Caute, David, *Sixty-Eight: The Year of the Barricades*, Hamish Hamilton, London, 1988.

Chambers, Colin, *The Story of Unity Theatre*, Lawrence and Wishart, London, 1989.

Cockburn, Alexander, and Blackburn, Robin, eds., *Student Power: Problems, Diagnosis, Action*, Penguin, Harmondsworth, 1969.

Cooper, David, ed., *The Dialectics of Liberation*, Penguin, Harmondsworth, 1968.

Duff, Peggy, *Left, Left, Left: A Personal Account of Six Protest Campaigns 1945–65*, Allison and Busby, London, 1971.

DuPlessis, Rachel Blau, and Snitow, Ann, eds., *The Feminist Memoir Project: Voices from Women's Liberation*, Three Rivers Press, New York, 1998.

Evans, Mary, *Simone de Beauvoir: A Feminist Mandarin*, Tavistock, London, 1985.

Faithfull, Marianne, with David Dalton, *Faithfull*, Penguin, Harmondsworth, 1995.

Fountain, Nigel, *Underground: The London Alternative Press 1966–1974*, Routledge, London, 1988.

Fraser, Ronald, *1968: A Student Generation in Revolt*, Chatto and Windus, London, 1988.

Gilbert, Stephen W., *Fight and Kick and Bite: The Life and Work of Dennis Potter*, Hodder and Stoughton, London, 1995.

Gombin, Richard, *The Origins of Modern Leftism*, Penguin, Harmondsworth, 1975.

Gould, Tony, *Inside Outsider: The Life and Times of Colin MacInnes*, Chatto and Windus, London, 1983.

Green, Jonathan, *Days in the Life: Voices from the English Underground 1961–1971*, Pimlico, London, 1998.

Gresty, Hilary, ed., *1965 to 1972: When Attitudes Became Form*, Kettle's Yard, Cambridge, 1984.

Griffiths, Trevor R., and Llewellyn-Jones, Margaret, *British and Irish Women Dramatists Since 1958: A Critical Handbook*, Open University Press, Buckingham, 1993.

Hardy, Phil, and Laing, Dave, *The Faber Companion to 20th-century Popular Music*, Faber and Faber, London, 1995.

Hewison, Robert, *Too Much: Art and Society in the Sixties, 1960–1975*, Methuen, London, 1986.

Hitchens, Christopher, 'Children of 68', *Vanity Fair*, June 1998.

Hobsbawm, Eric, *Age of Extremes: The Short Twentieth Century 1914–1991*, Michael Joseph, London, 1994.

—'May 1968', in Hobsbawm, Eric, ed., *Uncommon People: Resistance, Rebellion and Jazz*, Weidenfeld and Nicolson, London, 1998.

Hunt, Marsha, *Real Life*, HarperCollins, London, 1995.

Katsiaficas, G. N. *The Imagination of the New Left: A Global Analysis of 1968*, South End Press, Boston, 1987.

Kenny, Michael, *The First New Left: British Intellectuals After Stalin*, Lawrence and Wishart, London, 1995.

Laing, Adrian, *R. D. Laing: A Biography*, Peter Owen, London, 1994.

Larkin, Colin, ed., *The Guinness Who's Who of Sixties Music*, Guinness Publishing, London, 1992.

Leonard, Alison, *Telling Our Stories: Wrestling with a Fresh Language for the Spiritual Journey*, Darton, Longman and Todd, London, 1995.

Lessing, Doris, *The Golden Notebook*, Penguin, Harmondsworth, 1964.

—*Walking in the Shade: Volume Two of My Autobiography 1949–1962*, HarperCollins, London, 1998.

Macdonald, Ian, *Revolution in the Head: The Beatles' Records and the Sixties*, Pimlico, London, 1995.

Maitland, Sara, *Very Heaven: Looking Back at the 1960s*, Virago, London, 1988.

Marks, Howard, *Mr Nice: An Autobiography*, Minerva, London, 1997.

Marsh, Graham, and Lewis, Barrie, eds., *The Blues: Album Cover Art*, Collins and Brown, London, 1996.

Marwick, Arthur, *The Sixties: The Cultural Revolution in Britain, France, Italy and the United States* c. 1958–c. 1974, Oxford University Press, Oxford, 1998.

Murphy, Robert, *Sixties British Cinema*, BFI Publishing, London, 1992.

Neville, Richard, *Hippie Hippie Shake: The Dreams, the Trips, the Trials, the Love-ins, the Screw-ups . . . The Sixties*, Bloomsbury, London, 1995.

Newfield, Jack, *A Prophetic Minority: The American New Left*, Anthony Blond, London, 1967.

Newton, Francis, *The Jazz Scene*, Penguin, Harmondsworth, 1961.

Okely, Judith, *Simone de Beauvoir: A Re-reading*, Virago, London, 1986.

Panitch, Leo, and Leys, Colin, *The End of Parliamentary Socialism: From New Left to New Labour*, Verso, London, 1997.

Papastergiadis, Nikos, *Modernity as Exile: The Stranger in John Berger's Writing*, Manchester University Press, Manchester, 1993.

Peck, Abe, *Uncovering the Sixties: The Life and Times of the Underground Press*, Pantheon Books, New York, 1985.

Phillips, Charlie, and Phillips, Mike, *Notting Hill in the Sixties*, Lawrence and Wishart, London, 1991.

Pimlott, Ben, *Harold Wilson*, HarperCollins, London, 1992.

Quant, Mary, *Quant by Quant*, Cassell, London, 1965.

Sadler, Simon, *The Situationist City*, The MIT Press, Cambridge, Mass. and London, 1998.

Savage, Mike, 'Walter Benjamin's Urban Thought: A Critical Analysis', *Environment and Planning: Society and Space*, vol. 13, 1995.

Sebestyen, Amanda, ed., *'68, '78, '88: From Women's Liberation to Feminism*, Prism Press, Bridport, 1988.

Sked, Alan, and Cook, Chris, *Post-war Britain: A Political History 1945–1992*, Penguin, Harmondsworth, 1993.

Thompson, Dorothy, 'On the Trail of the New Left', *New Left Review*, no. 215, January–February 1996.

Thompson, E. P., 'Outside the Whale', in Thompson, E. P., ed., *The Poverty of Theory and Other Essays*, Merlin Press, London, 1978.

Tynan, Kathleen, *The Life of Kenneth Tynan*, Methuen, London, 1988.

Upshad, Michael, ed., *The Sixties*, Helicon Publishing, Oxford, 1994.

Wandor, Michelene, ed., *Once a Feminist: Stories of a Generation*, Virago, London, 1990.

Widgery, David, *The Left in Britain*, Penguin, Harmondsworth, 1975.

Williams, Raymond, ed., *May Day Manifesto 1968*, Penguin, Harmondsworth, 1968.

Wollen, Peter, 'The Situationist International: On the Passage of a Few People Through a Rather Brief Period of Time', in Wollen, Peter, ed., *Raiding the Icebox: Reflections on Twentieth-century Culture*, Verso, London, 1993.

I also consulted the following periodicals and journals: *Black Dwarf, Evergreen Review, Les Temps Moderne, New Left Review, New Reasoner, Oz, Radical Philosophy, Shrew, Socialist Register, Socialist Woman, Yorkshire Life.*